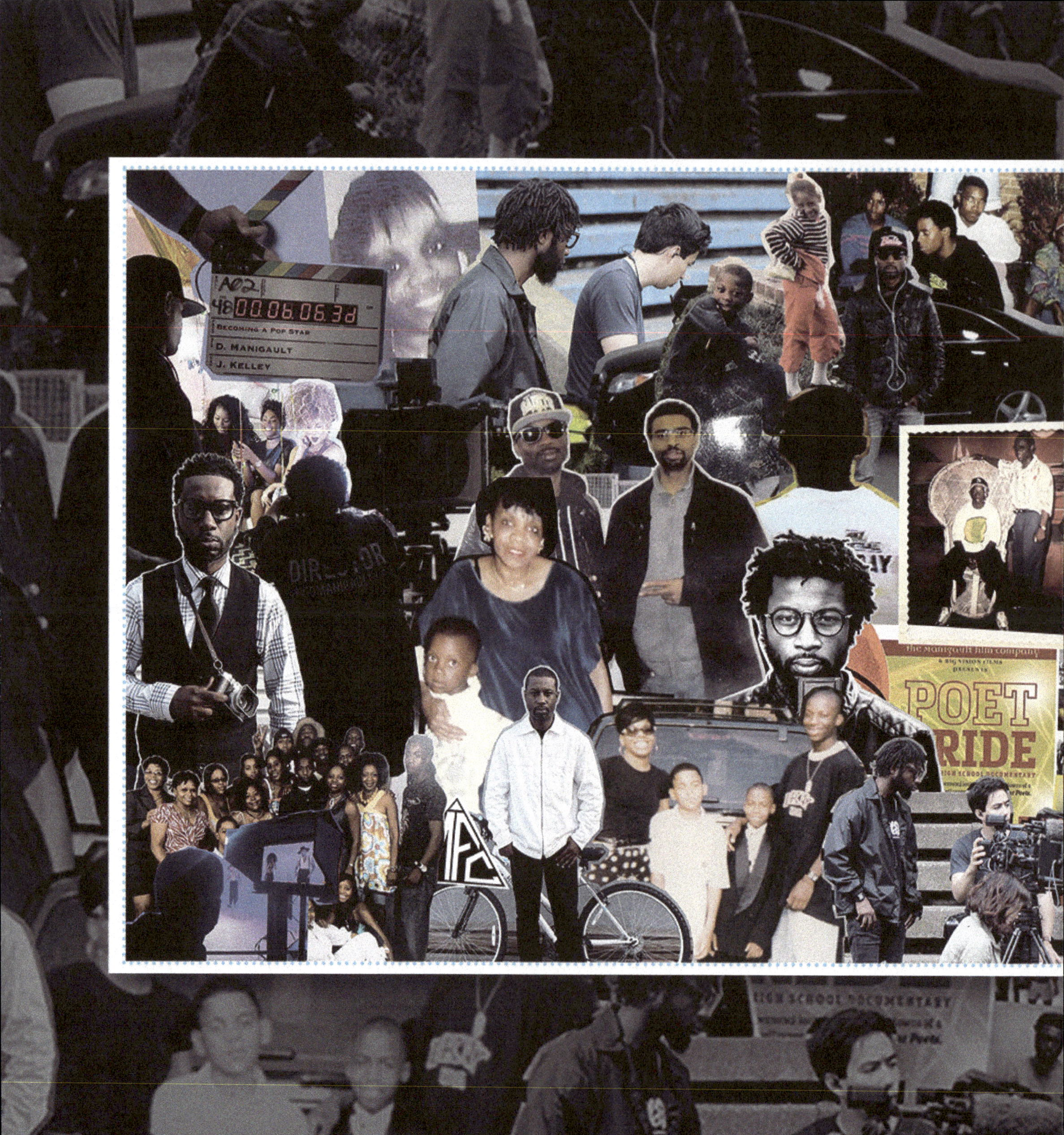

A02
48
BECOMING A POP STAR
D. MANIGAULT
J. KELLEY
POET
RIDE

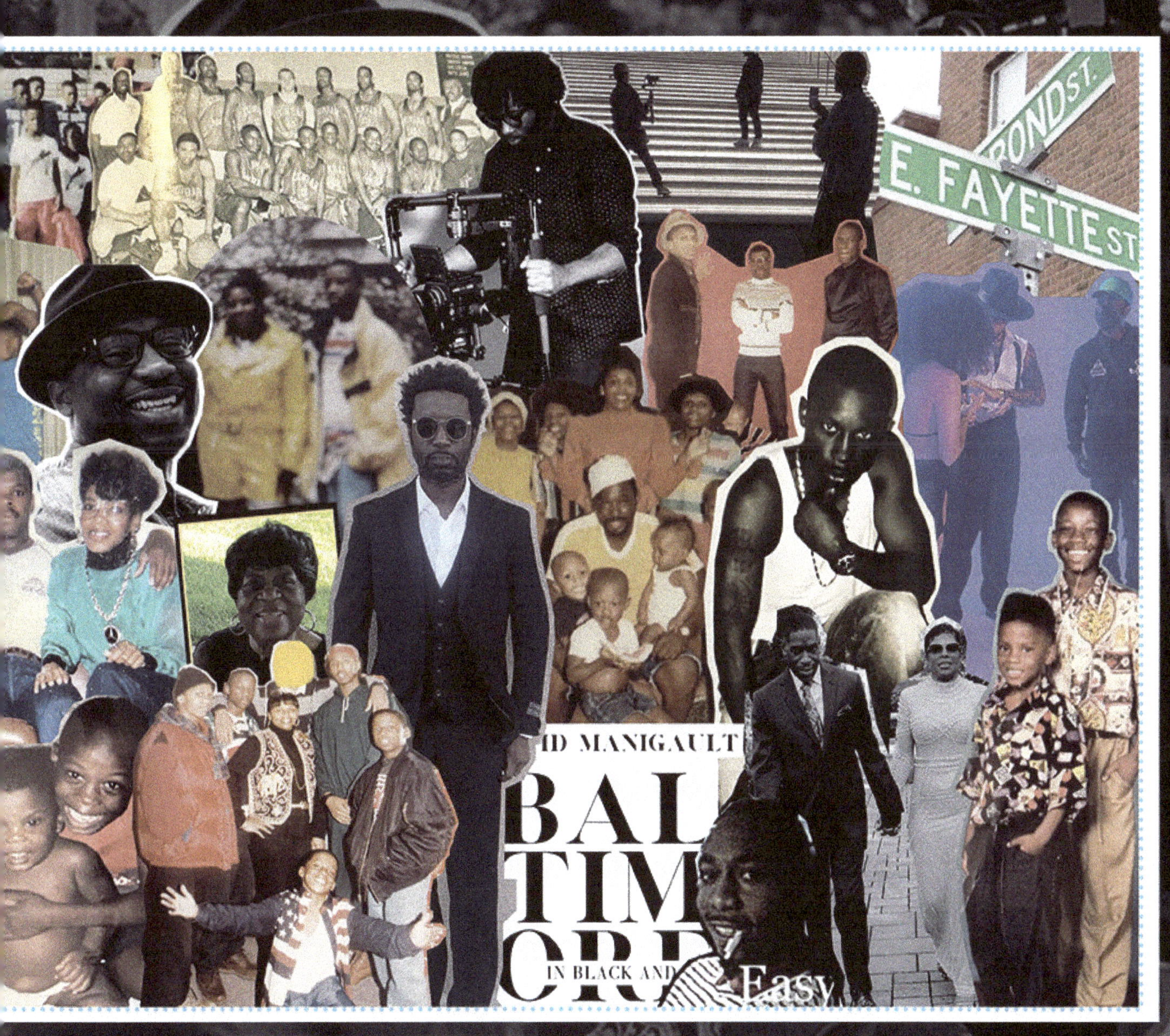

E. FAYETTE ST
ID MANIGAULT
BAL
TIM
IN BLACK AND
Easy

Library of Congress Cataloging-in-Publication Data.
ISBN: 978-0-578-83911-0

Printed in the United States of America.

Photographer David Manigault
Photo editing by Kamaria Jones
Cover Design by Destiny Productions
Book Production by Nikiea Redmond

INTRODUCTION

This coffee table book, "Black Body, Baltimore in Black and White" captured some of the most prolific images from the Baltimore uprisings of 2015, East vs West peace rally, and everyday life in Baltimore on the ground level. The east and west stop the violence rally that was captured show community leadership, resilience and unity from the people of Baltimore city followed by the death of Freddy Gray in police custody. Through the lens of renowned filmmaker and photographer David Manigault, this photo series celebrates black Baltimore while taking you on a journey through the city's tumultuous vibrant culture, and its resilient spirit. From the streets of Baltimore, this book captures the beauty and complexity of a city that has seen both tragedy and triumph. It is a testament to the strength of the people of Baltimore and a reminder of the power of collective action.

Manigault serves as an inspiration to others from similar backgrounds who may be facing similar obstacles, showing that with perseverance and hard work, anyone can overcome their circumstances and achieve their dreams. Through his photographs, Manigault paints a vivid picture of the city's past, present, and future, and the hope that lies within.

Understanding what has happened in the past stokes creative energy, giving photographers today the stimulus for art tomorrow. Manigault believes looking back over photography's past, our eyes are firmly on the expanding horizons of photography's future.

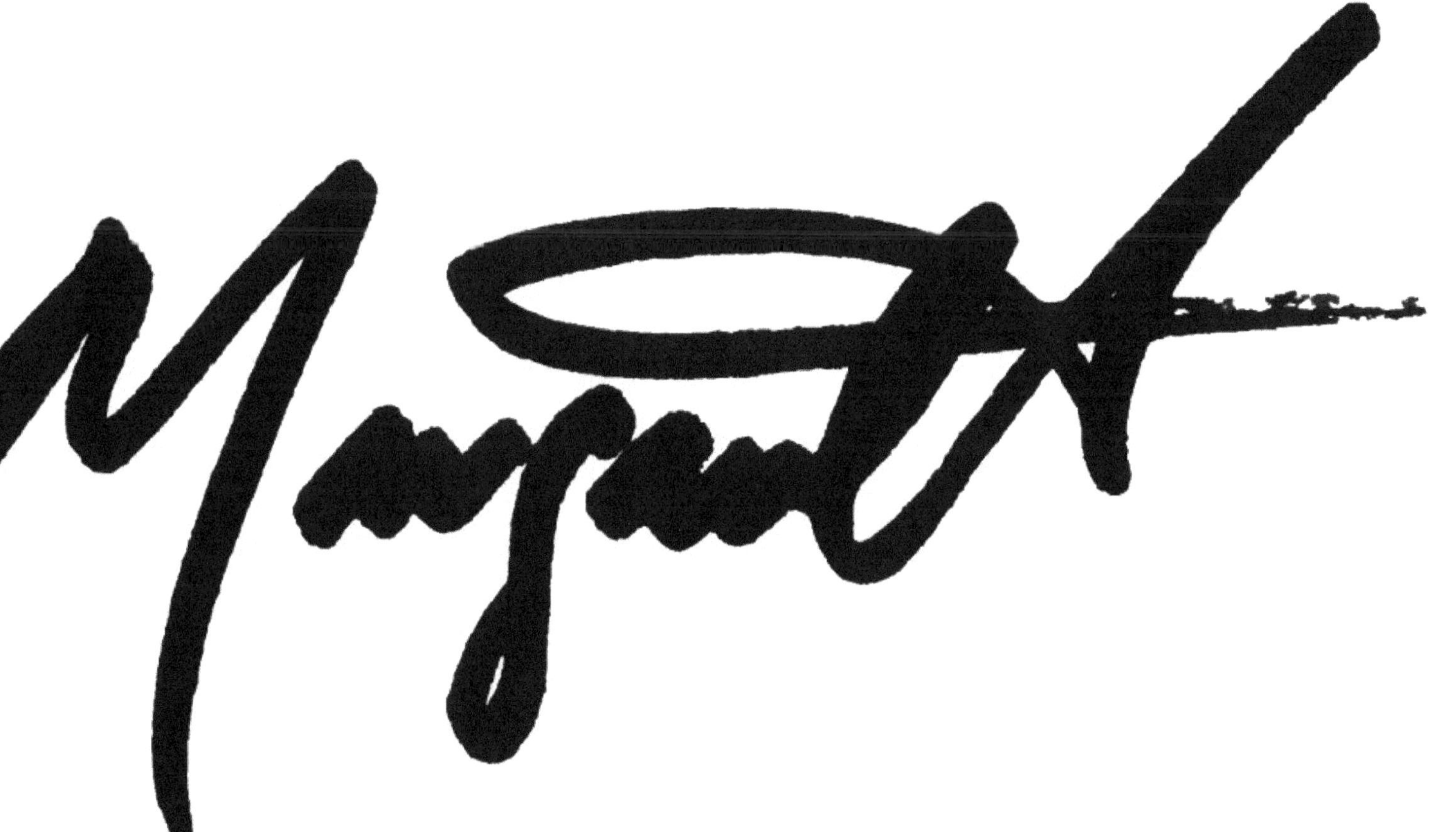

"BLACK BODY"

BALTIMORE IN BLACK AND WHITE

DAVID MANIGAULT

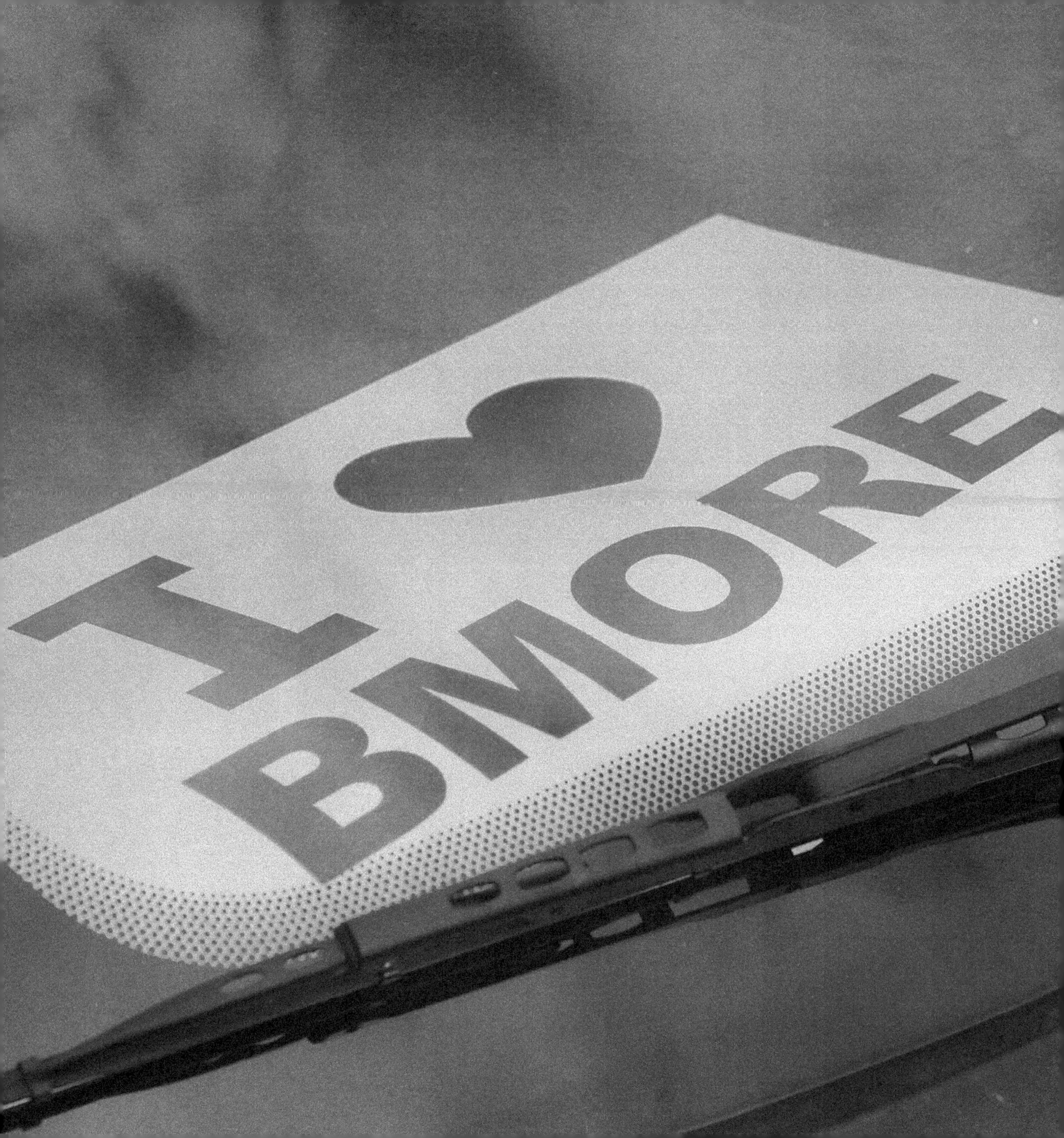
I
BMORE

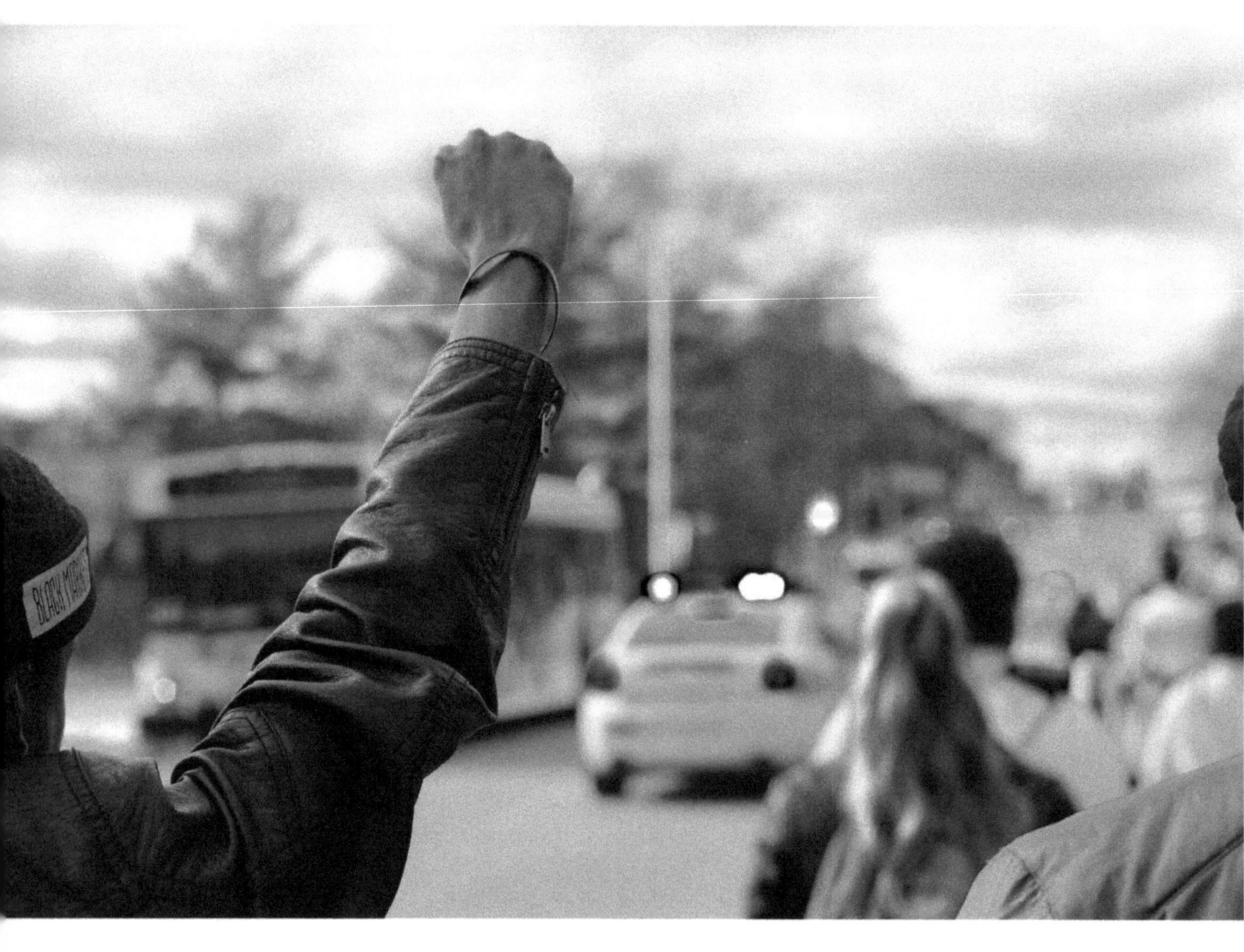
BLACK

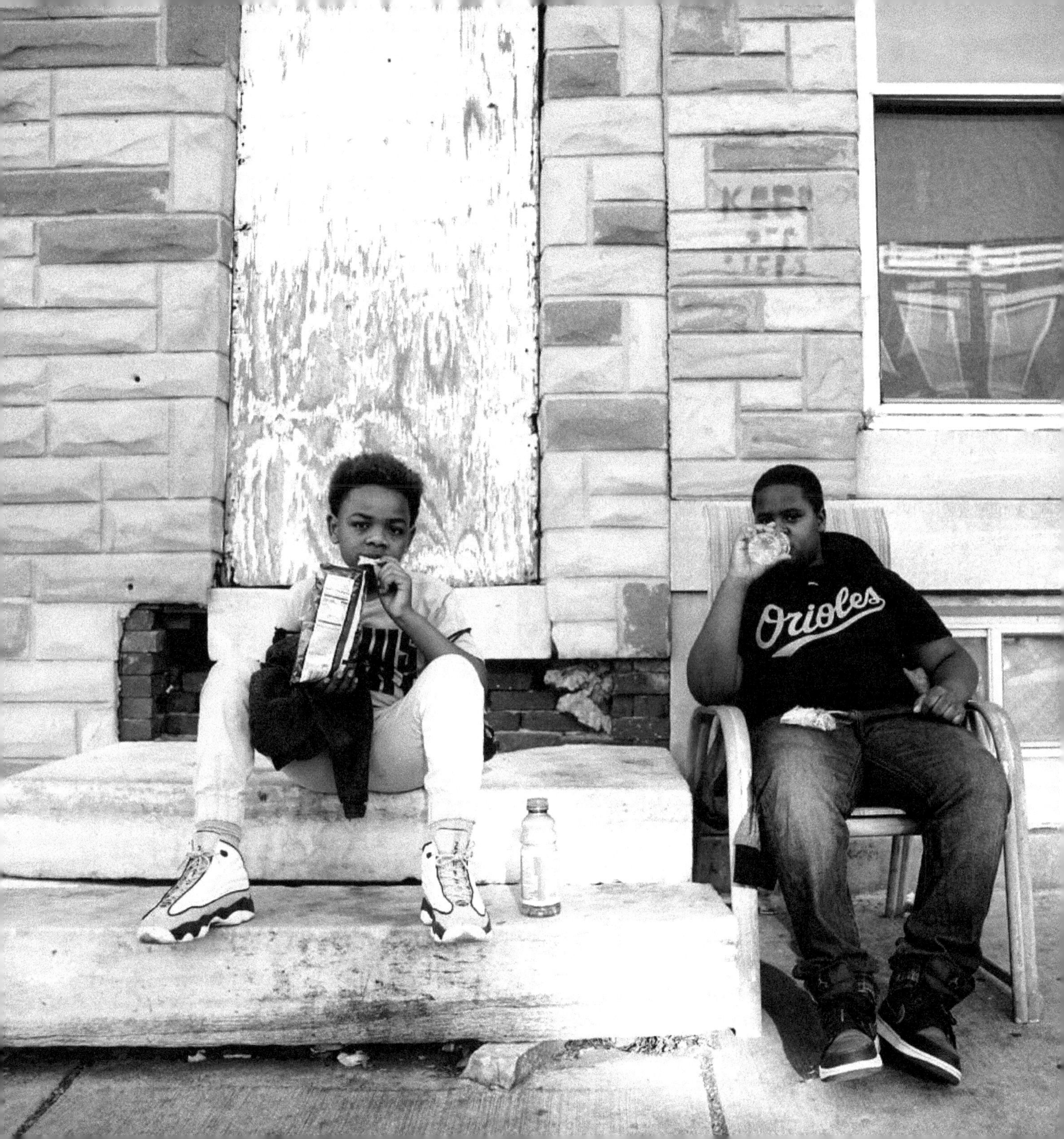
Orioles

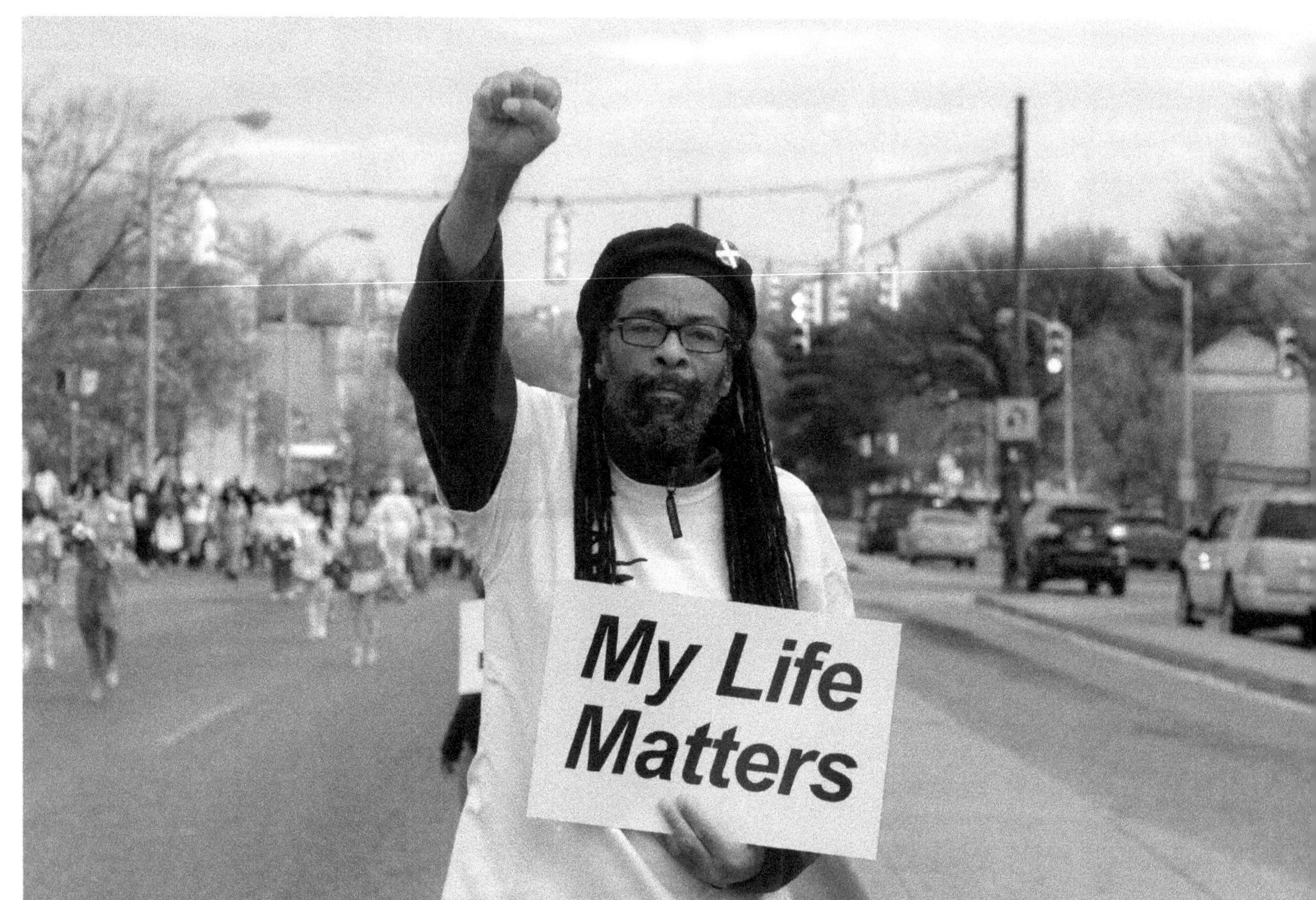
My Life
Matters

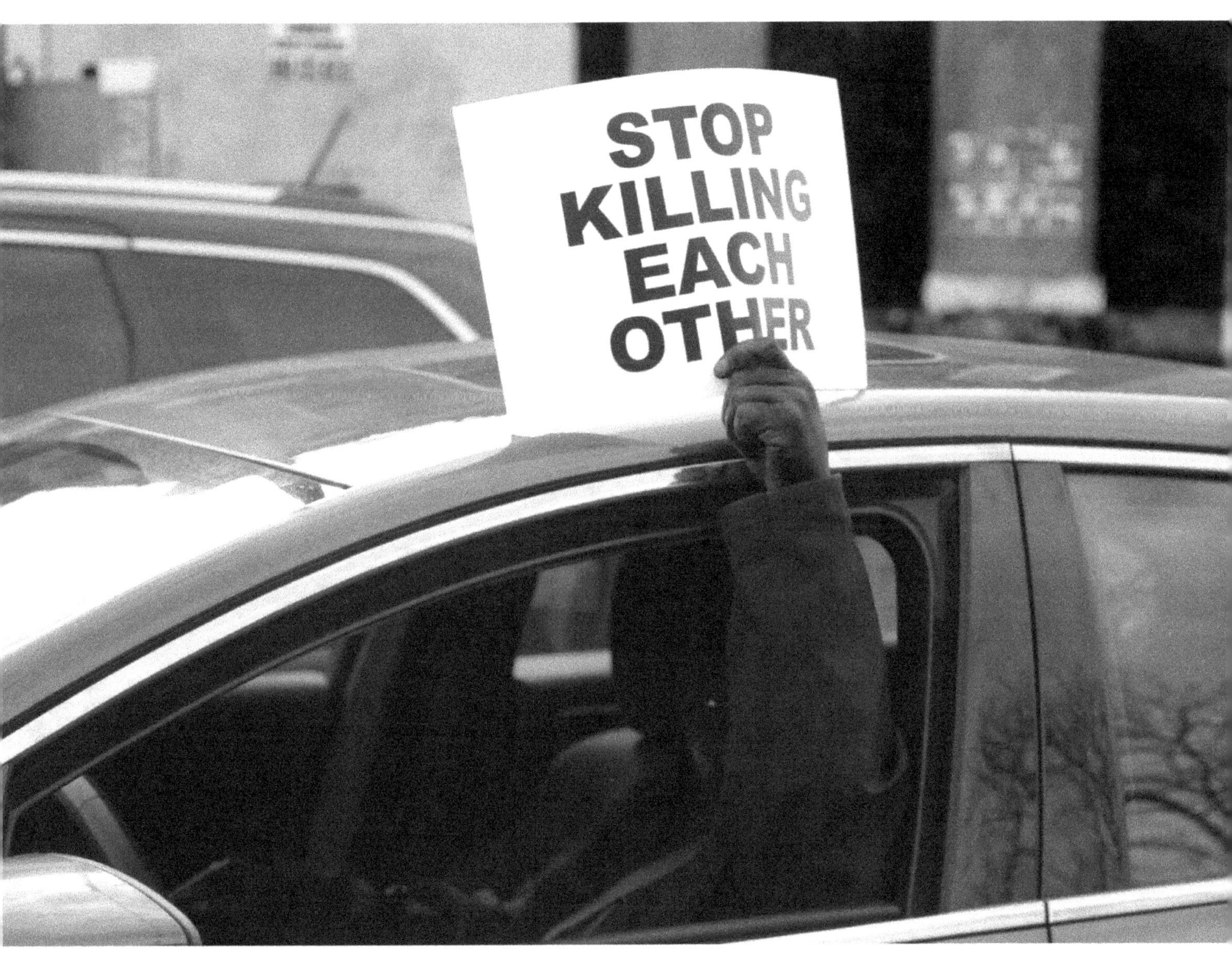
STOP
KILLING
EACH
OTHER

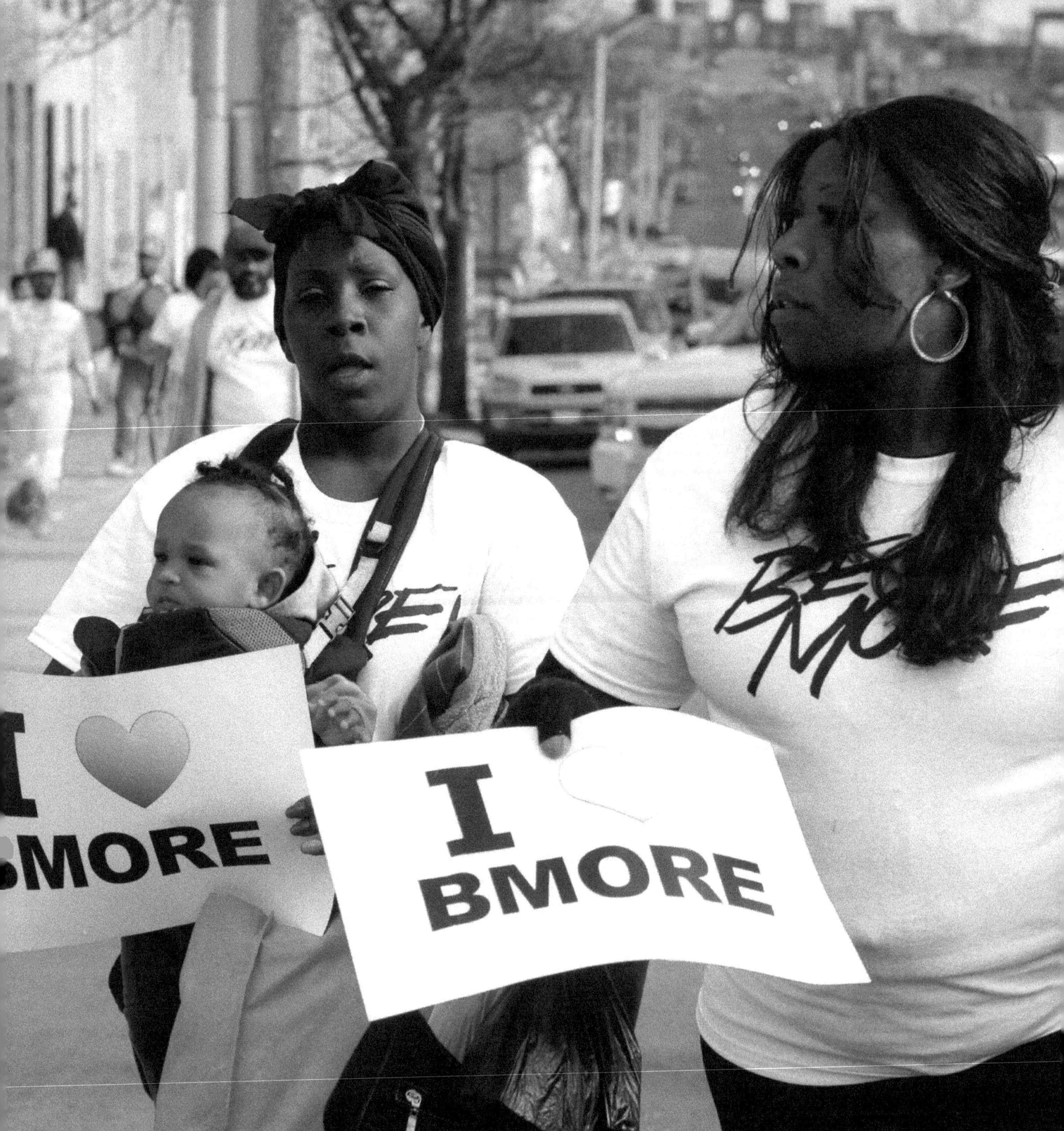
I
MORE
I
BMORE

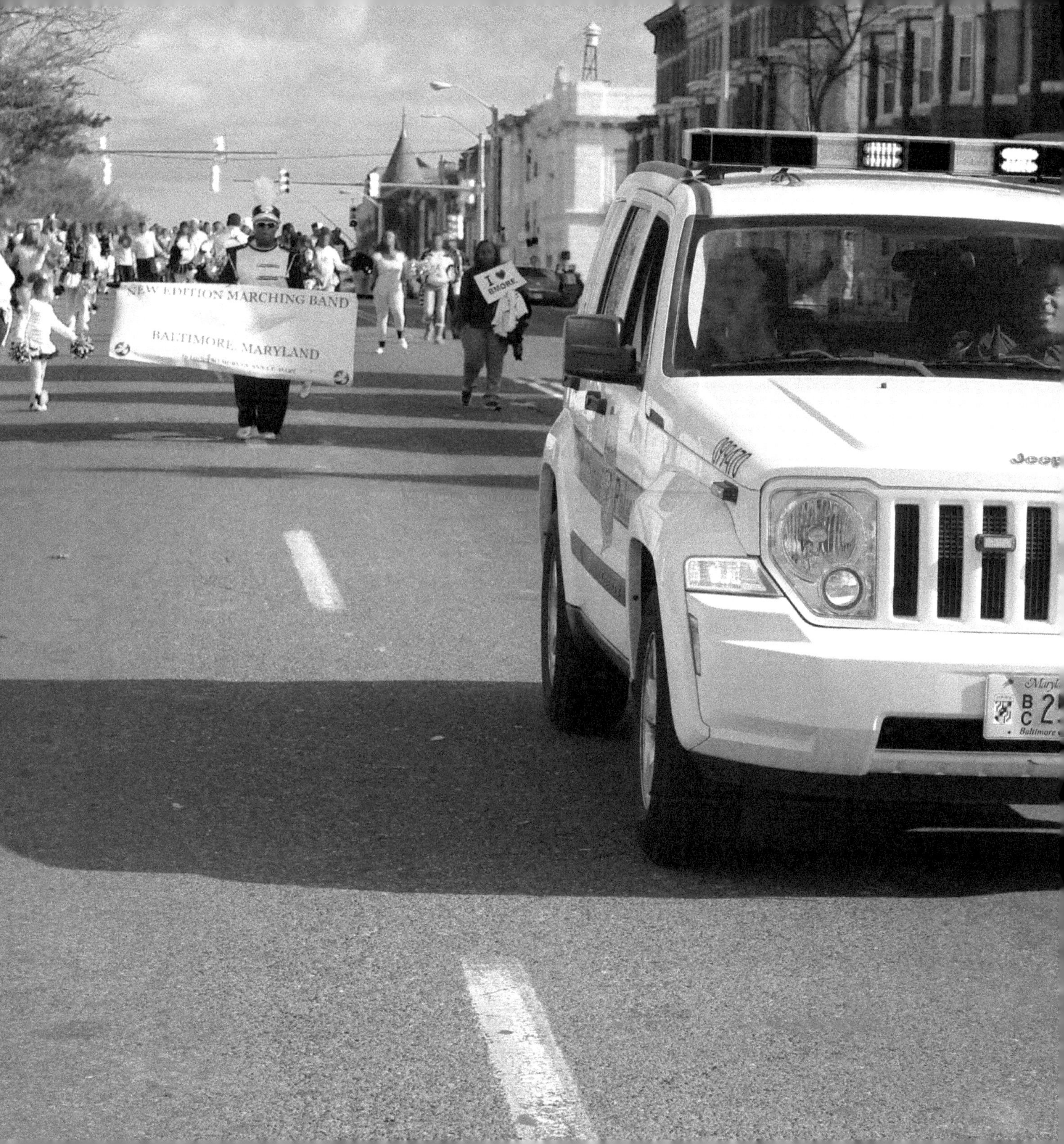
NEW EDITION MARCHING BAND
BALTIMORE, MARYLAND
I ♥ BMORE
Jeep

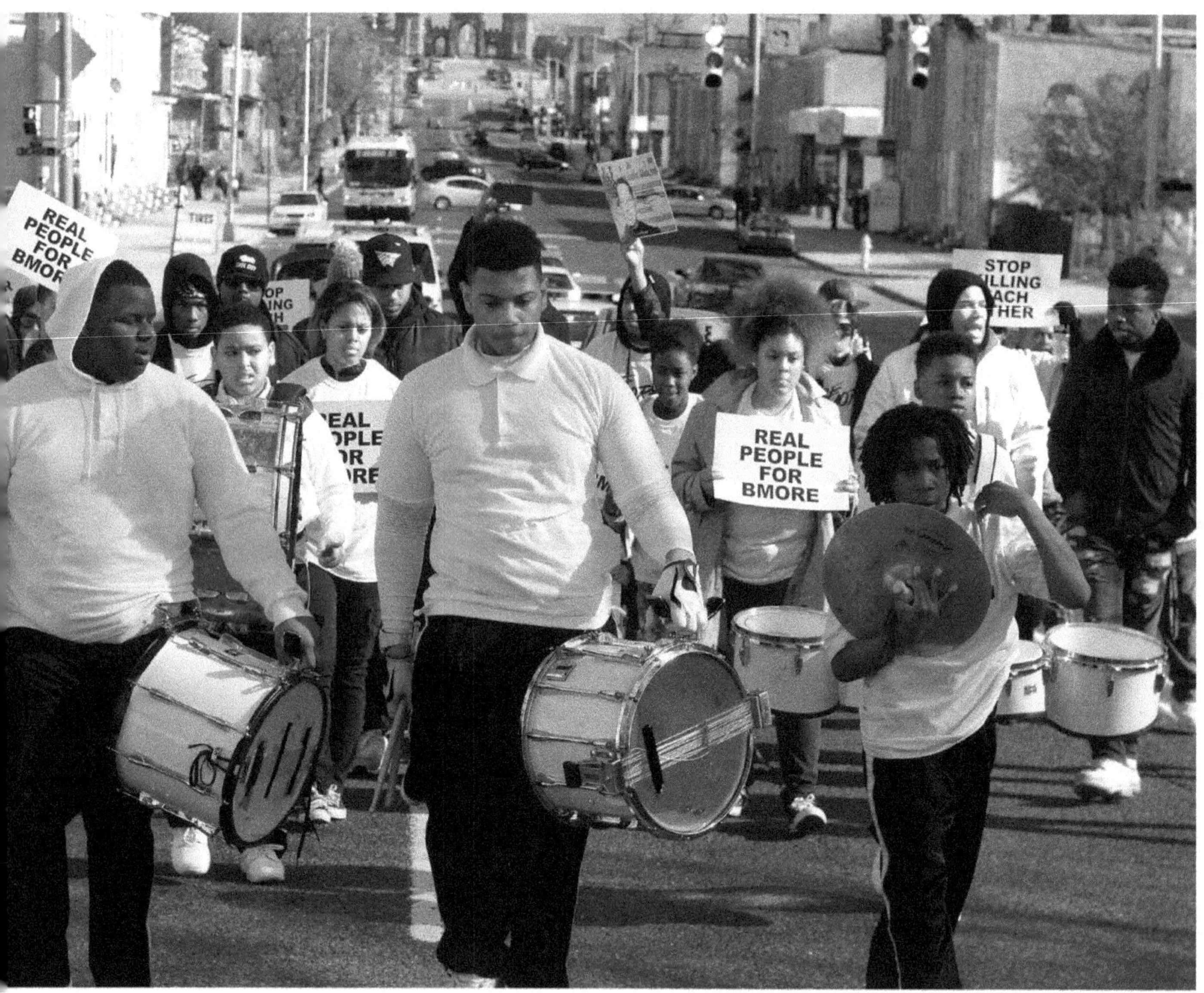
REAL PEOPLE FOR BMORE
STOP KILLING EACH OTHER
REAL PEOPLE FOR BMORE

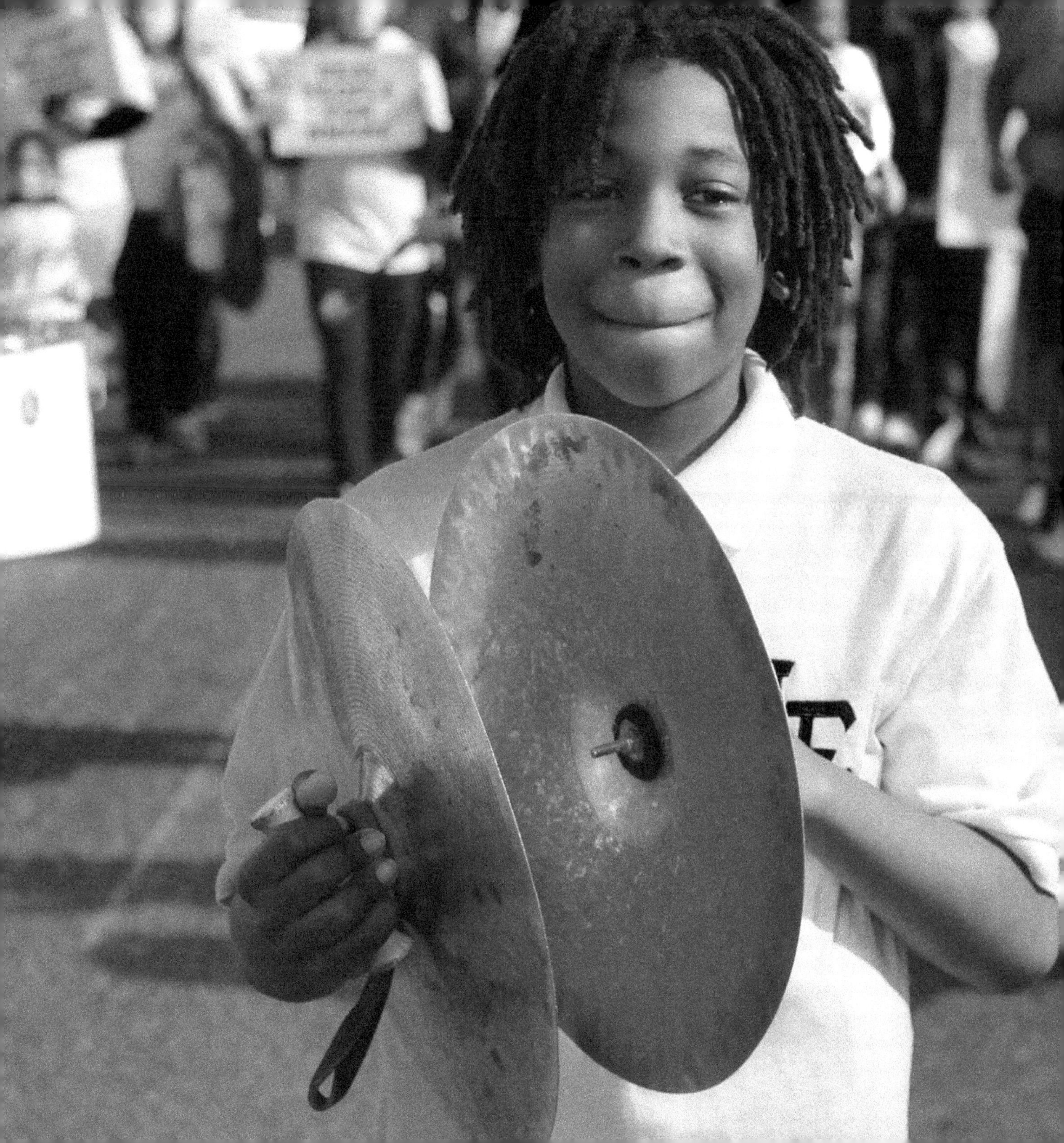

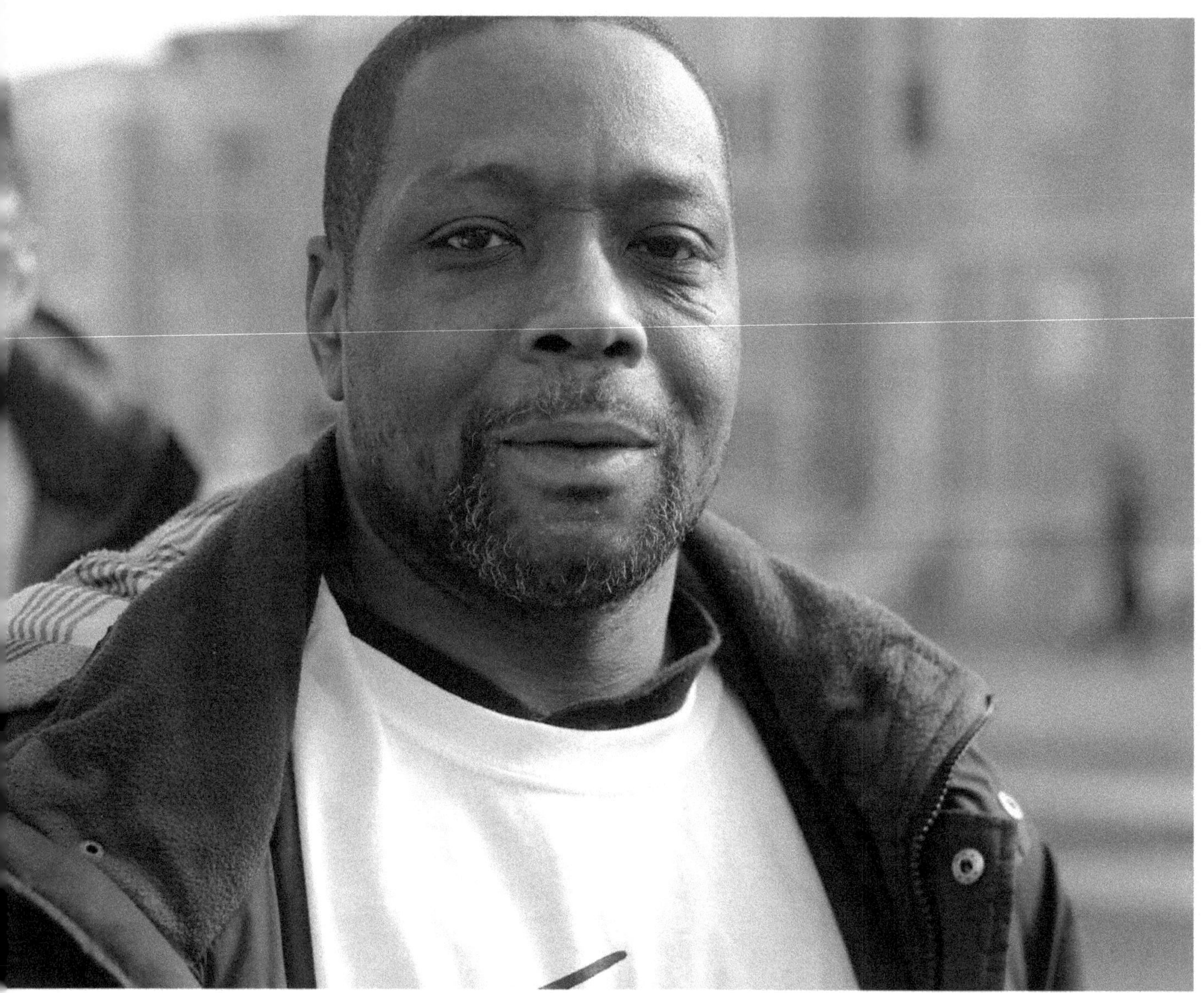

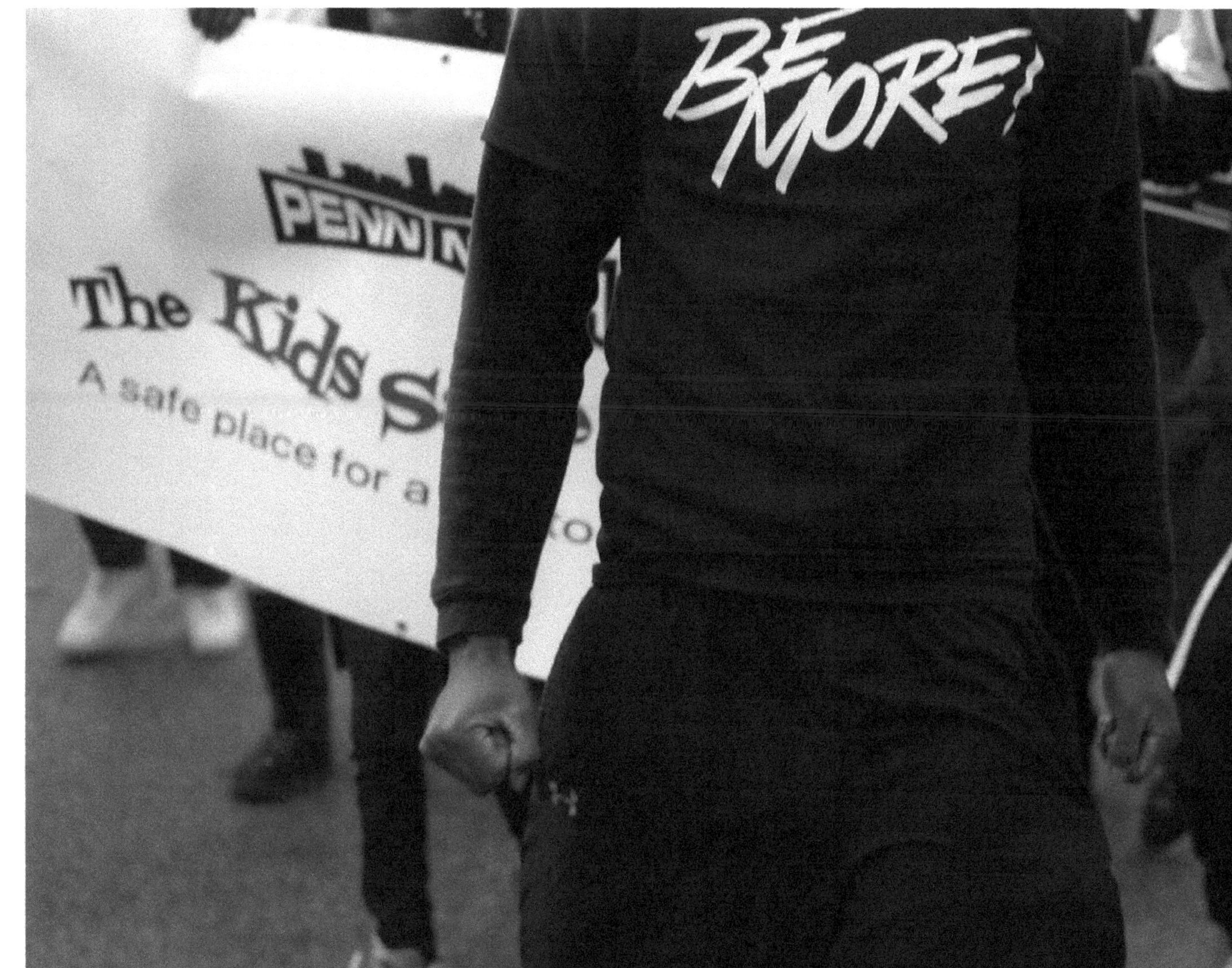

BE MORE
PENN
The Kids
A safe place for a

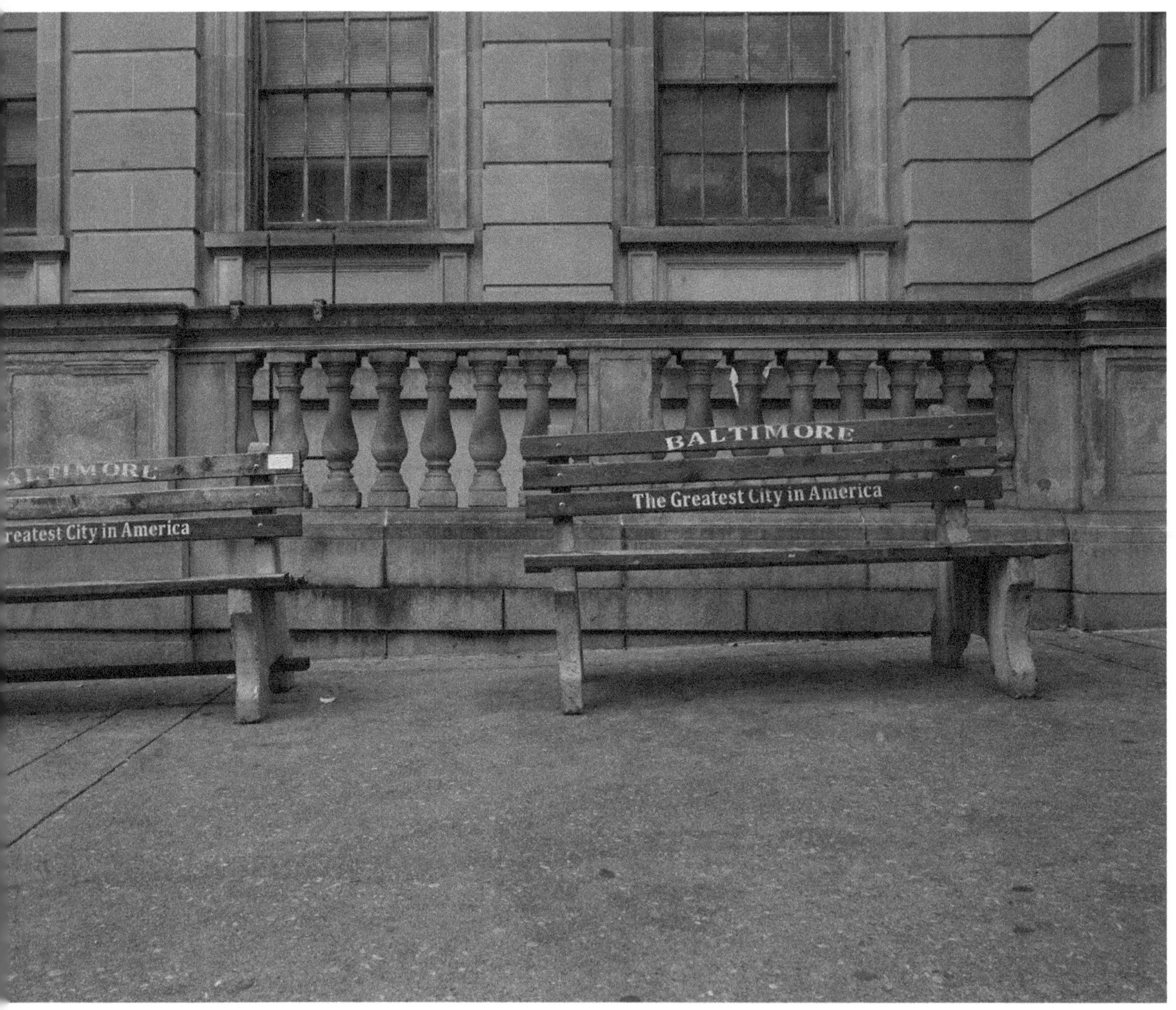
BALTIMORE
The Greatest City in America
reatest City in America

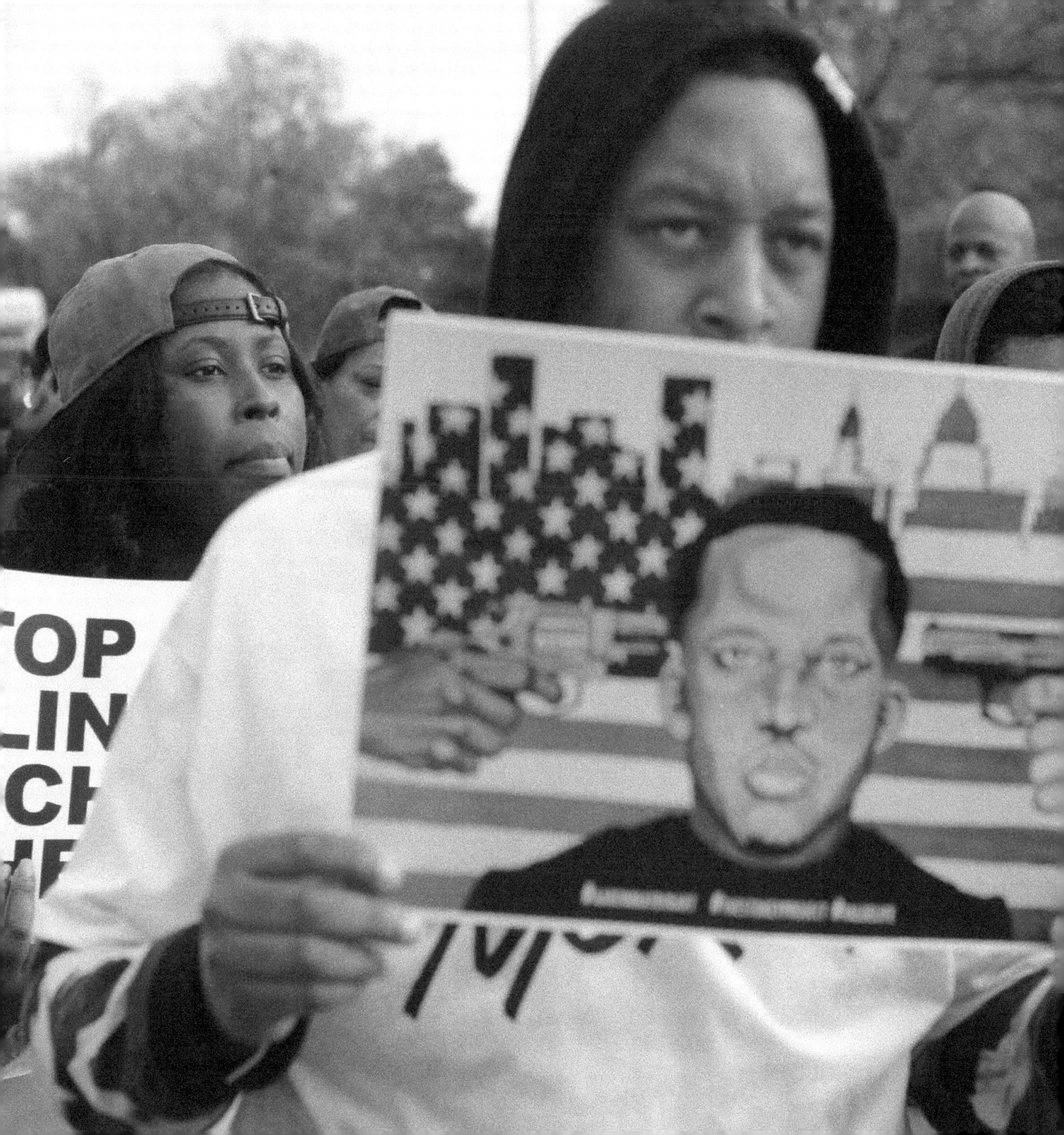

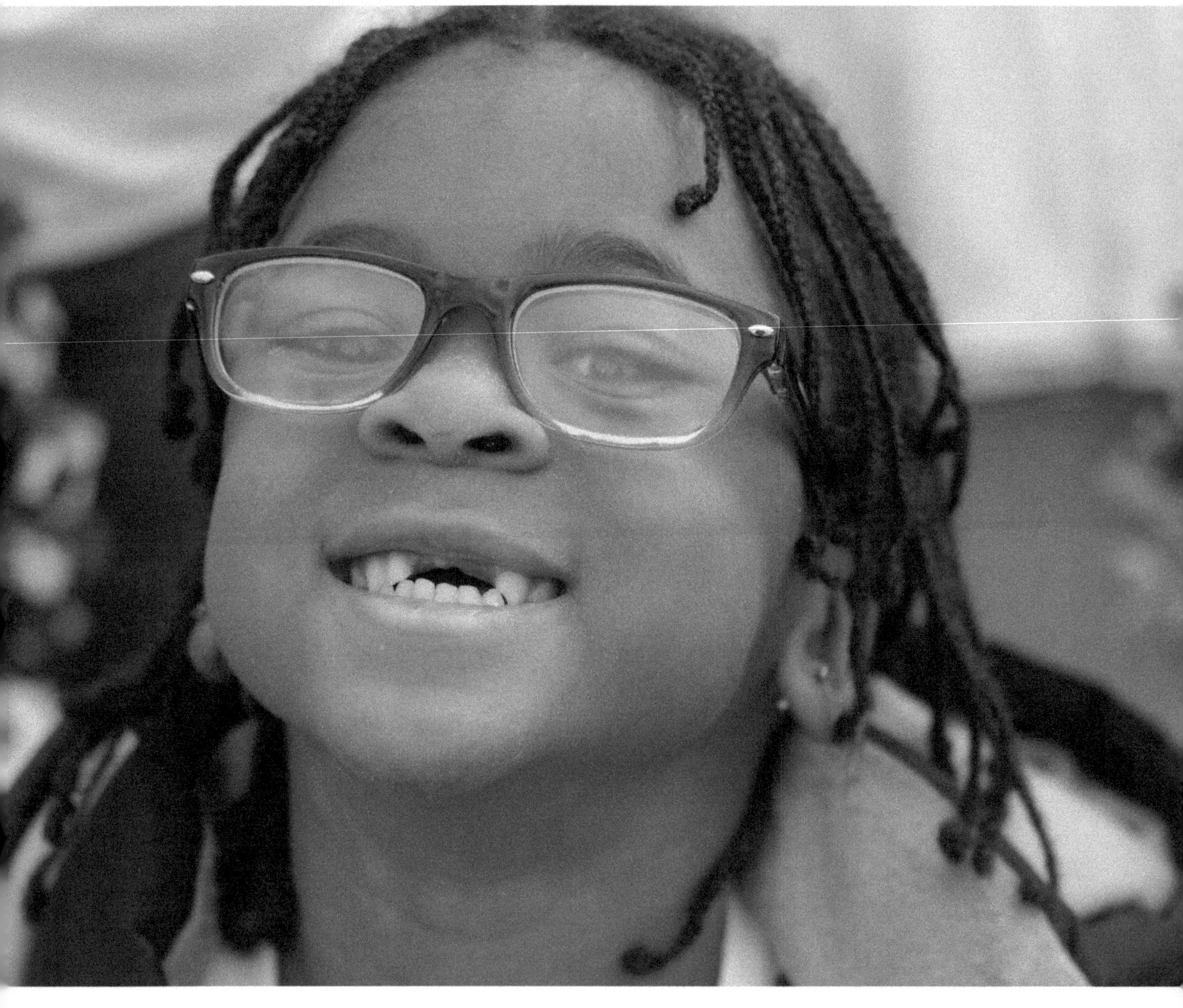

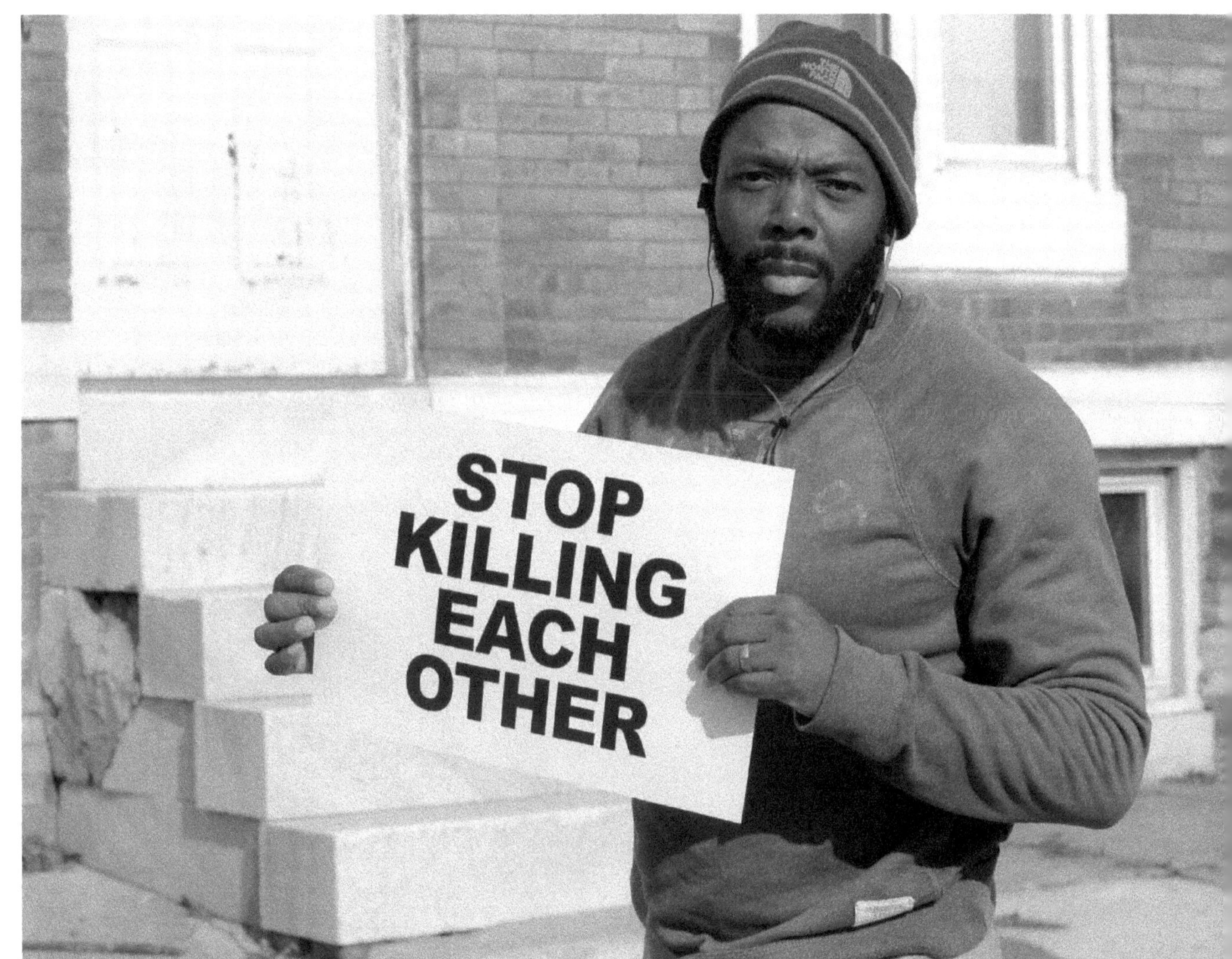
STOP
KILLING
EACH
OTHER

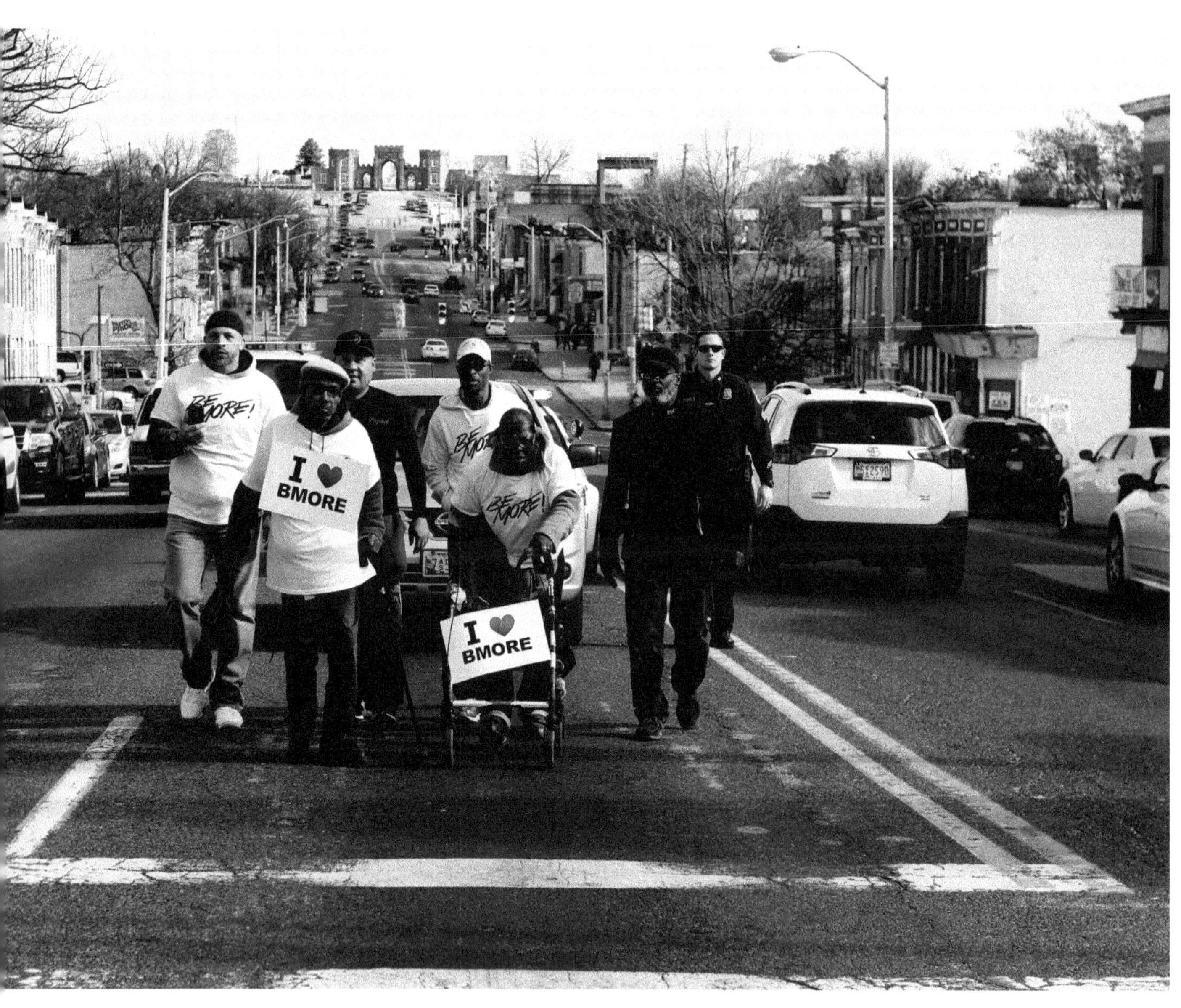
BE MORE!
I BMORE
BE MORE
I BMORE
BE MORE!
I BMORE

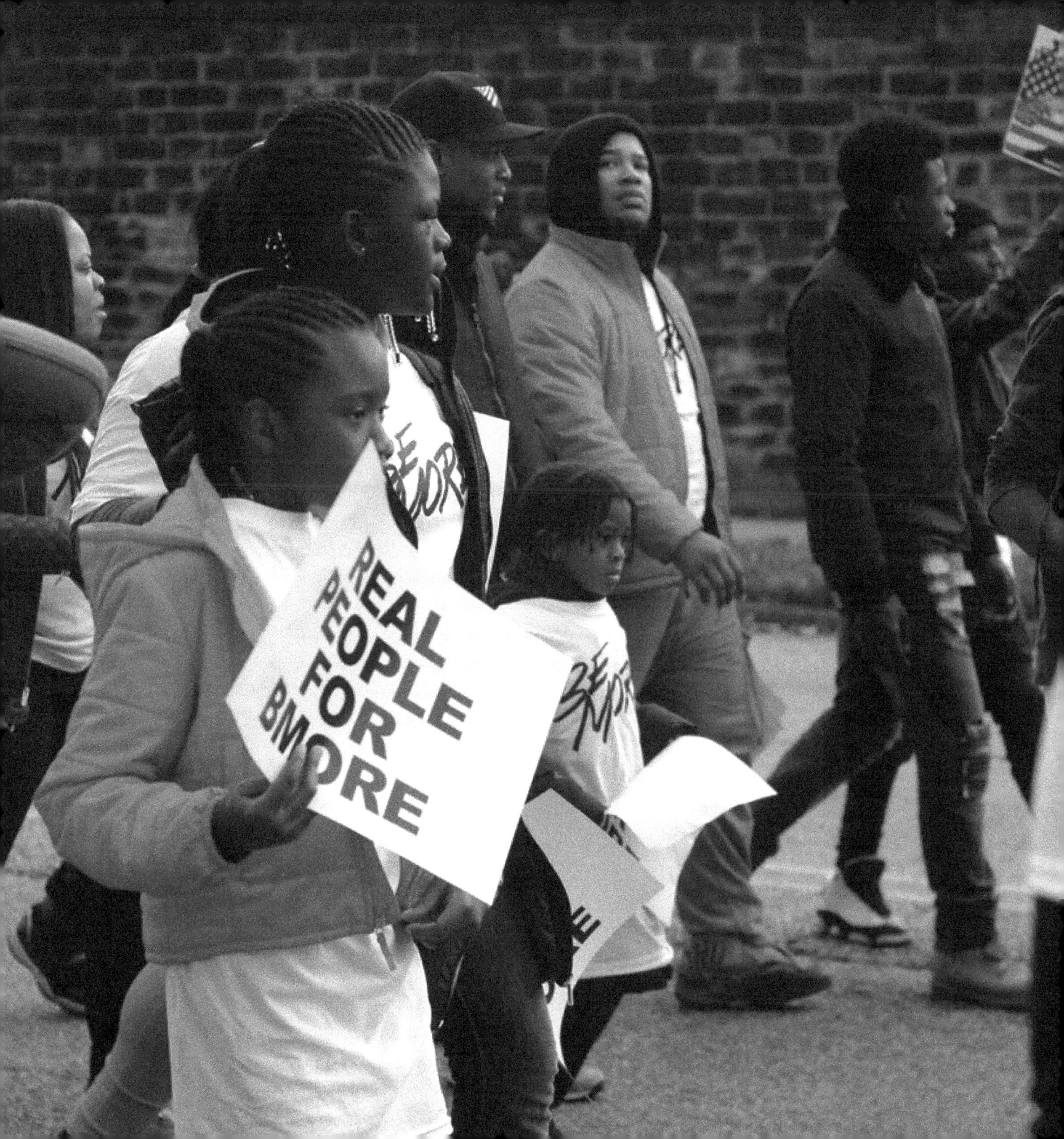
REAL
PEOPLE
FOR
BMORE

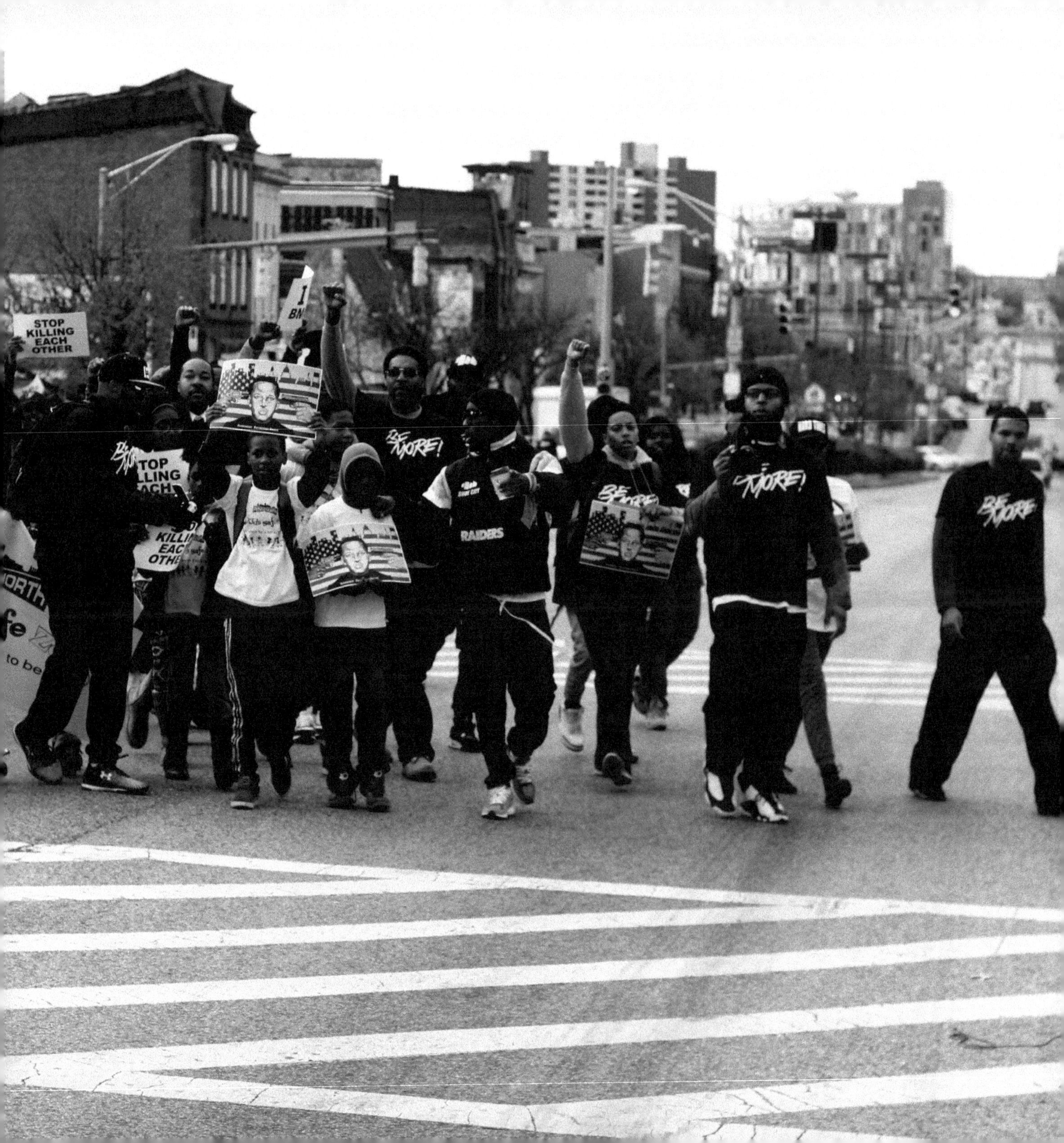

STOP KILLING EACH OTHER
STOP KILLING EACH
STOP KILLING EACH OTHER
BE MORE!
BE MORE!
RAIDERS
BE MORE!
BE MORE!

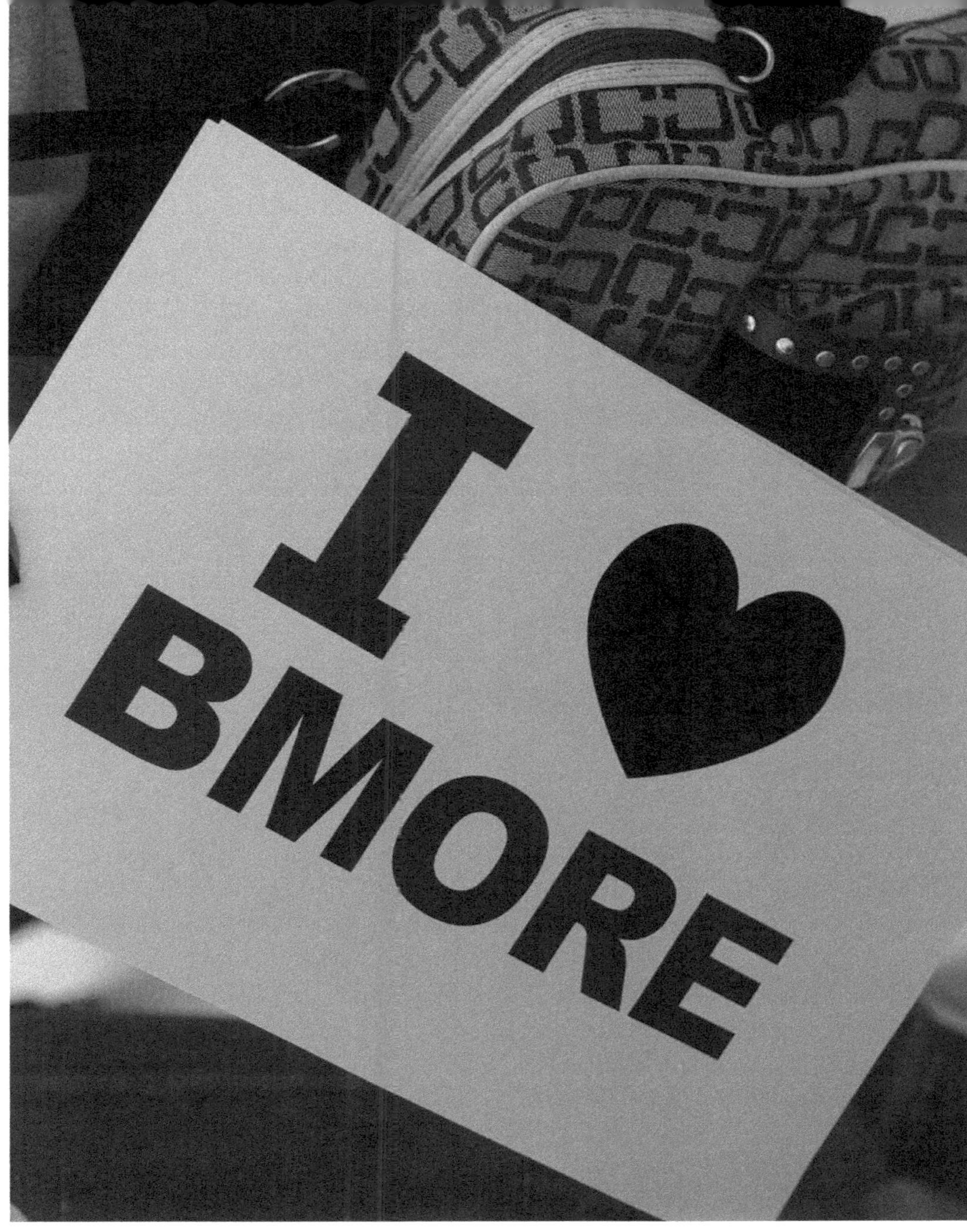
I
BMORE

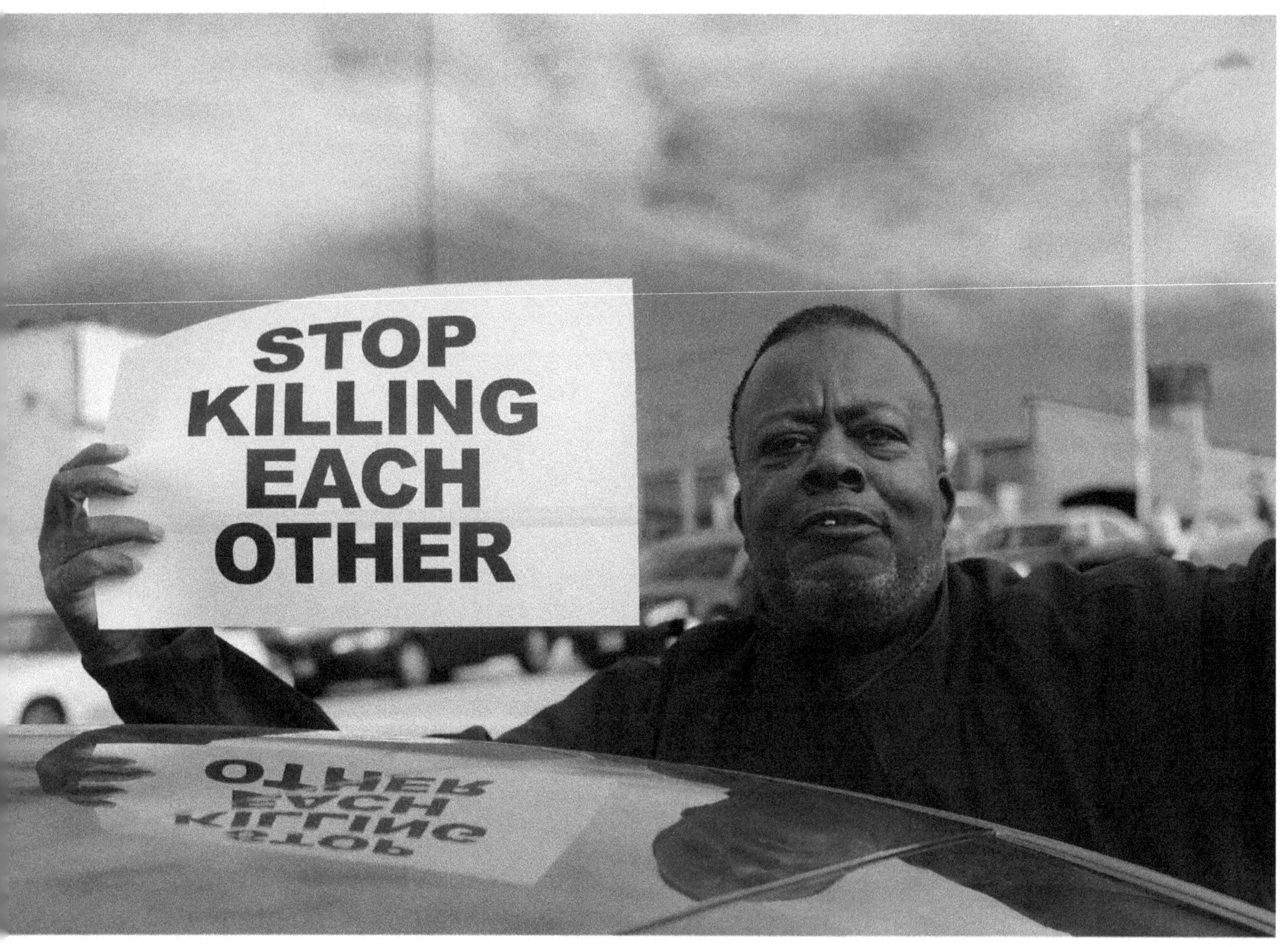
STOP
KILLING
EACH
OTHER

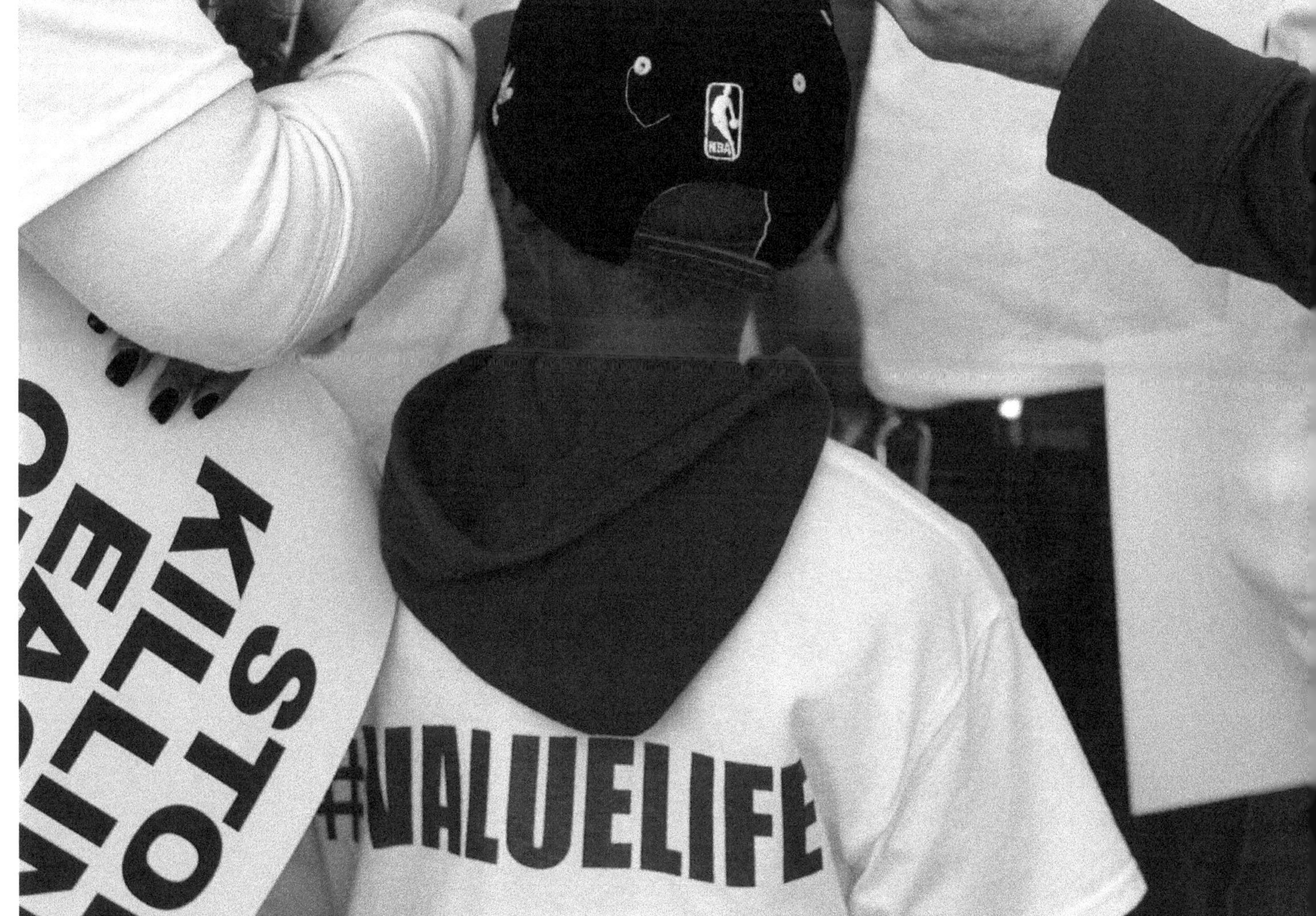
NBA
#VALUELIFE
THE

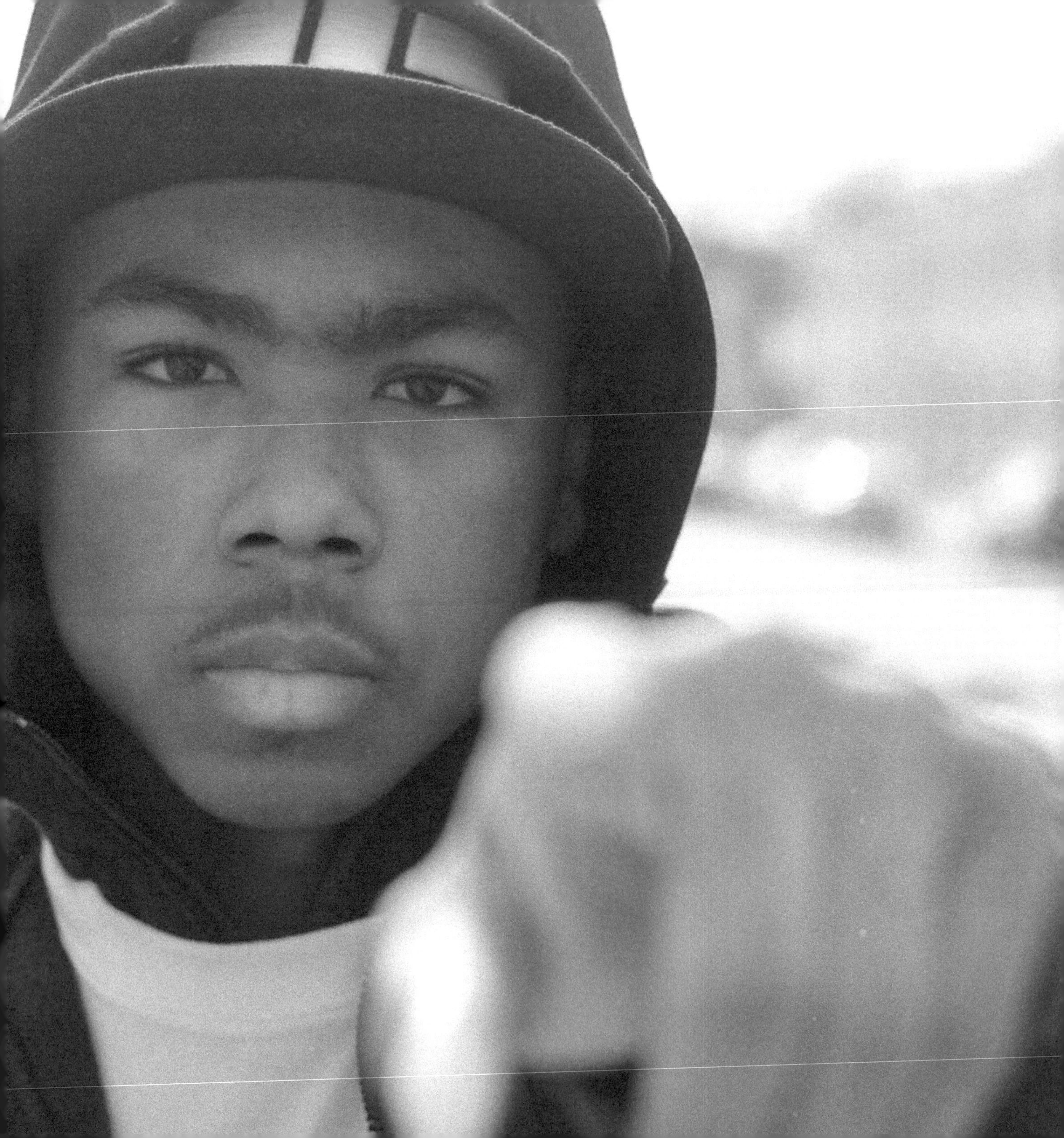

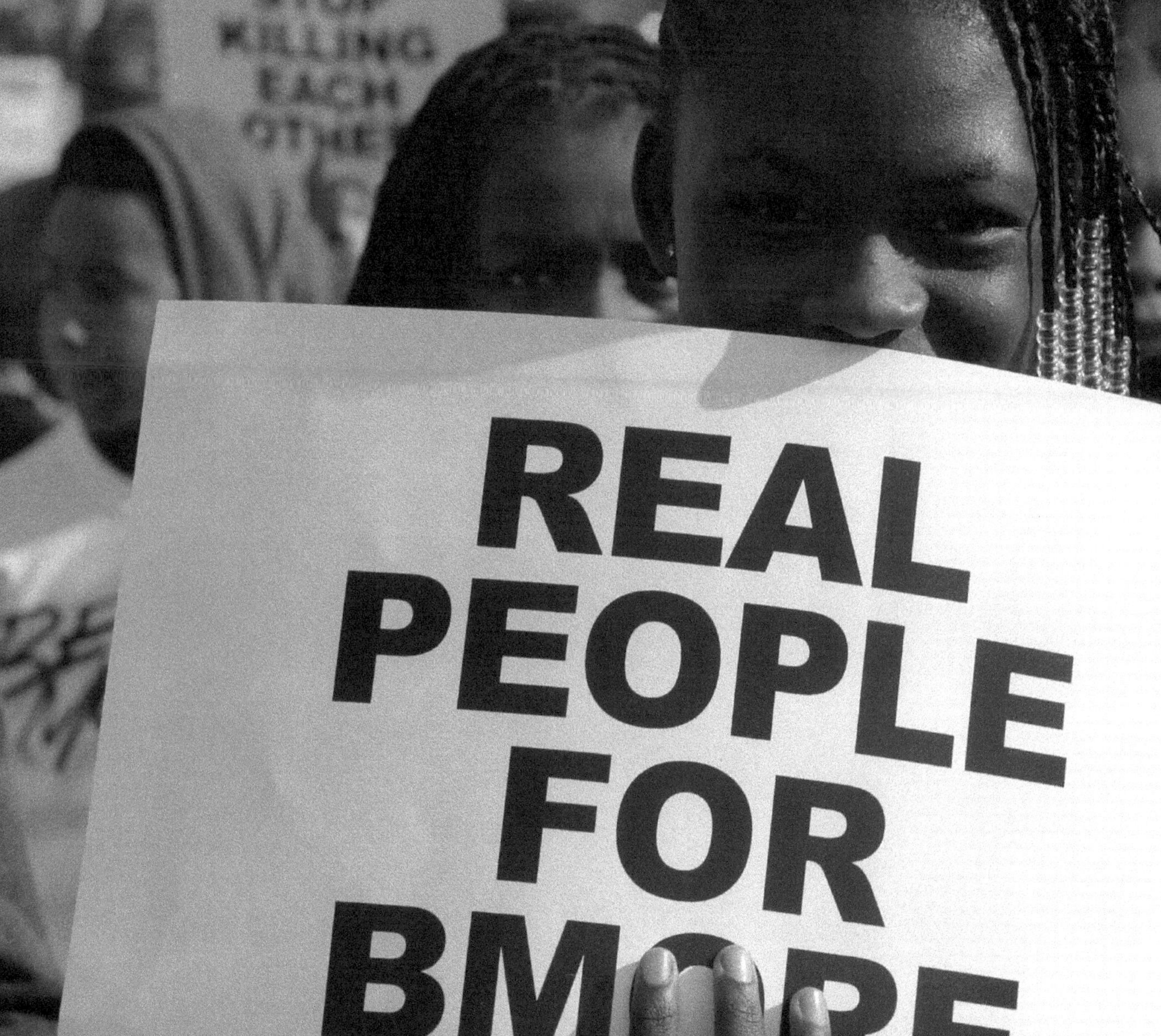
STOP
KILLING
EACH
REAL
PEOPLE
FOR
BMORE

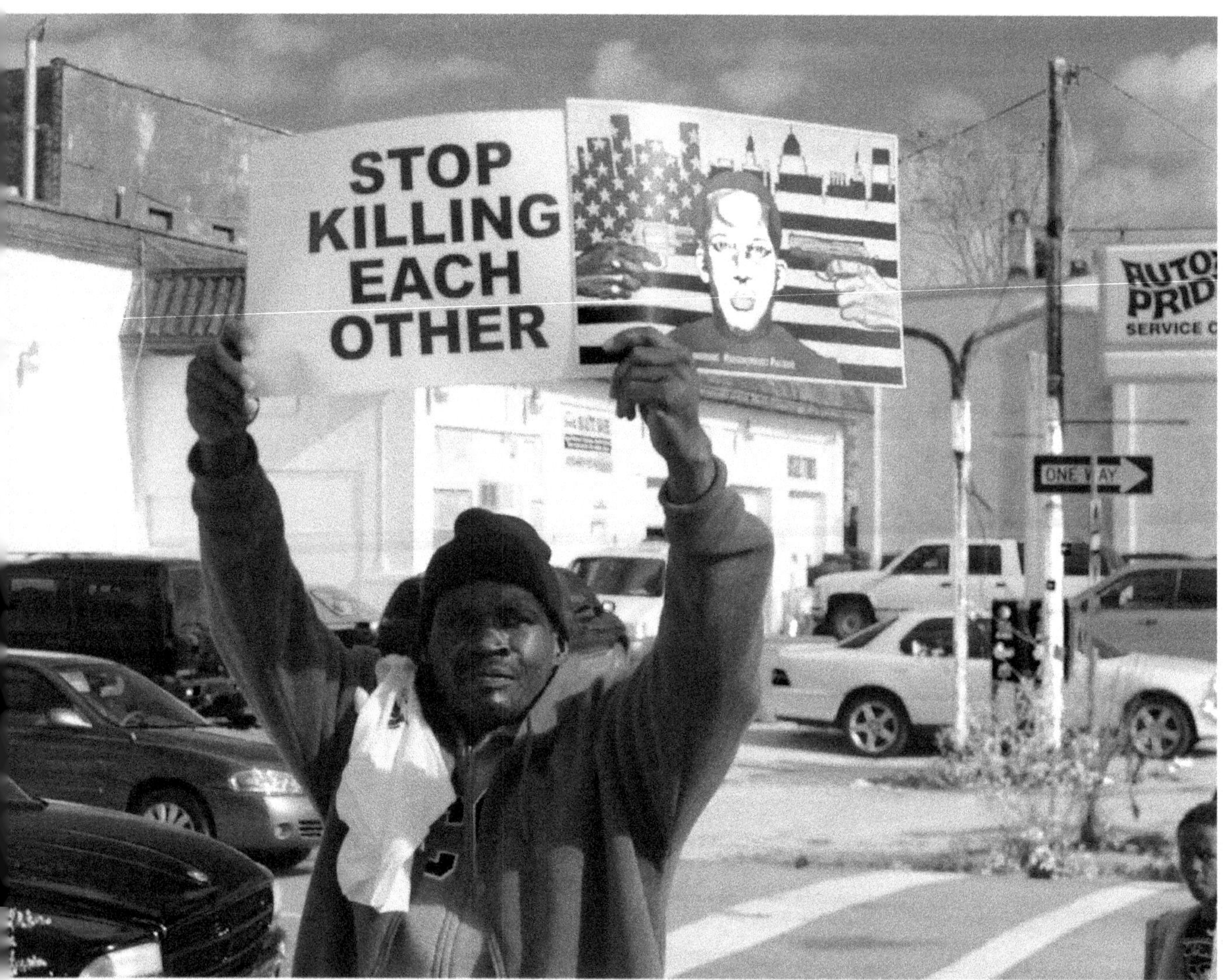
STOP
KILLING
EACH
OTHER
ONE WAY

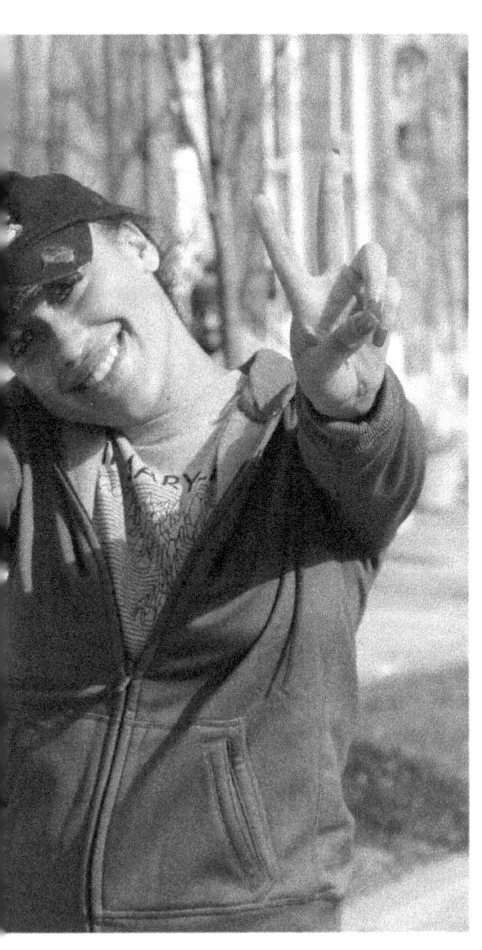

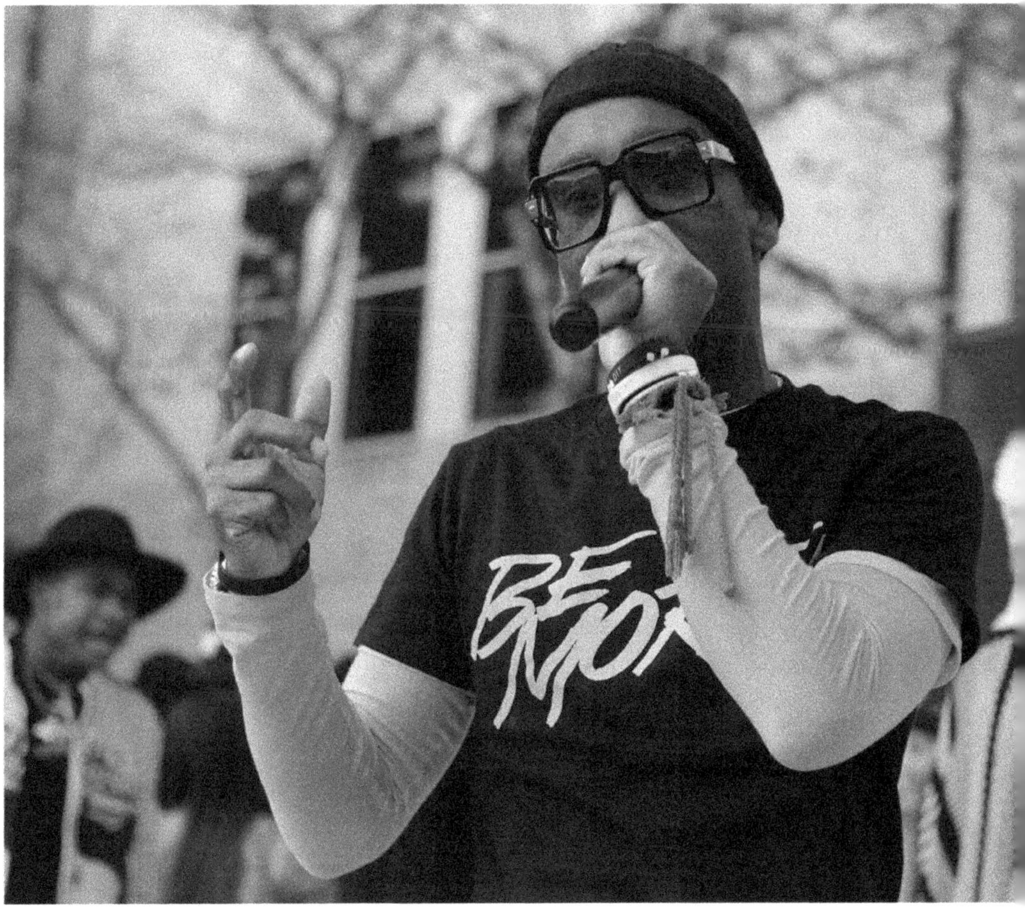

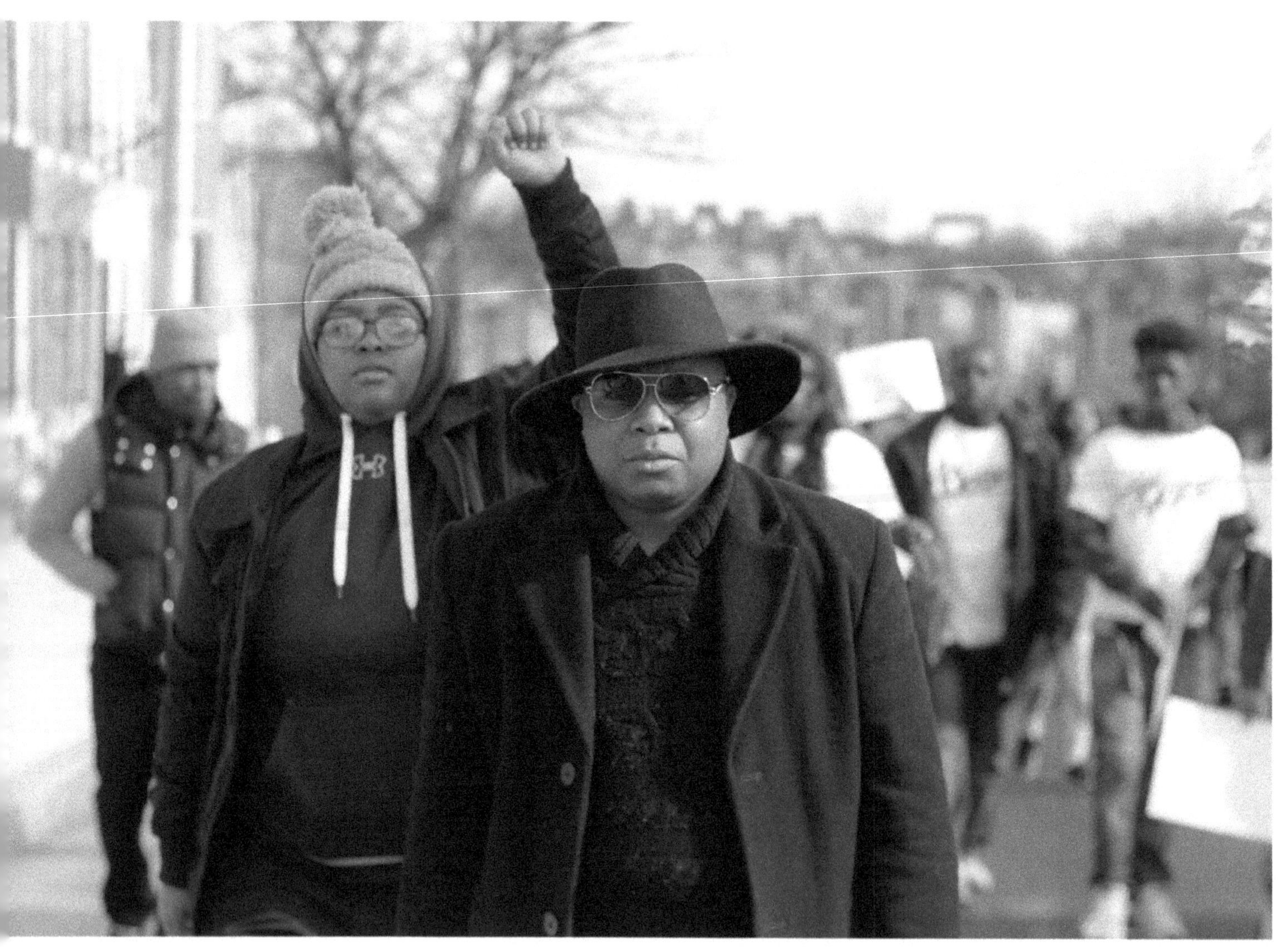

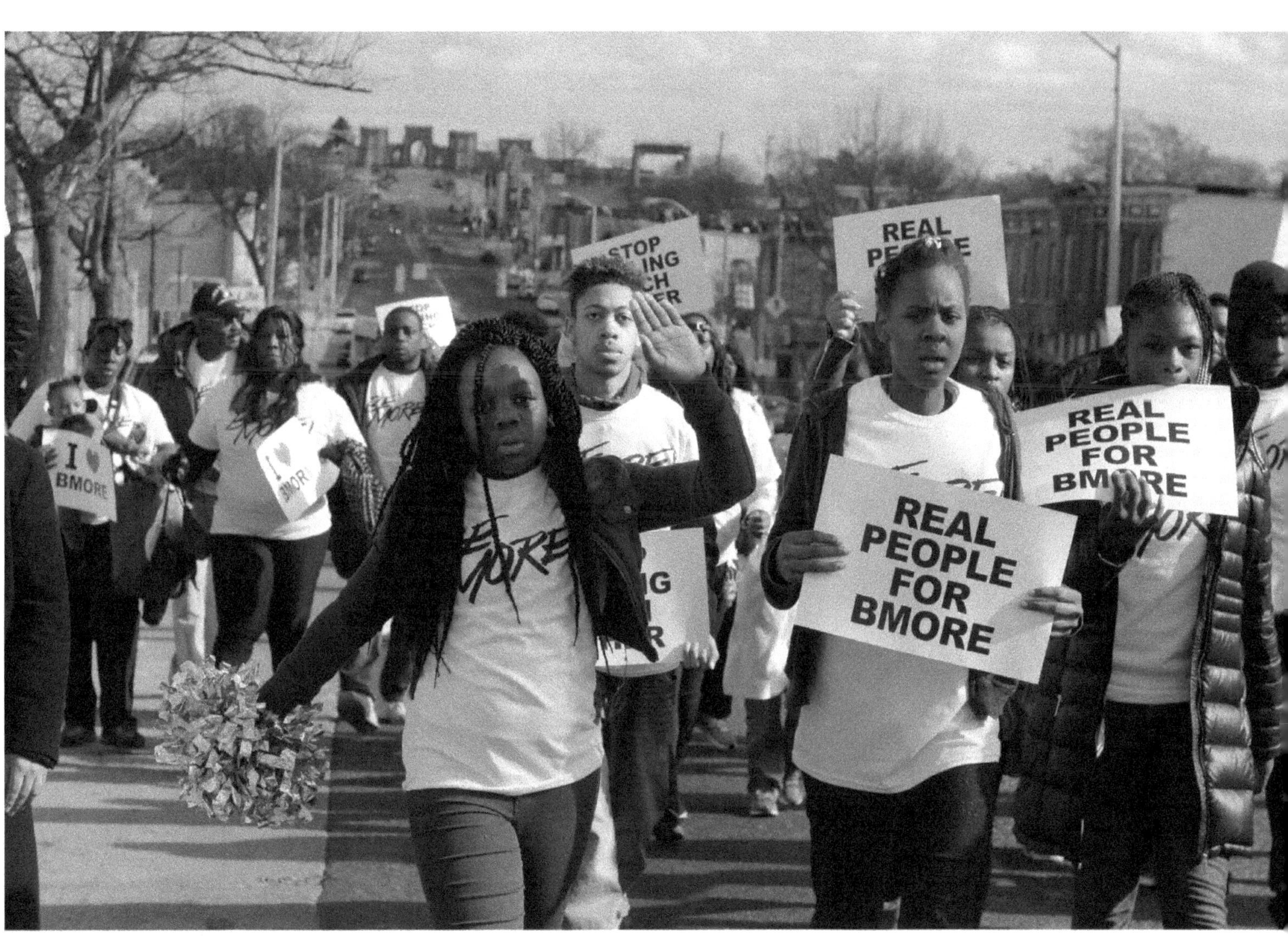
REAL PEOPLE FOR BMORE
REAL PEOPLE FOR BMORE
I ♥ BMORE

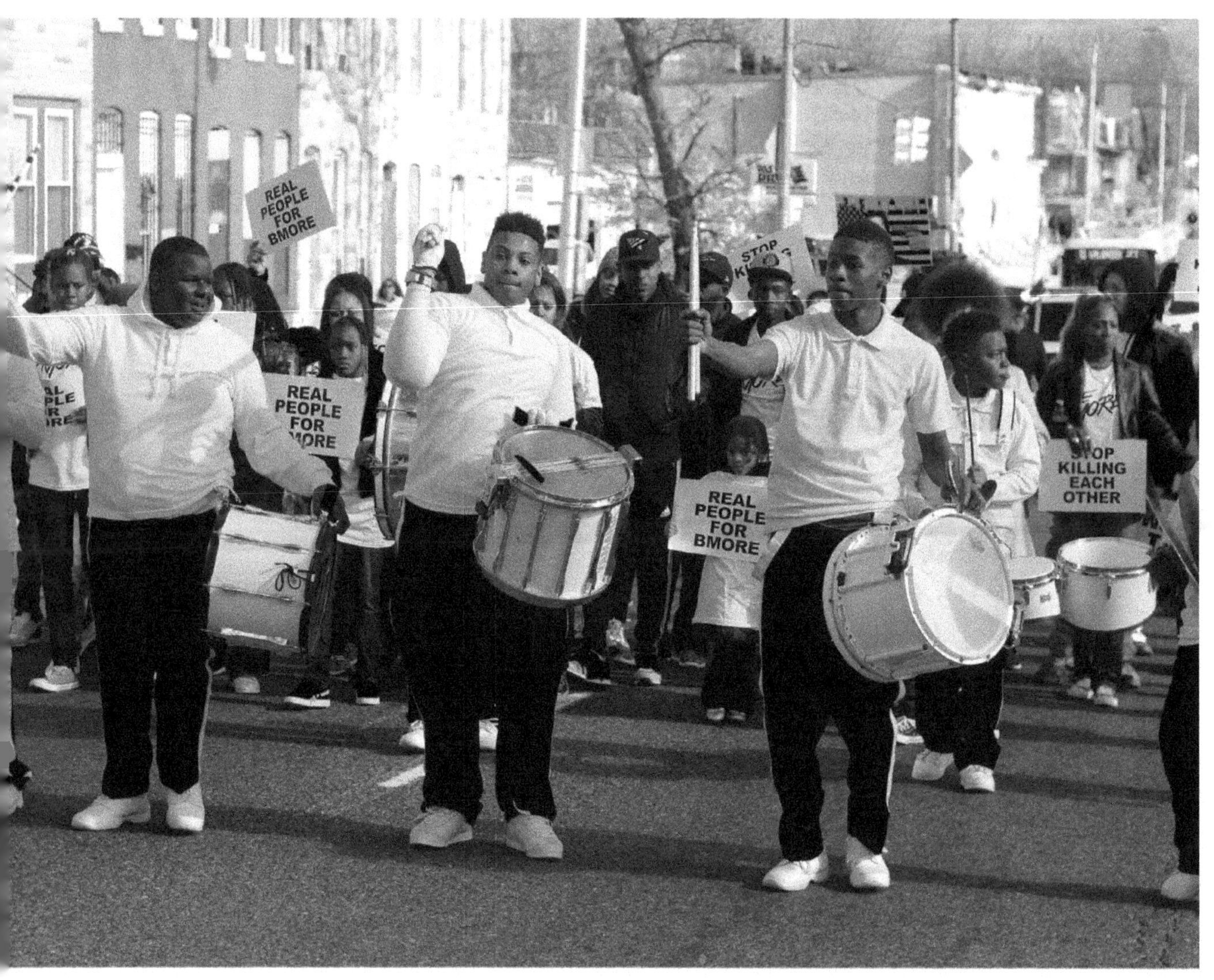
REAL PEOPLE FOR BMORE
REAL PEOPLE FOR BMORE
REAL PEOPLE FOR BMORE
STOP KILLING EACH OTHER

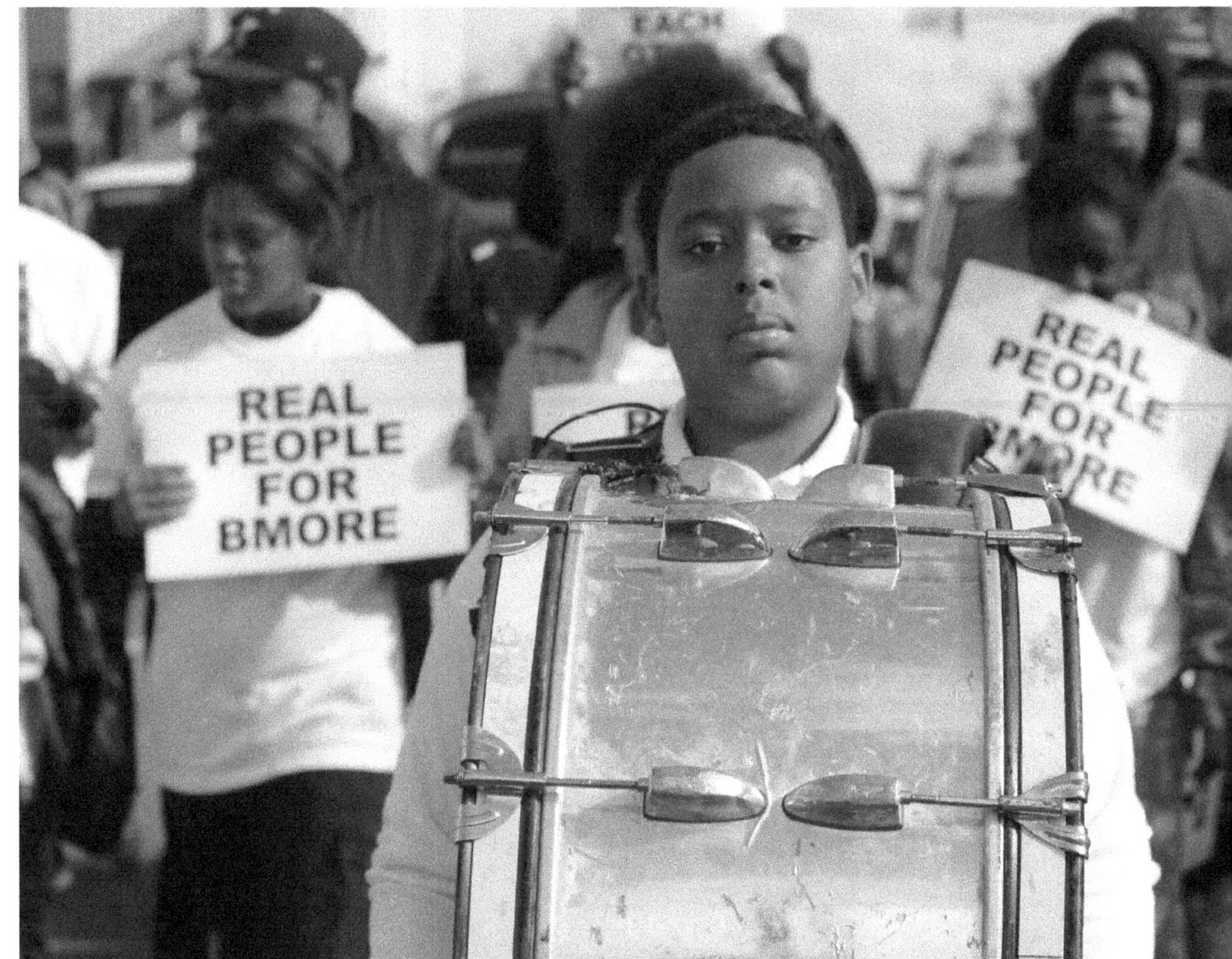
REAL
PEOPLE
FOR
BMORE
REAL
PEOPLE
FOR

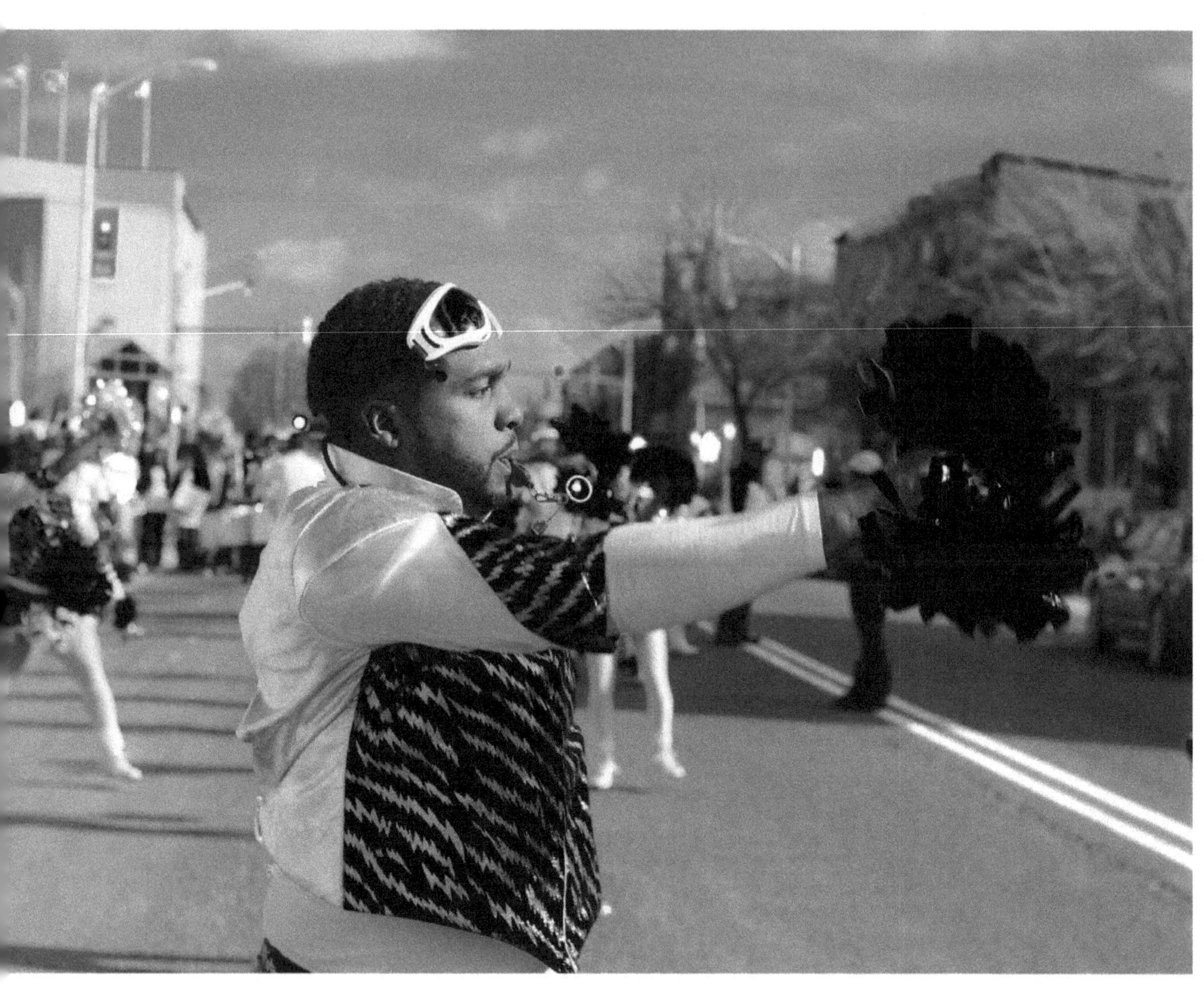

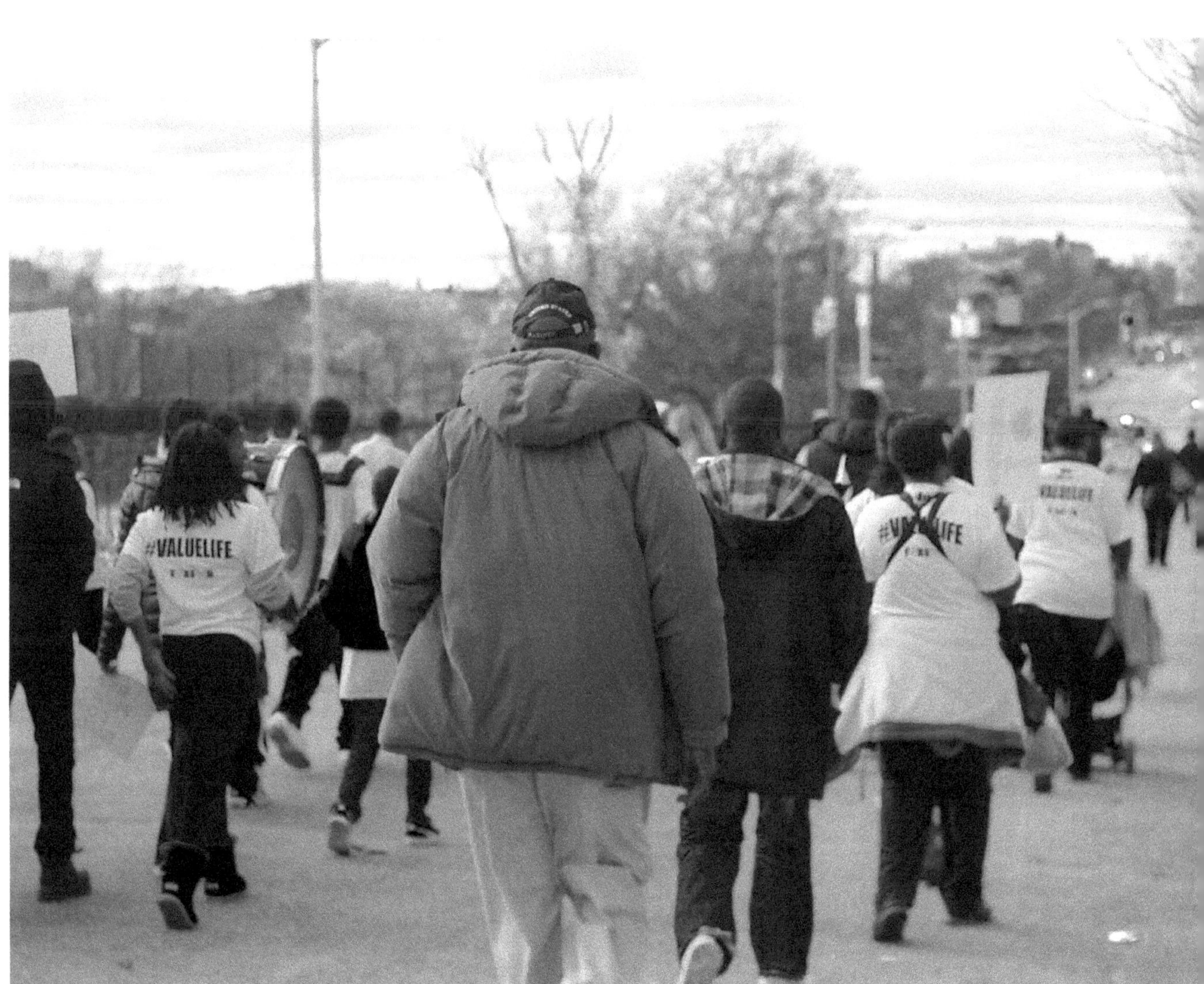
#VALUELIFE

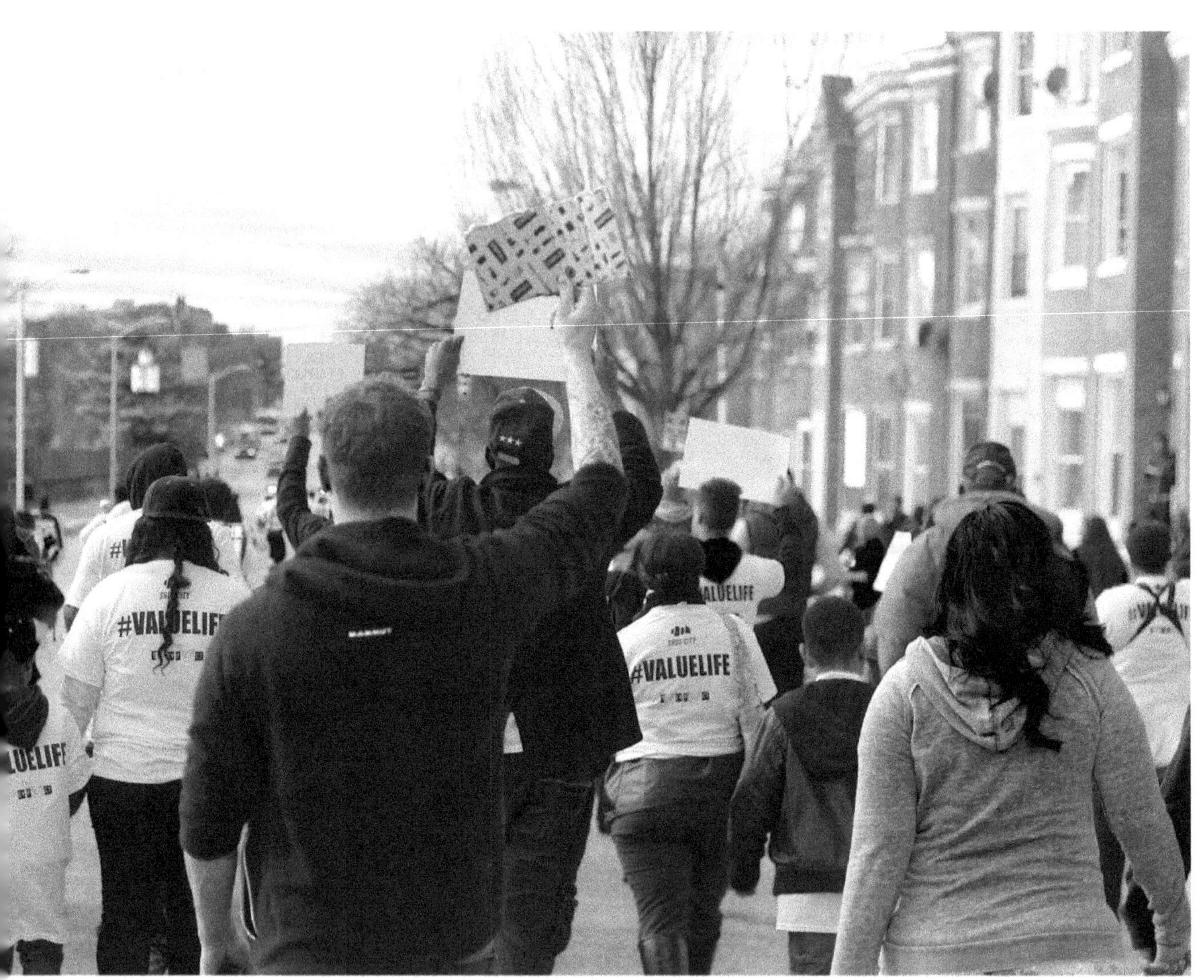
#VALUELIFE

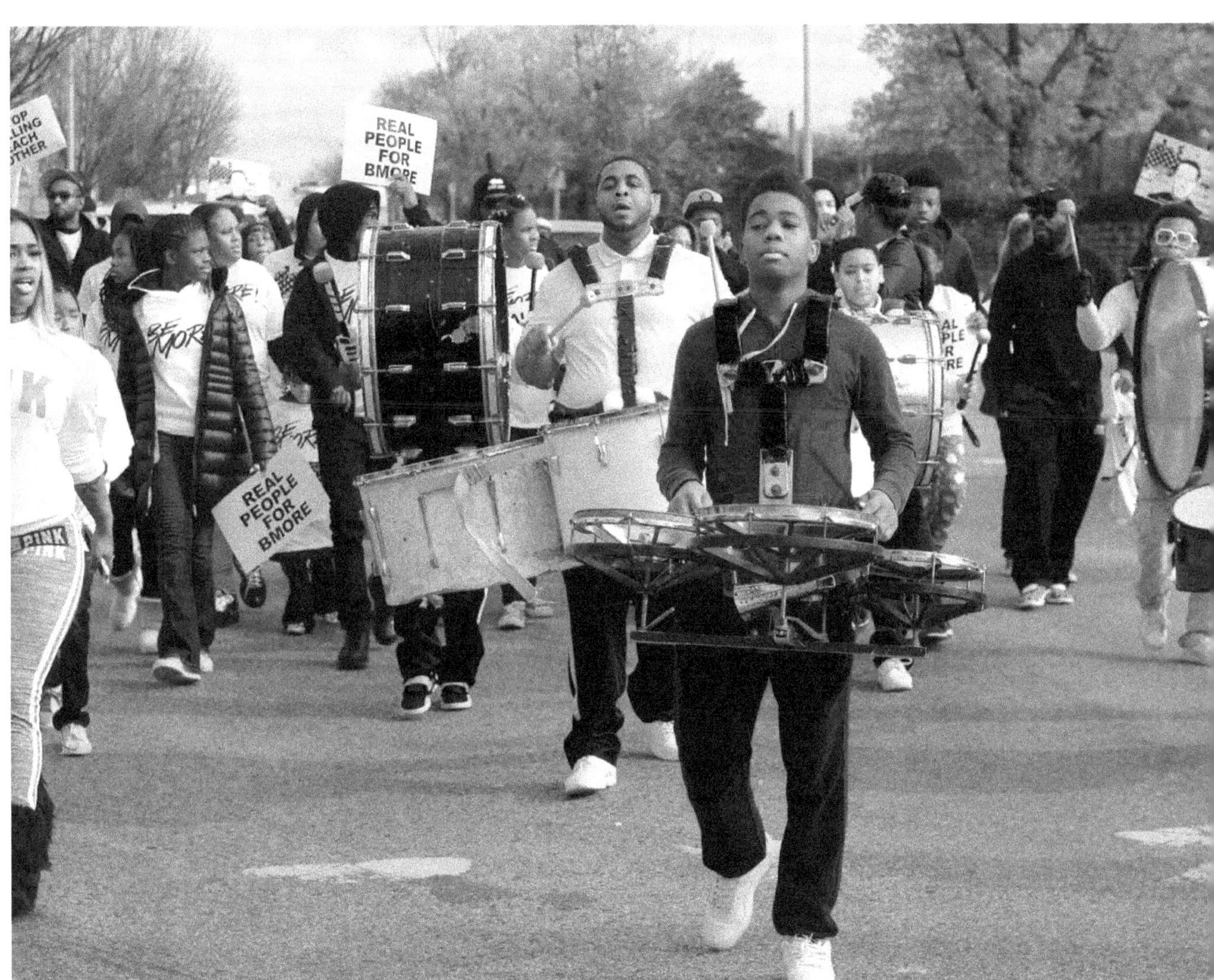
REAL
PEOPLE
FOR
BMORE
BE MORE
REAL
PEOPLE
FOR
BMORE
PINK

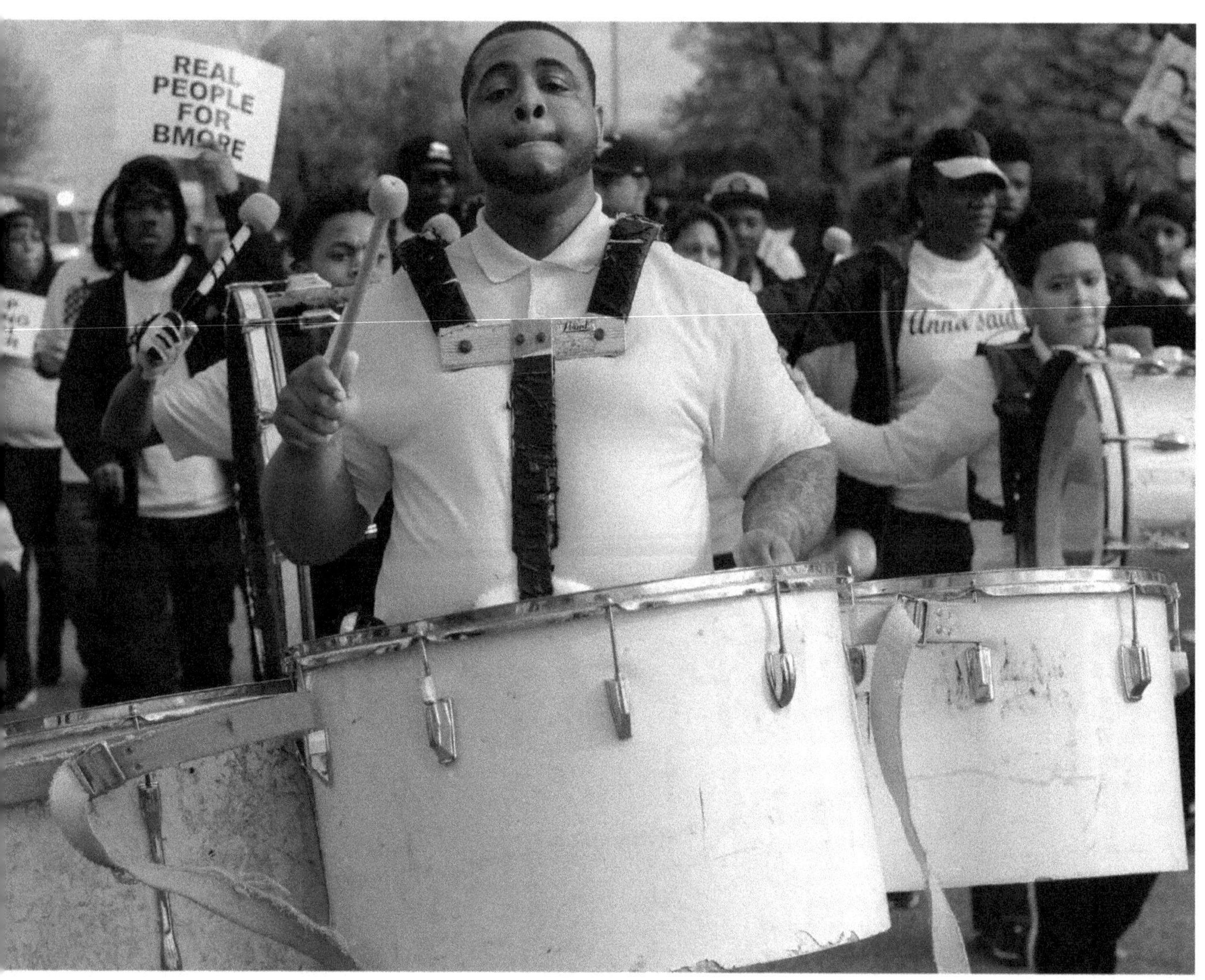
REAL
PEOPLE
FOR
BMORE

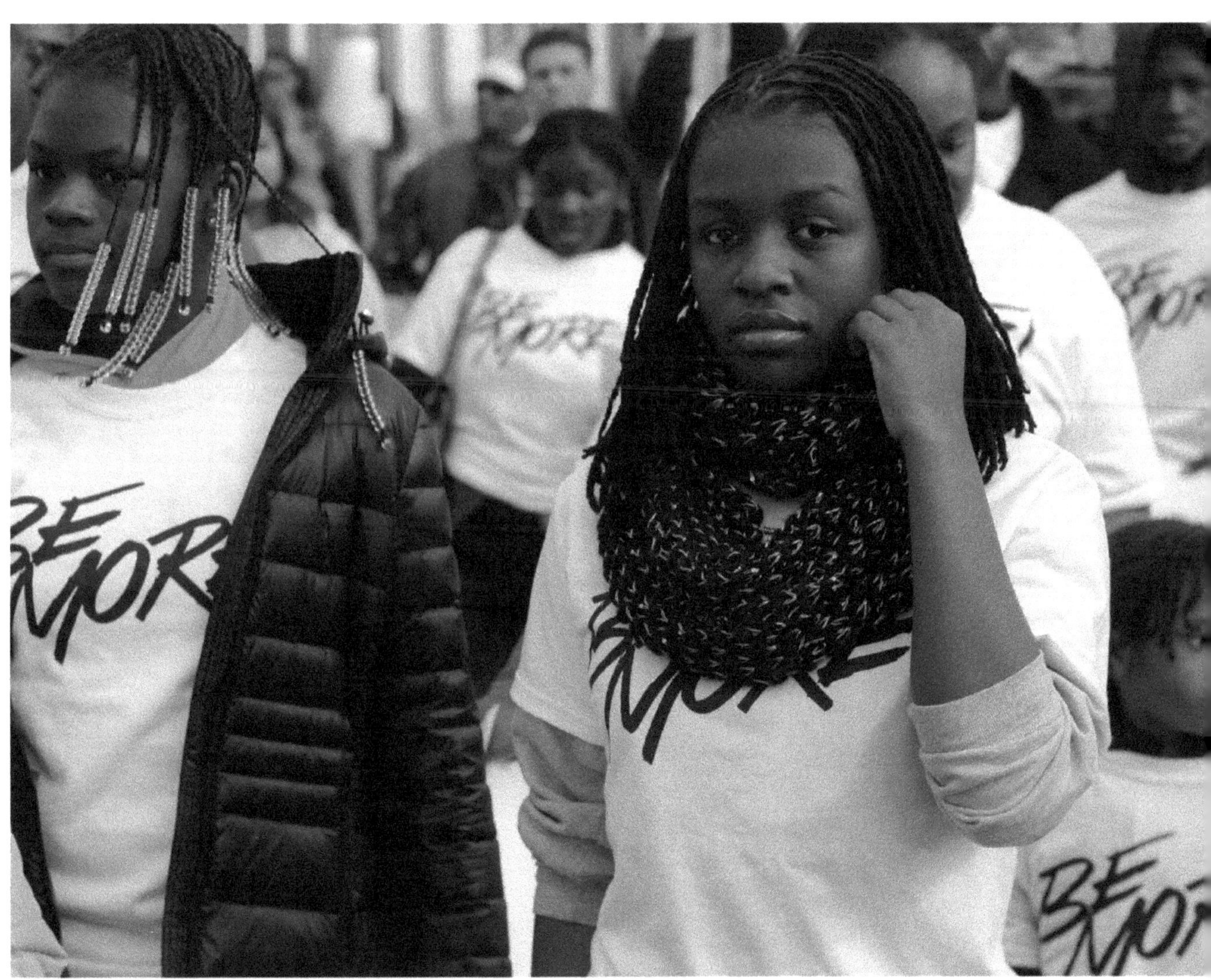
BE
MOR

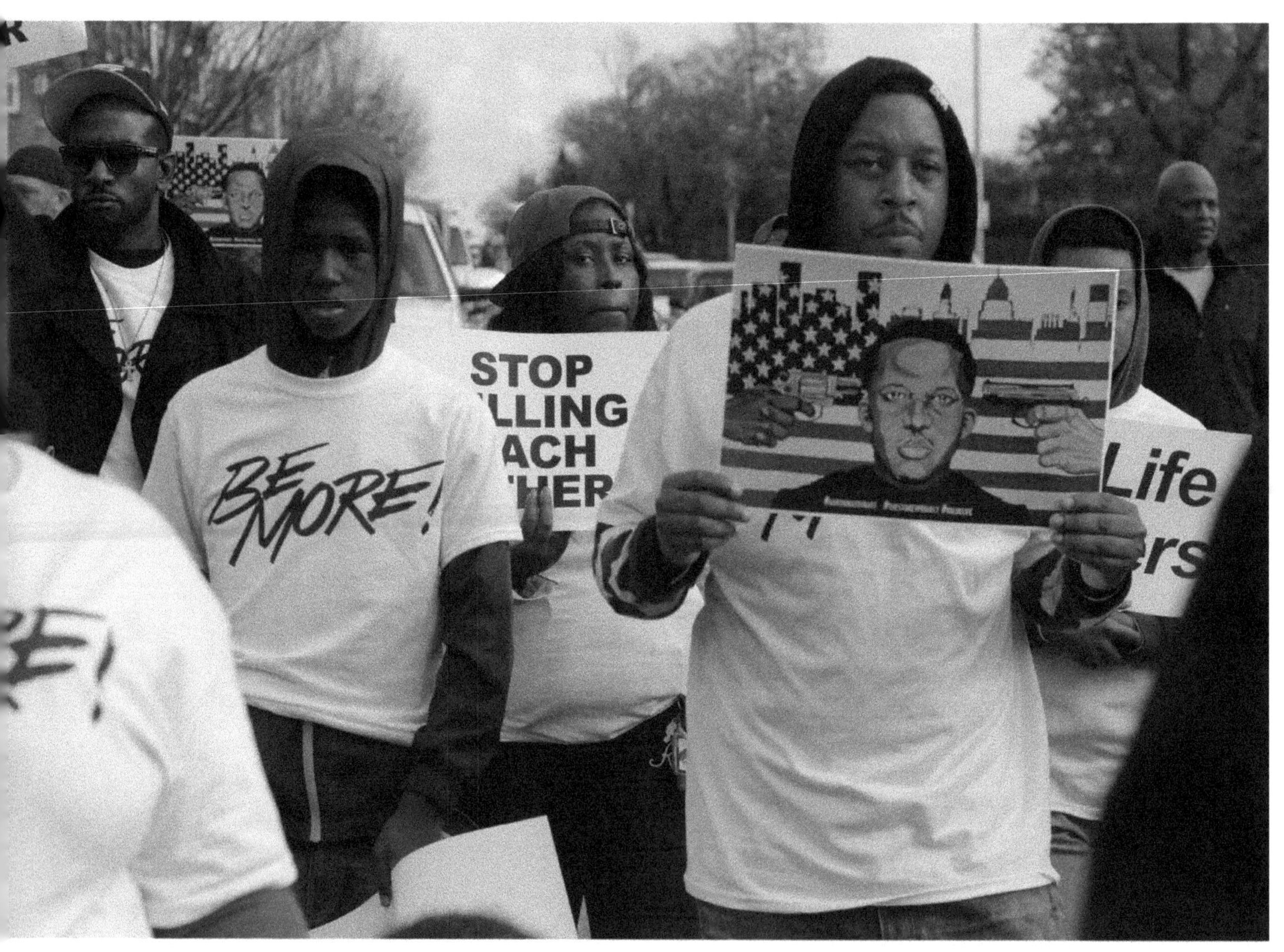
BE MORE!
STOP
Life

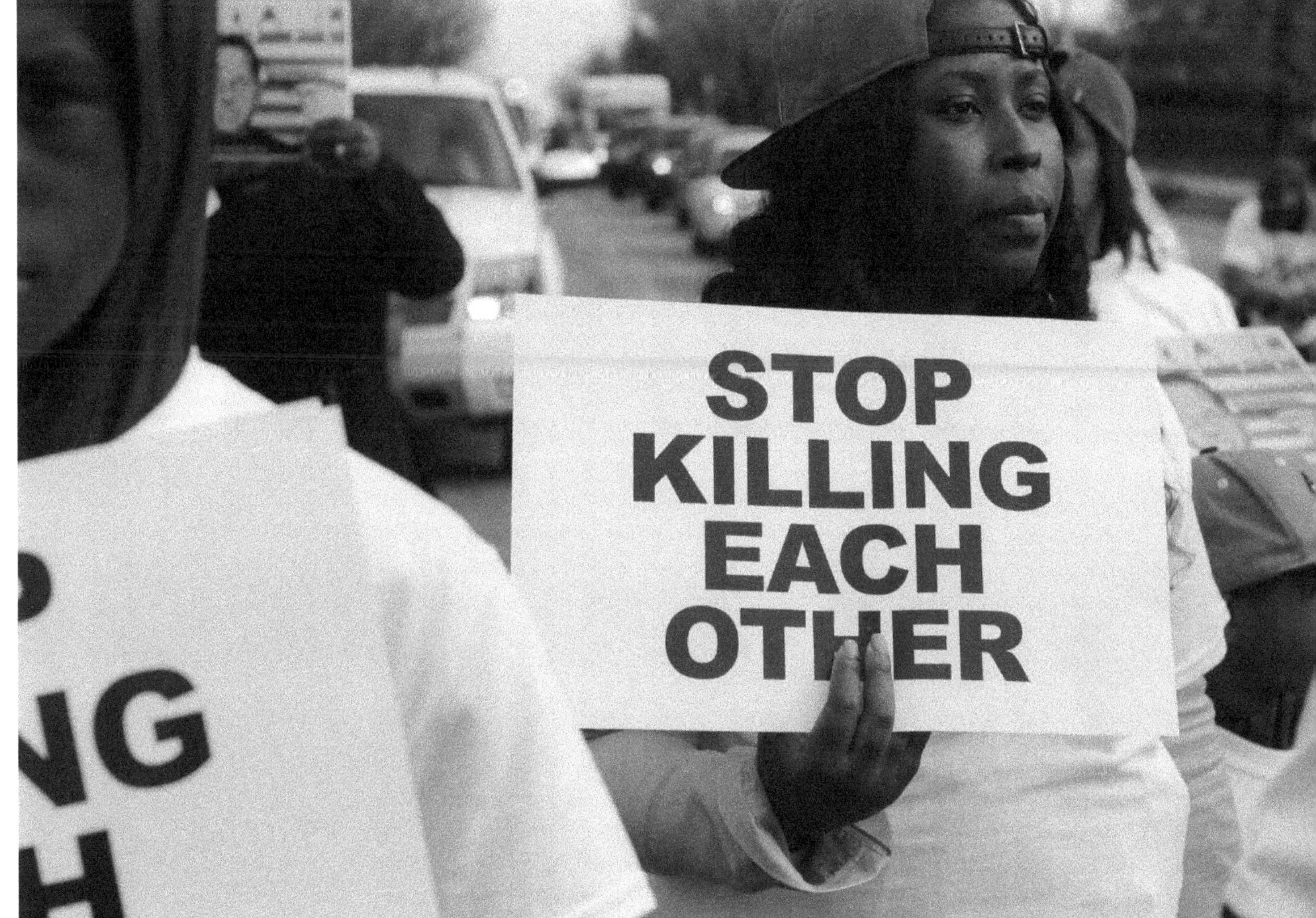
STOP
KILLING
EACH
OTHER

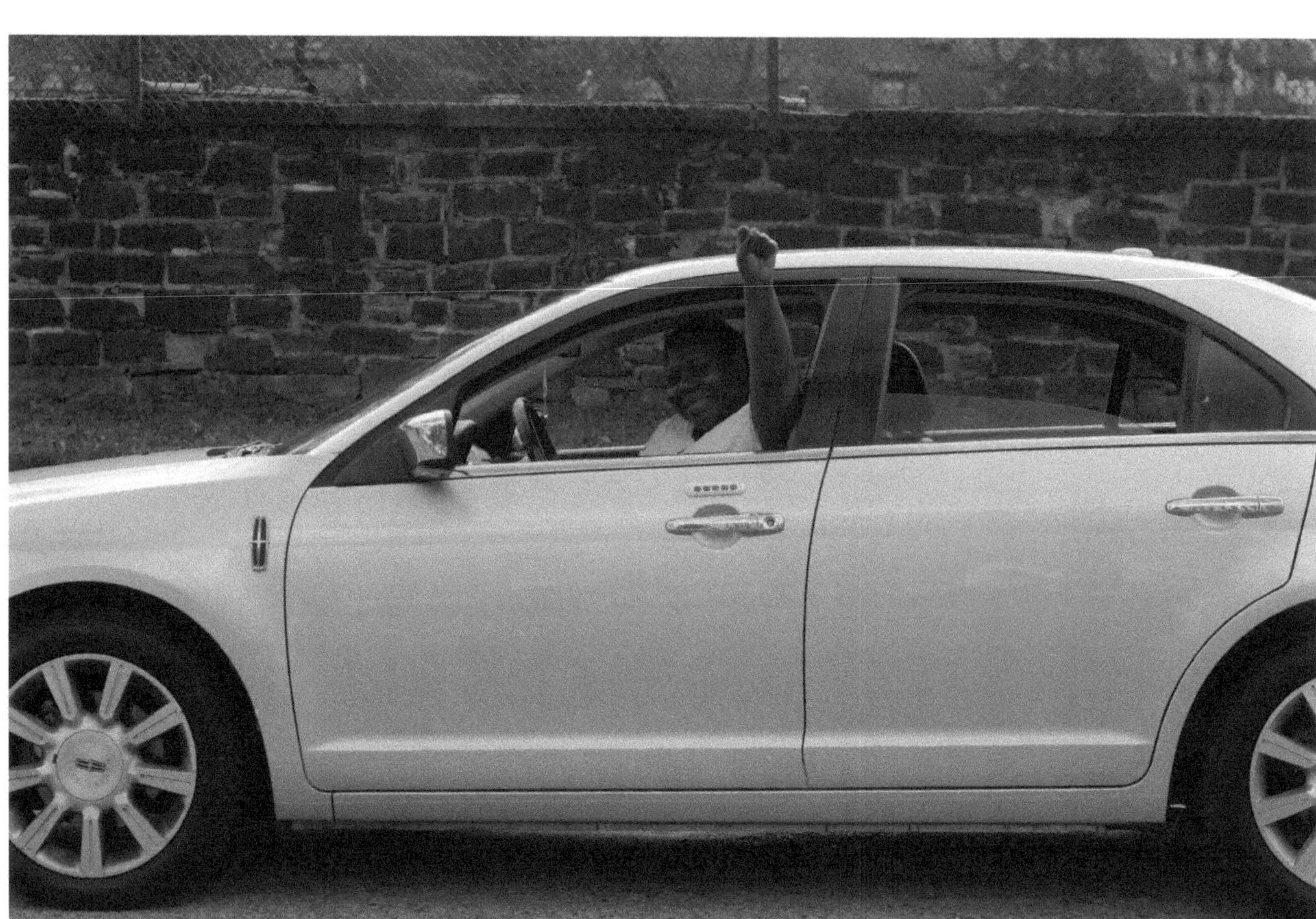

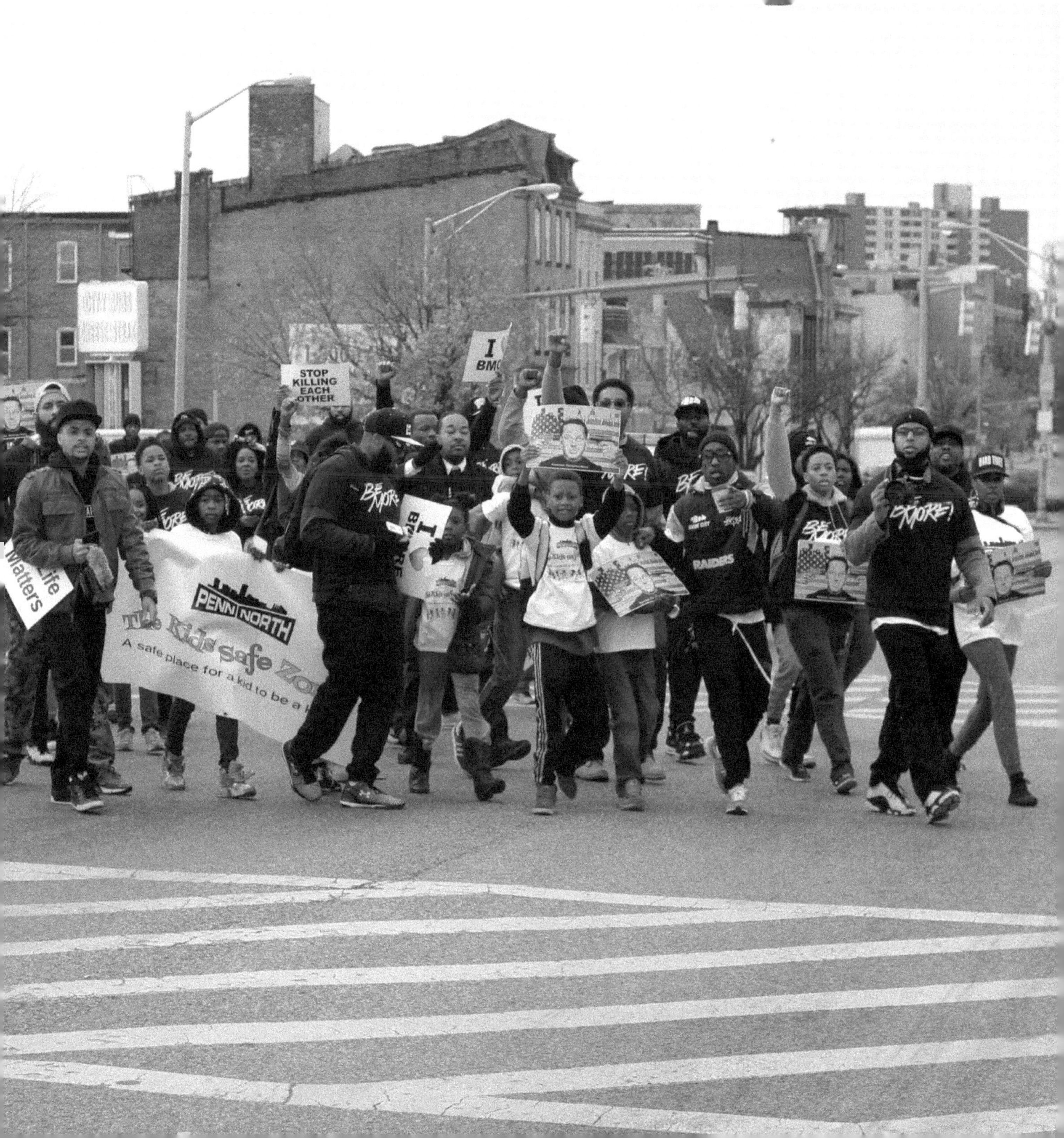
STOP KILLING EACH OTHER
PENN NORTH
BE MORE!
RAIDERS
Life
Matters

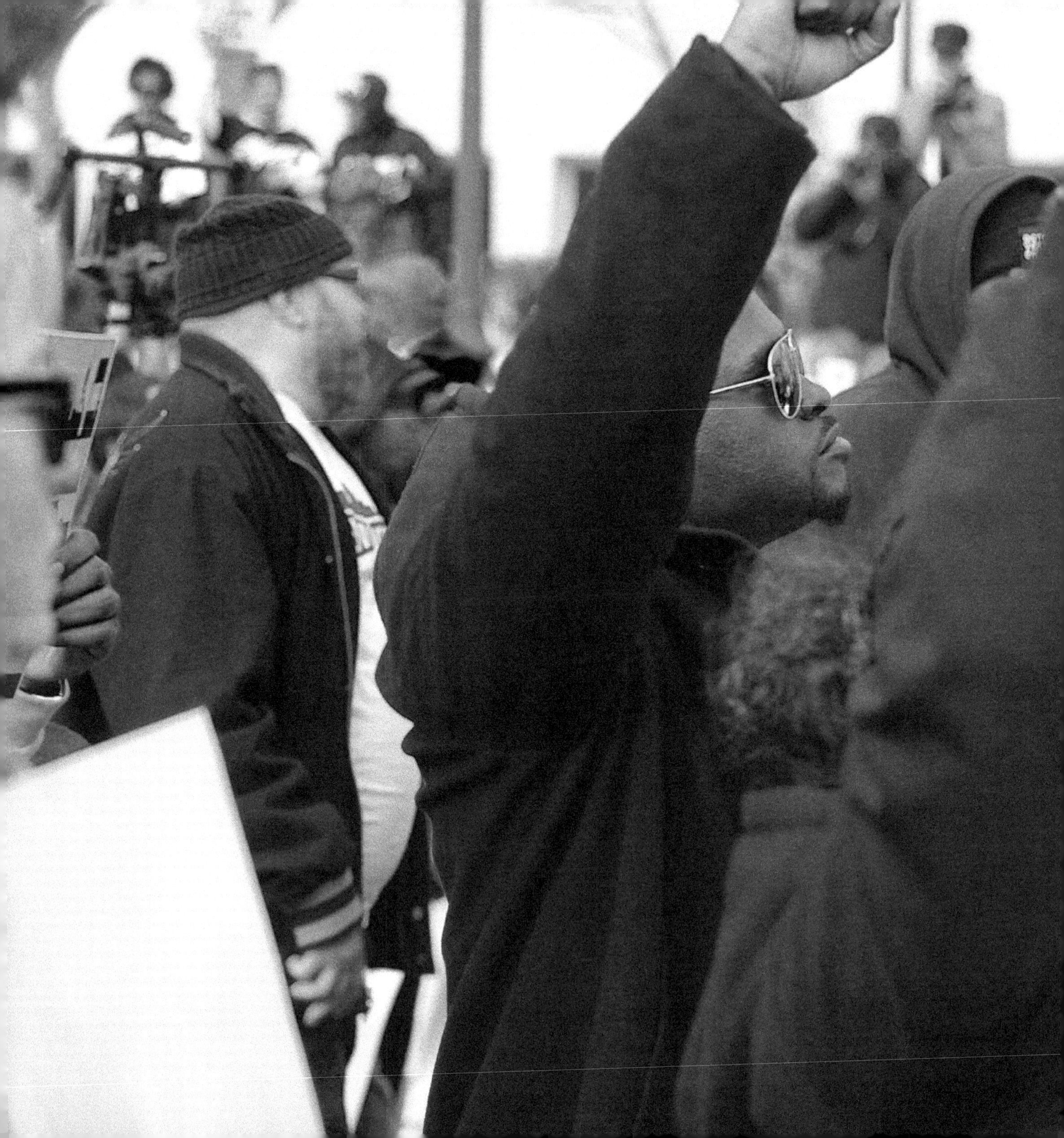

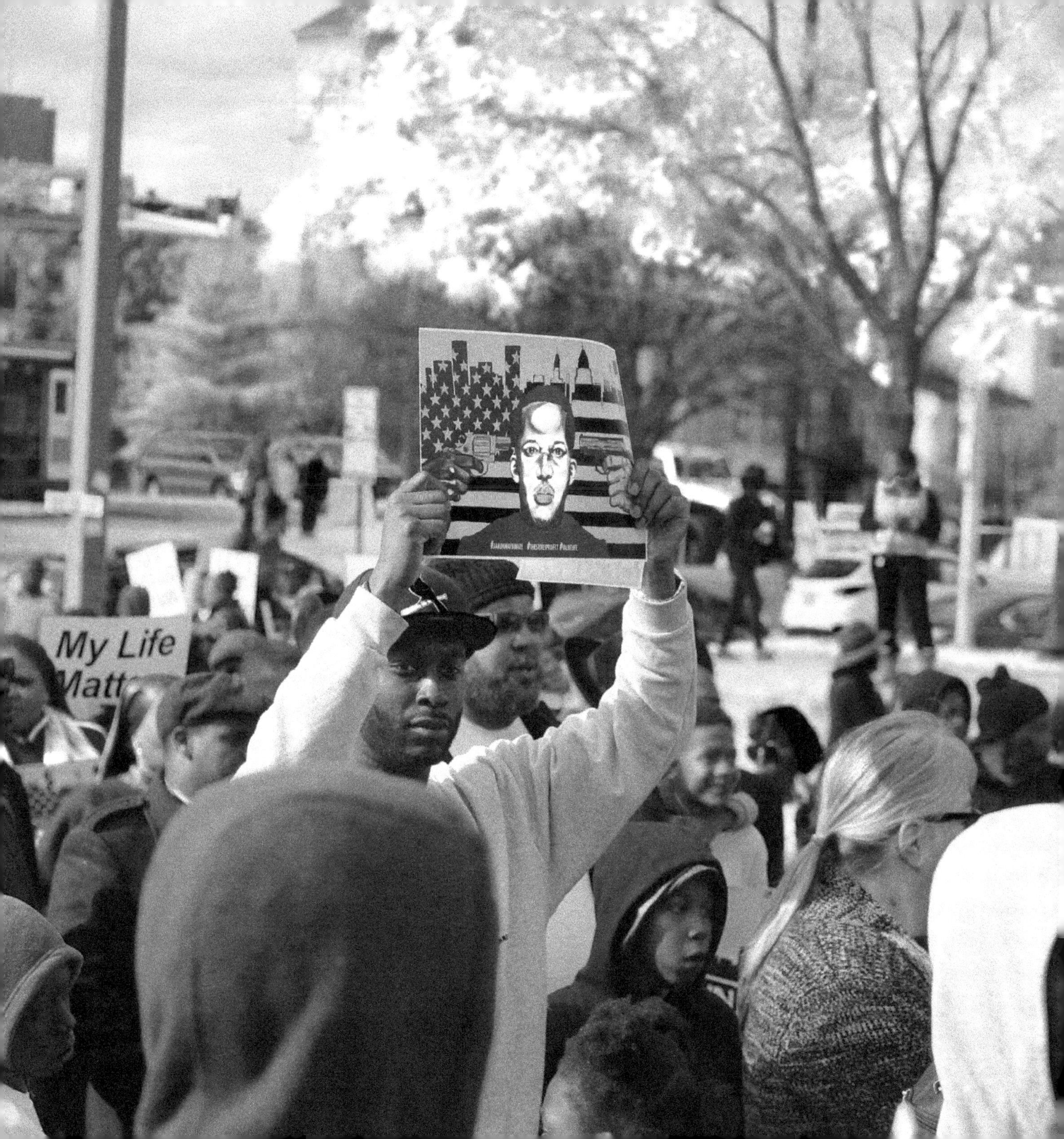
My Life

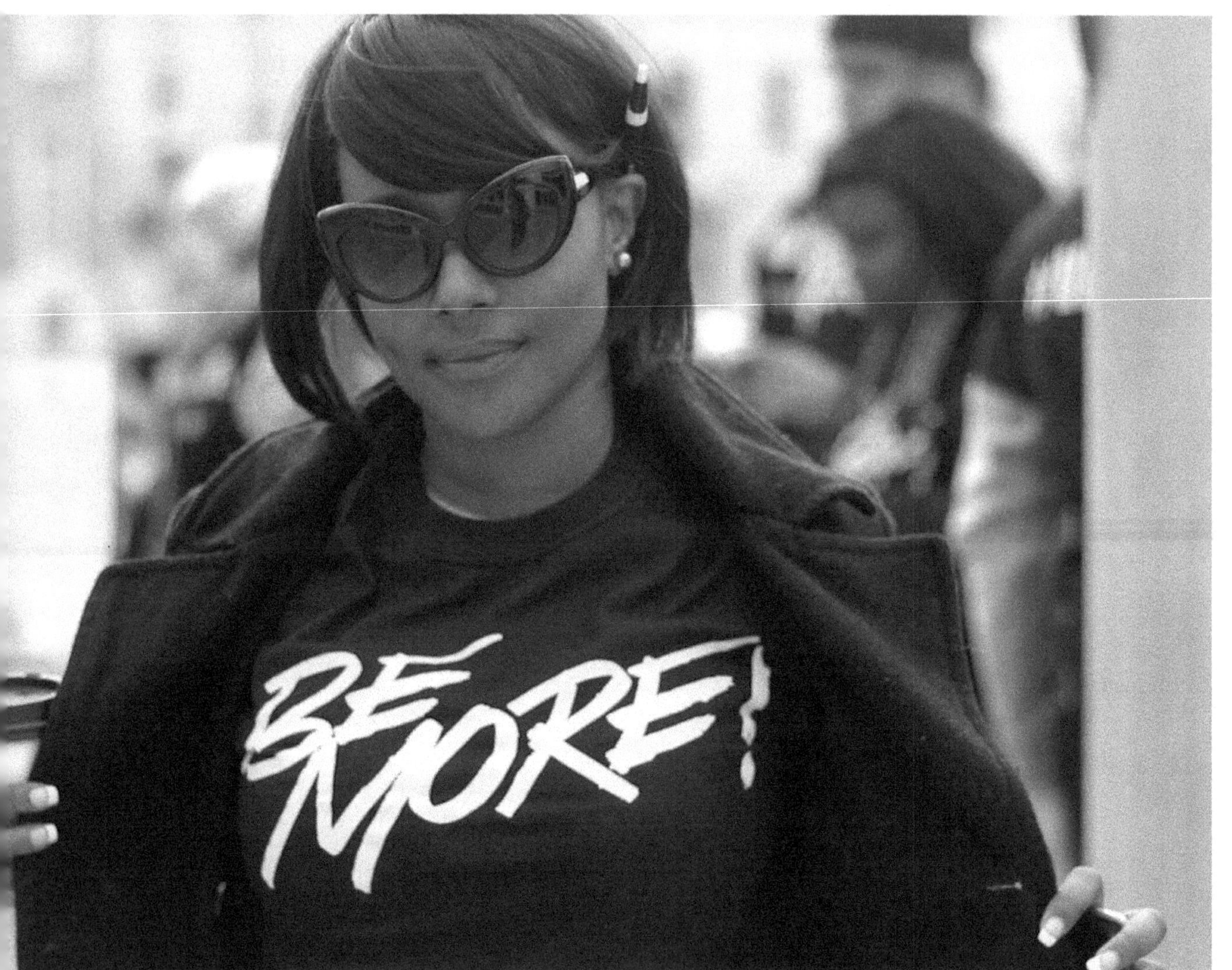
BE MORE!

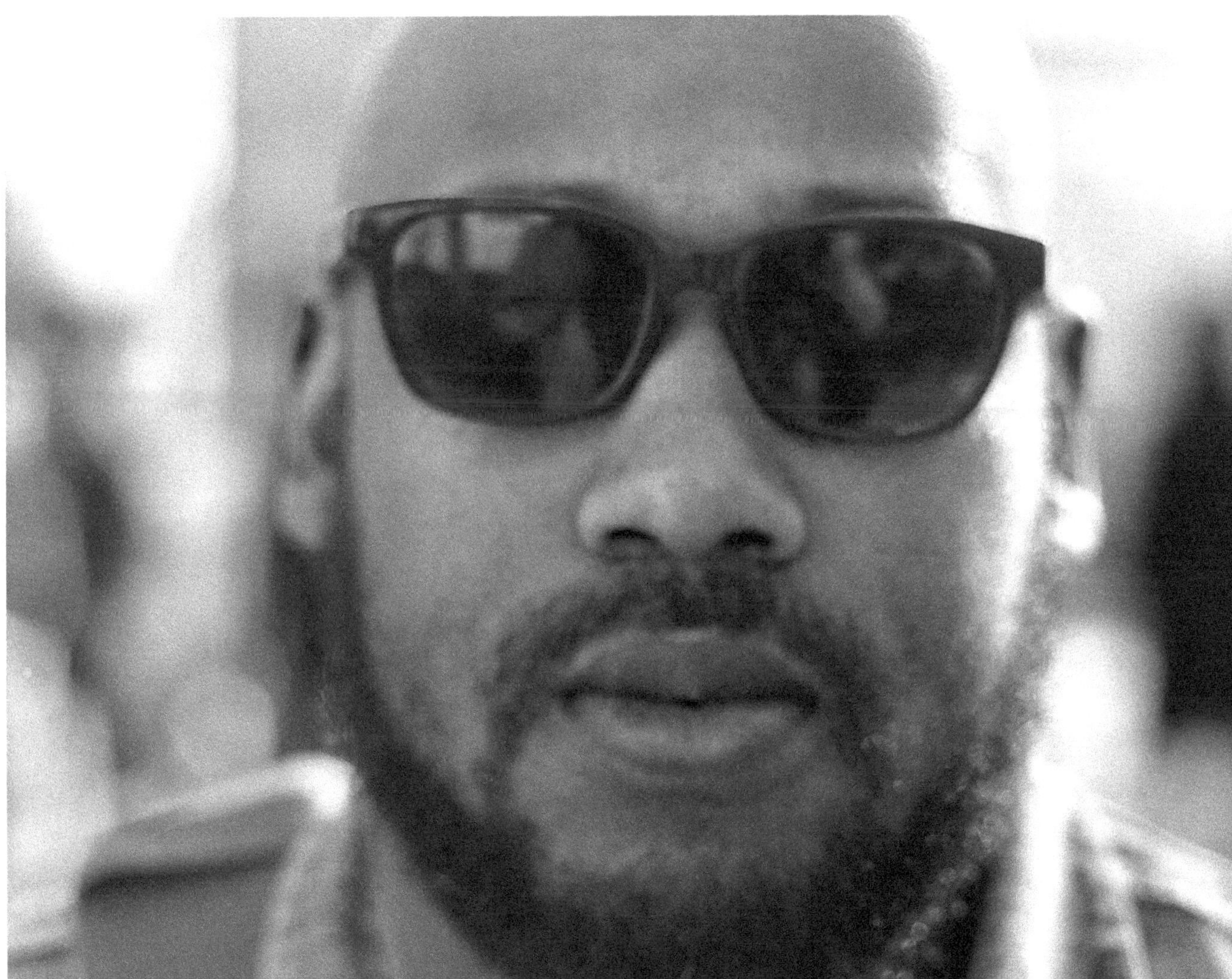

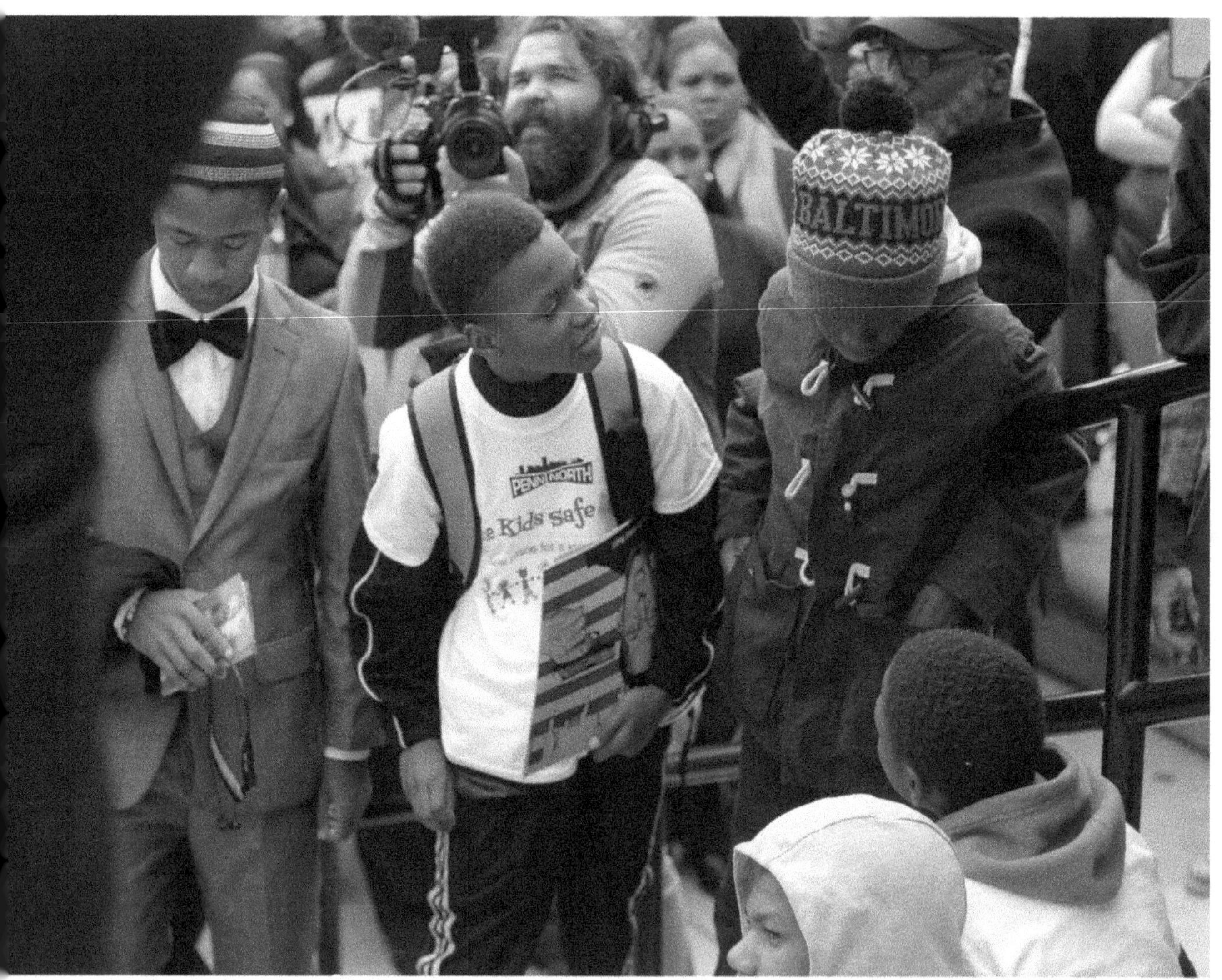
PENN NORTH
Kids Safe

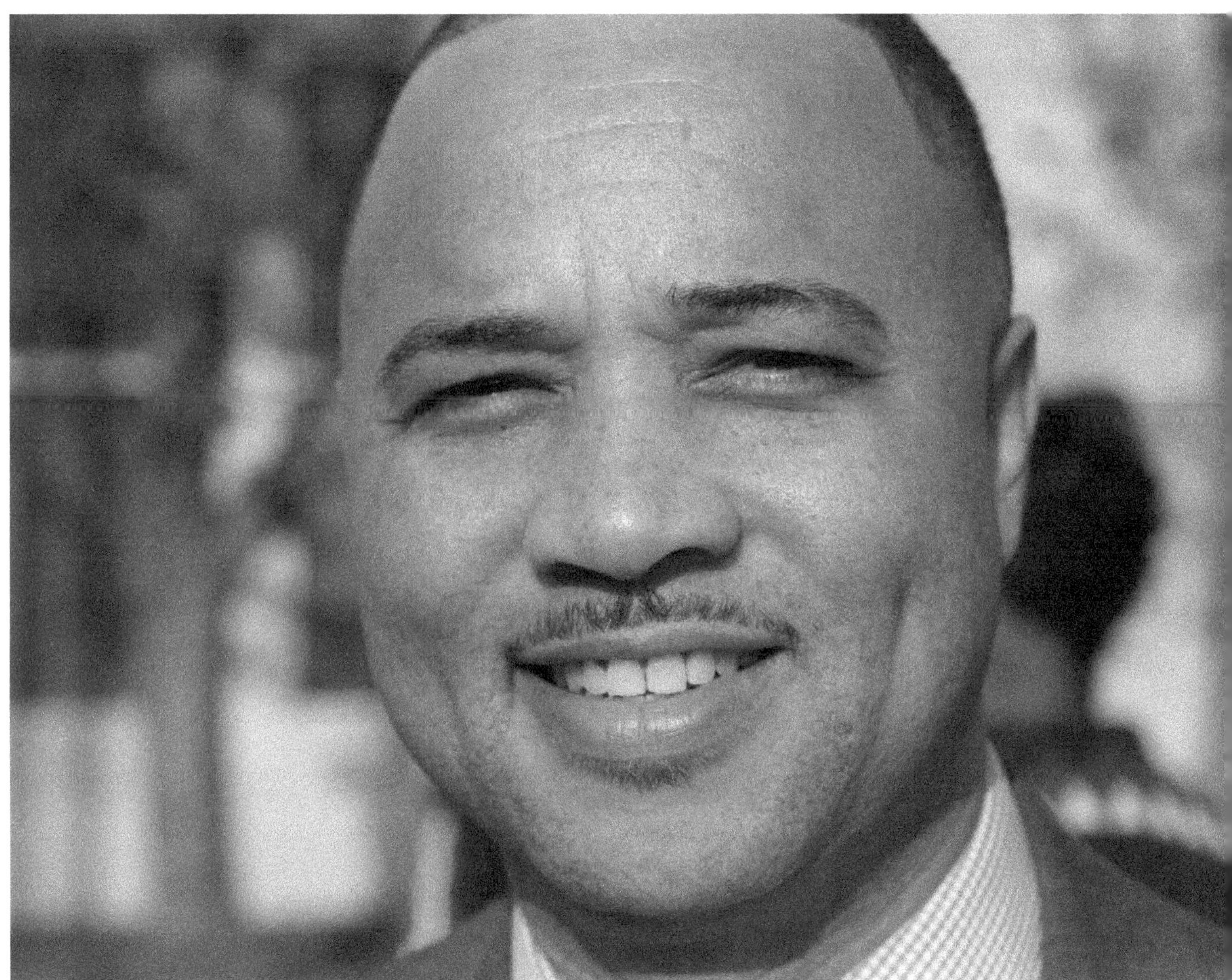

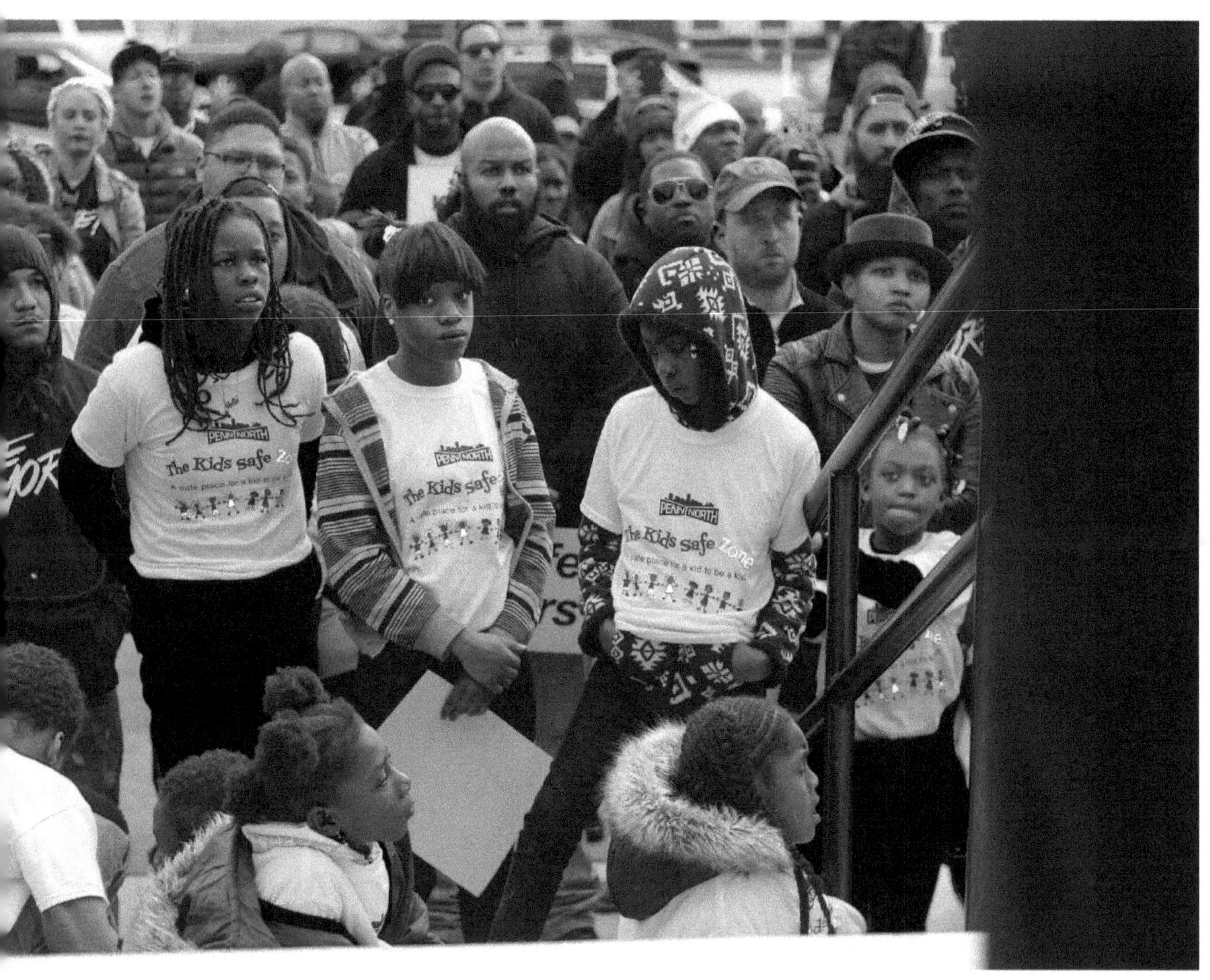
PENN NORTH
The Kids safe Zone

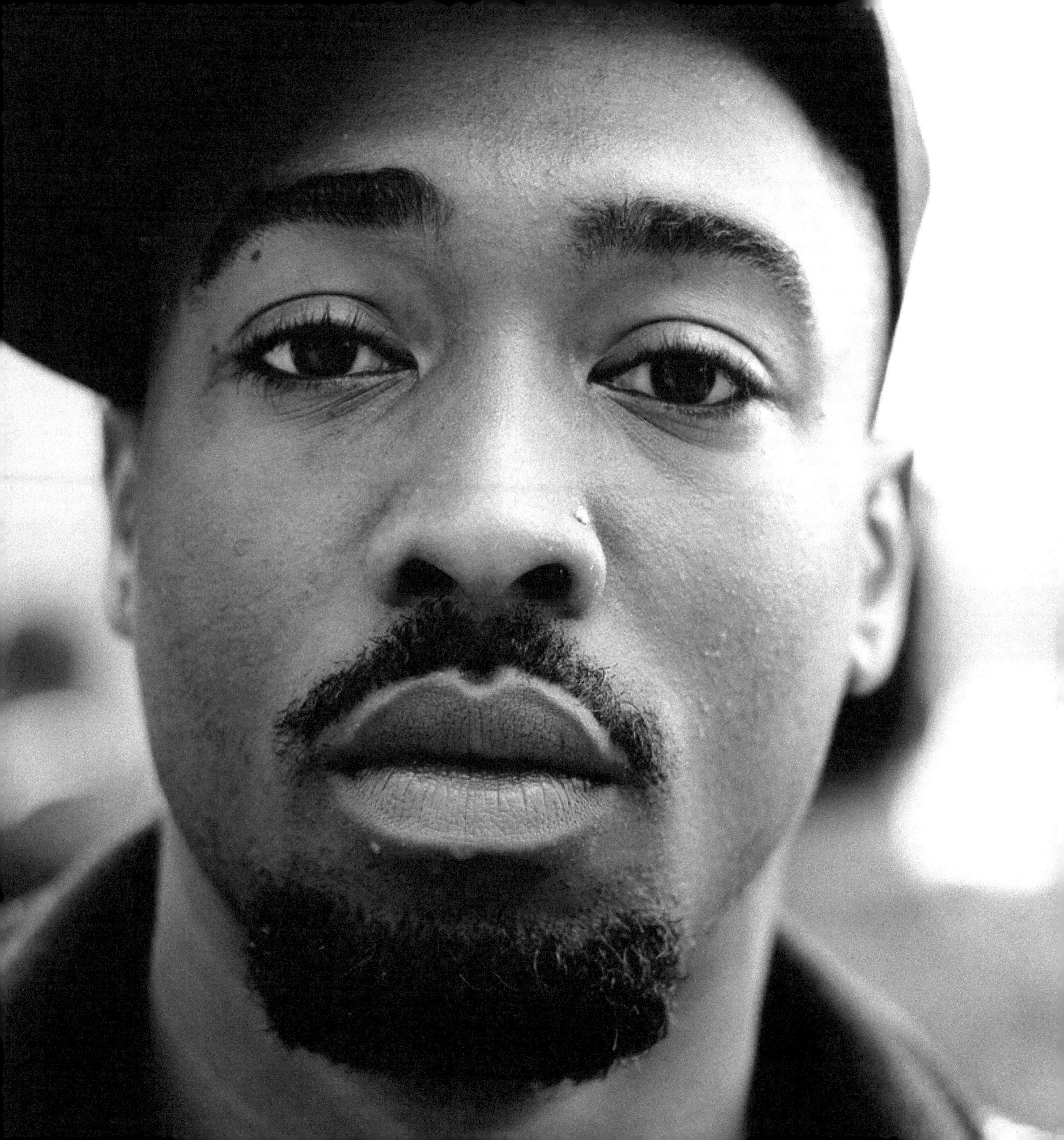

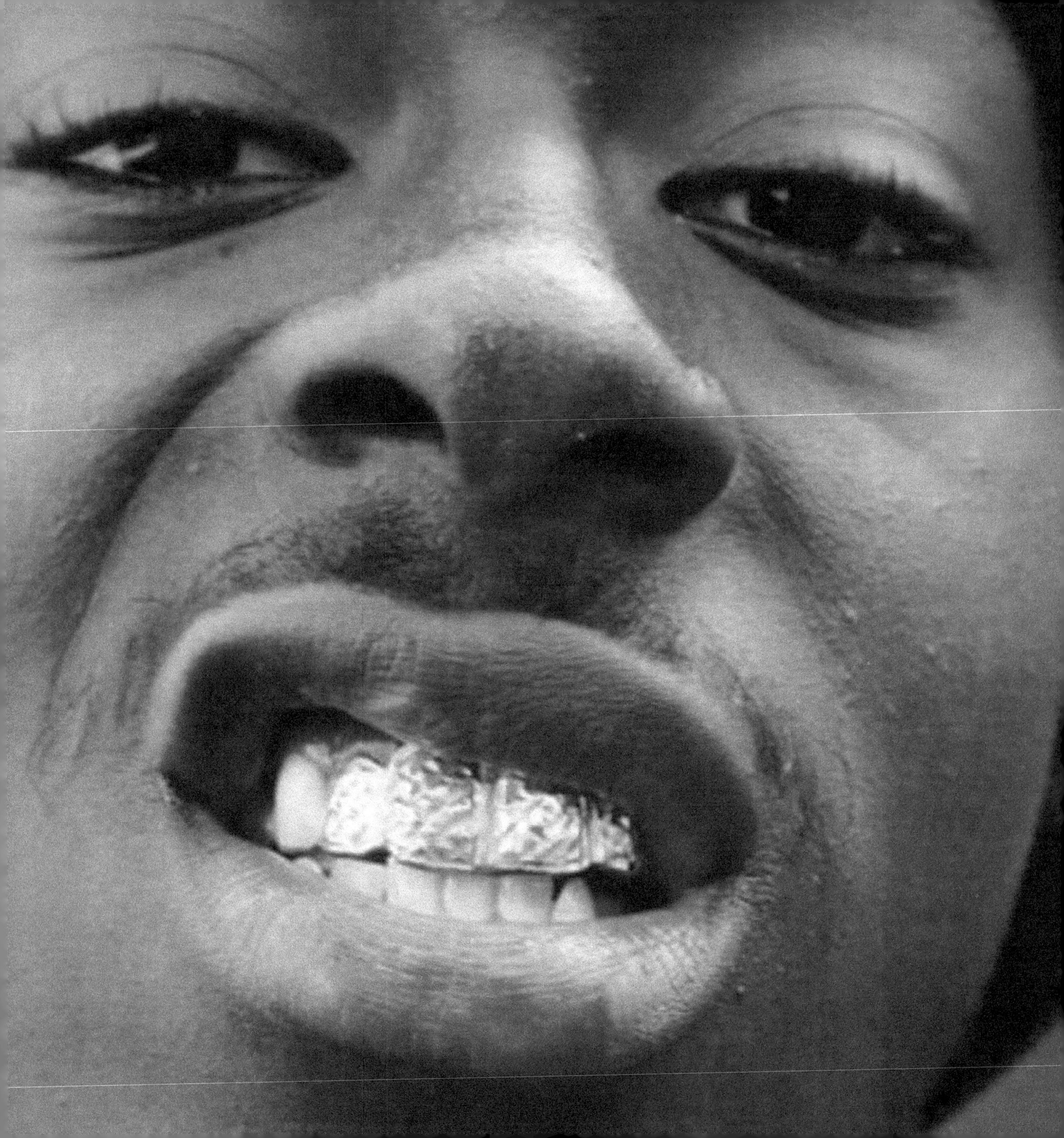

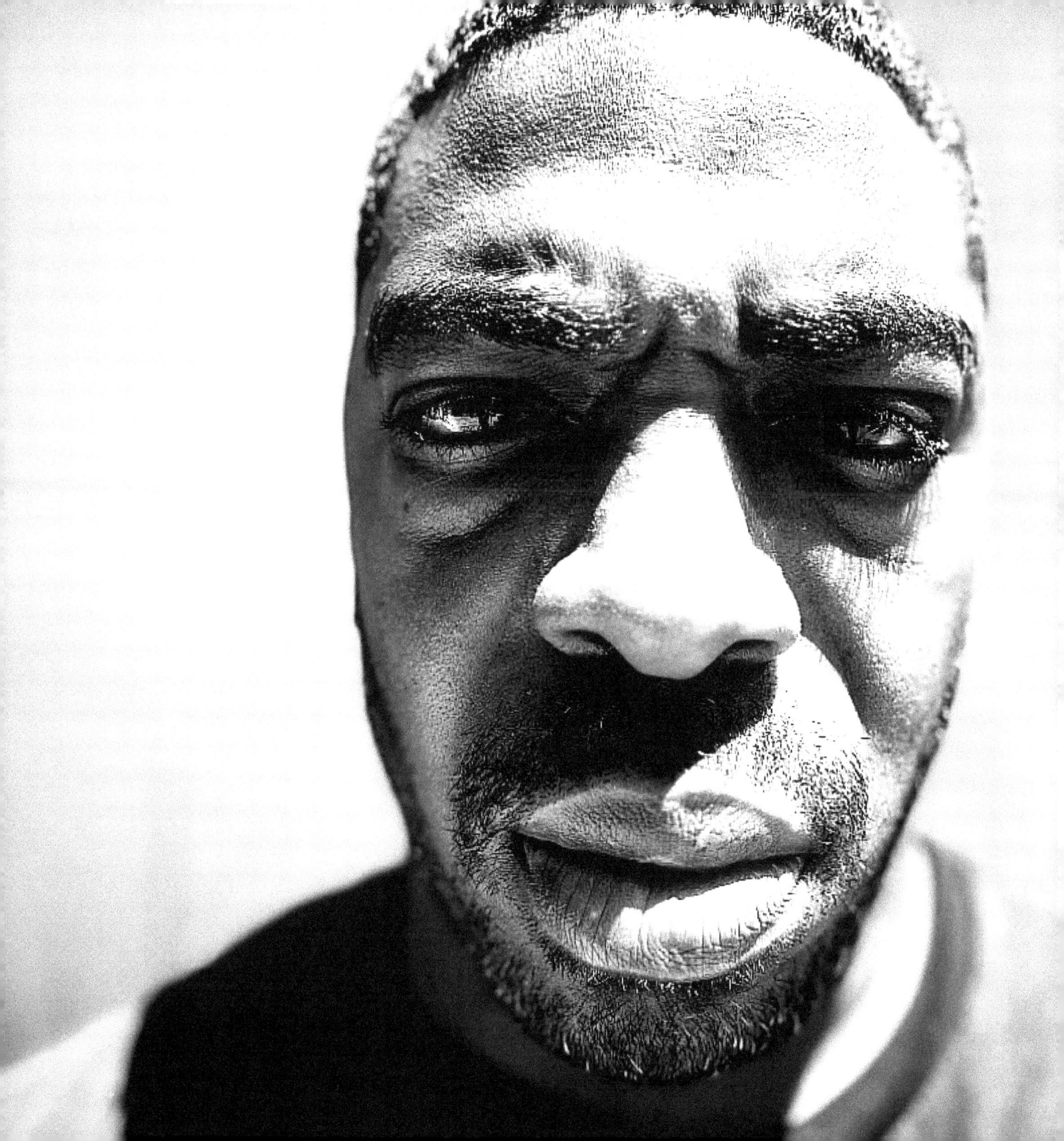

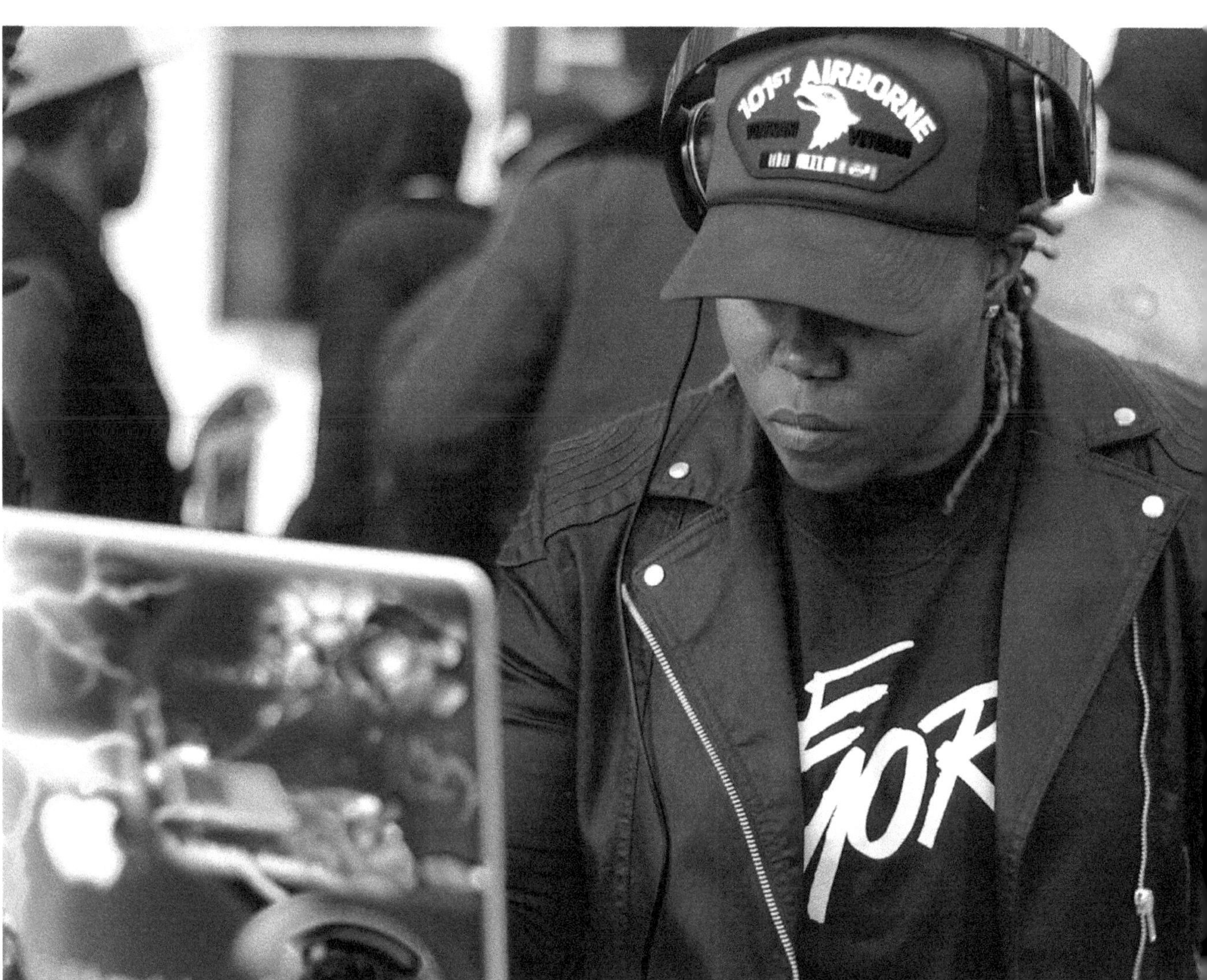
101ST AIRBORNE

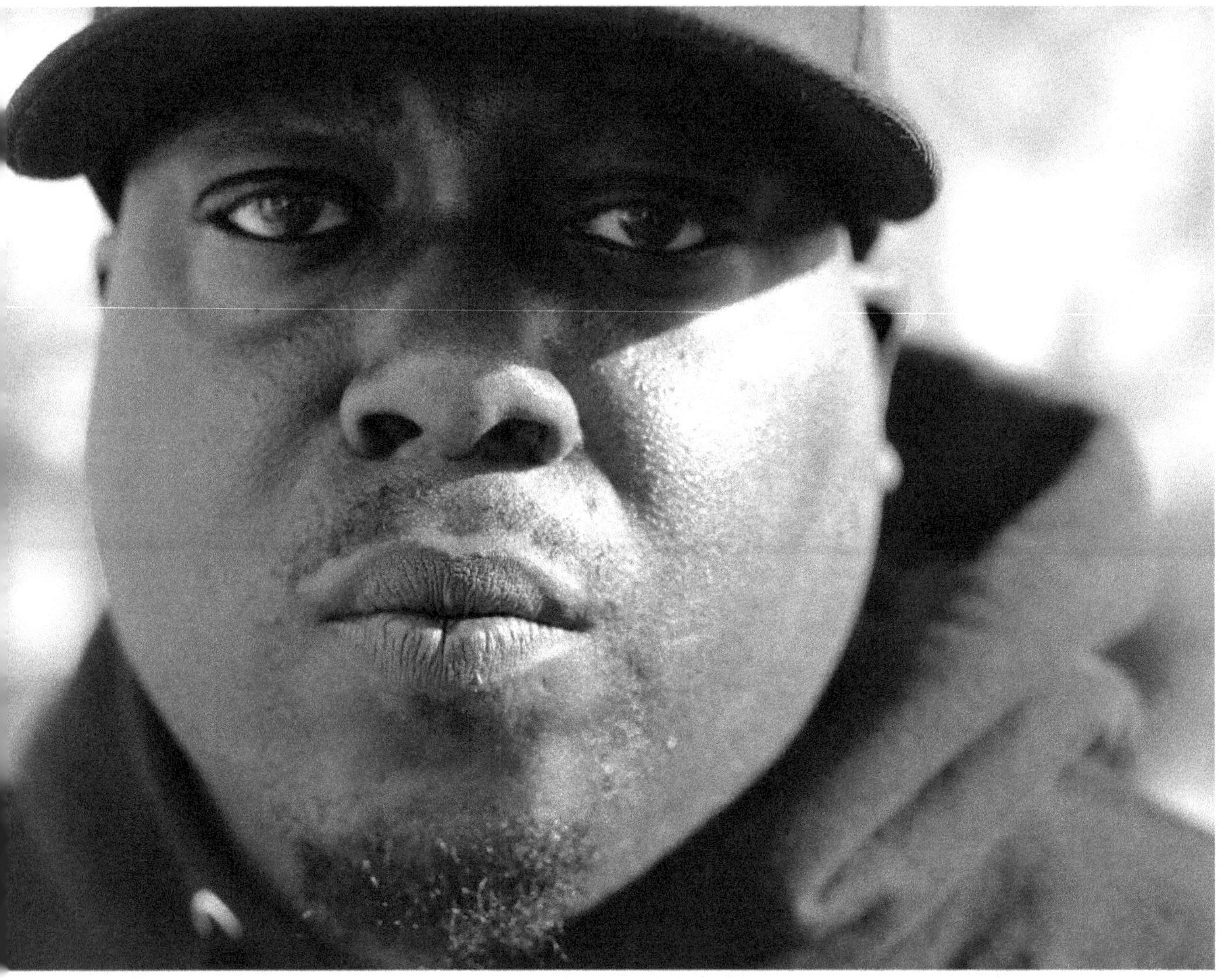

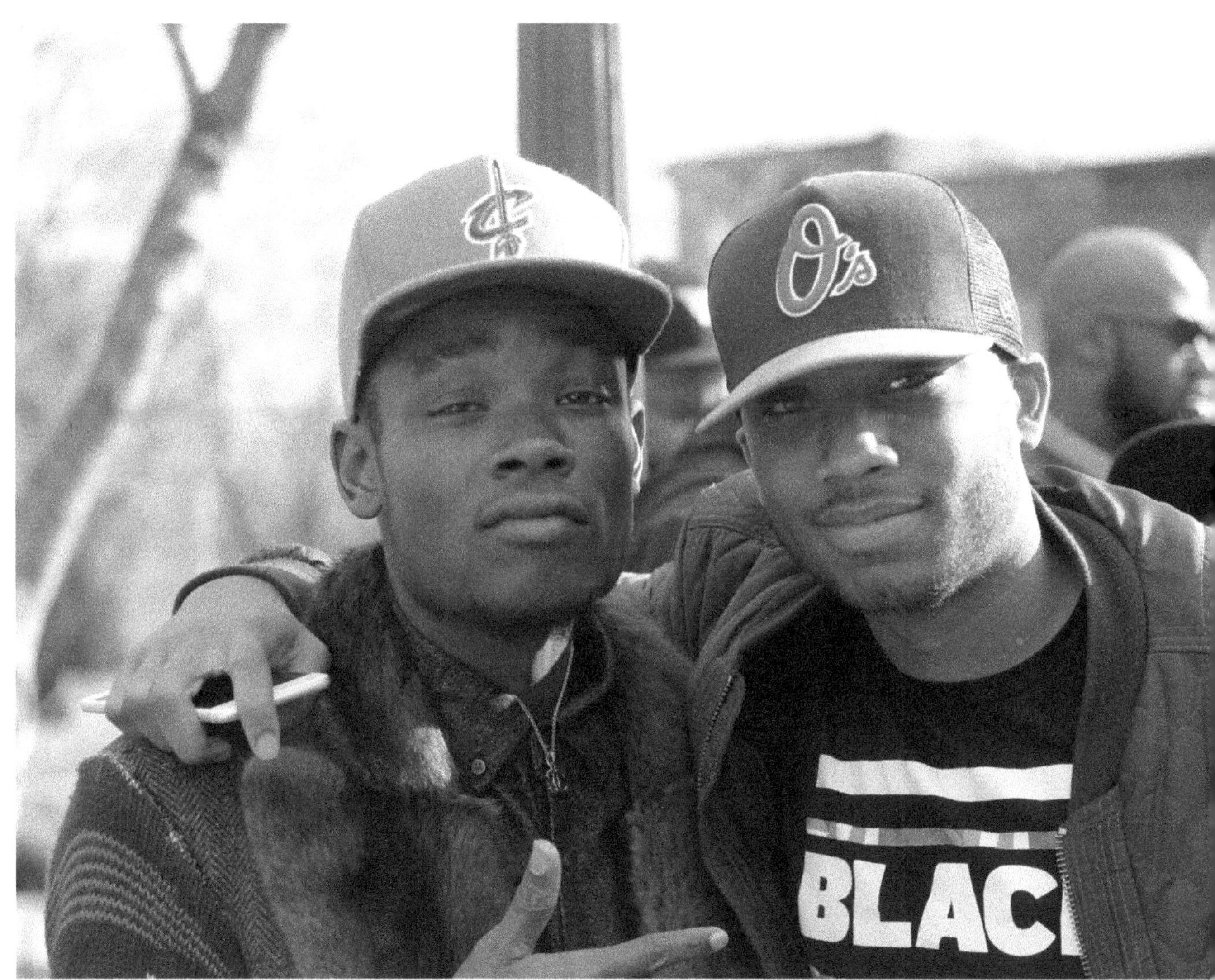
O's
BLAC

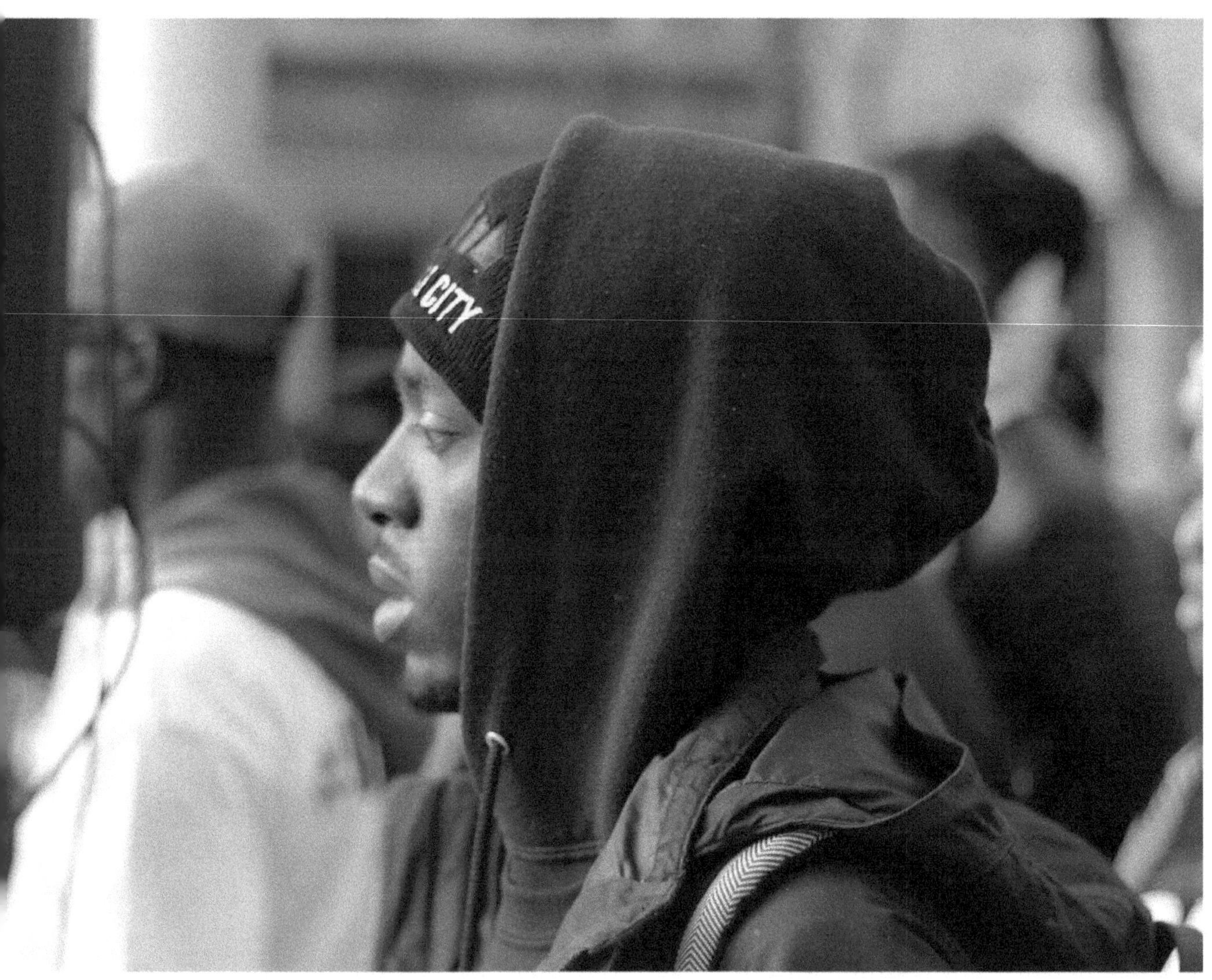
CITY

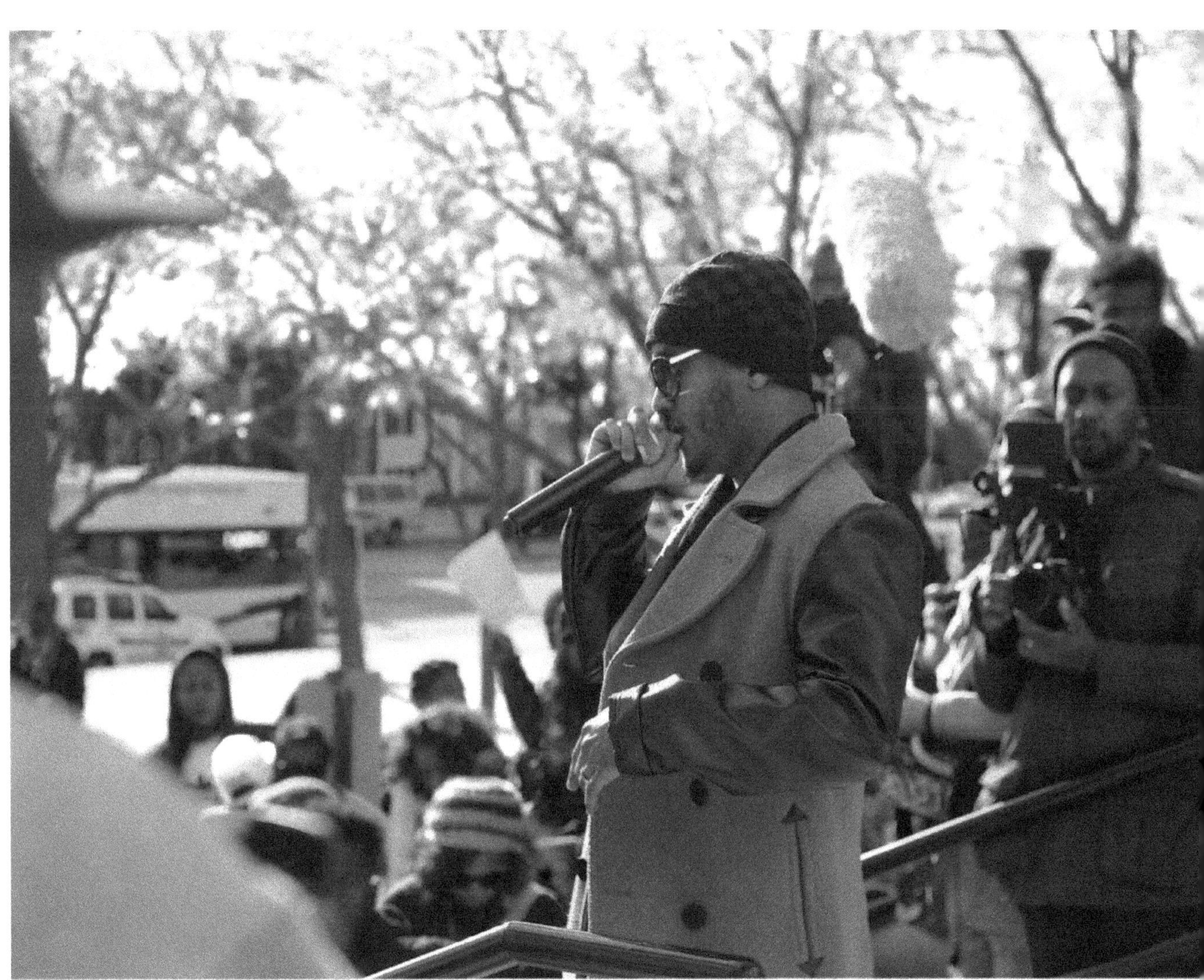

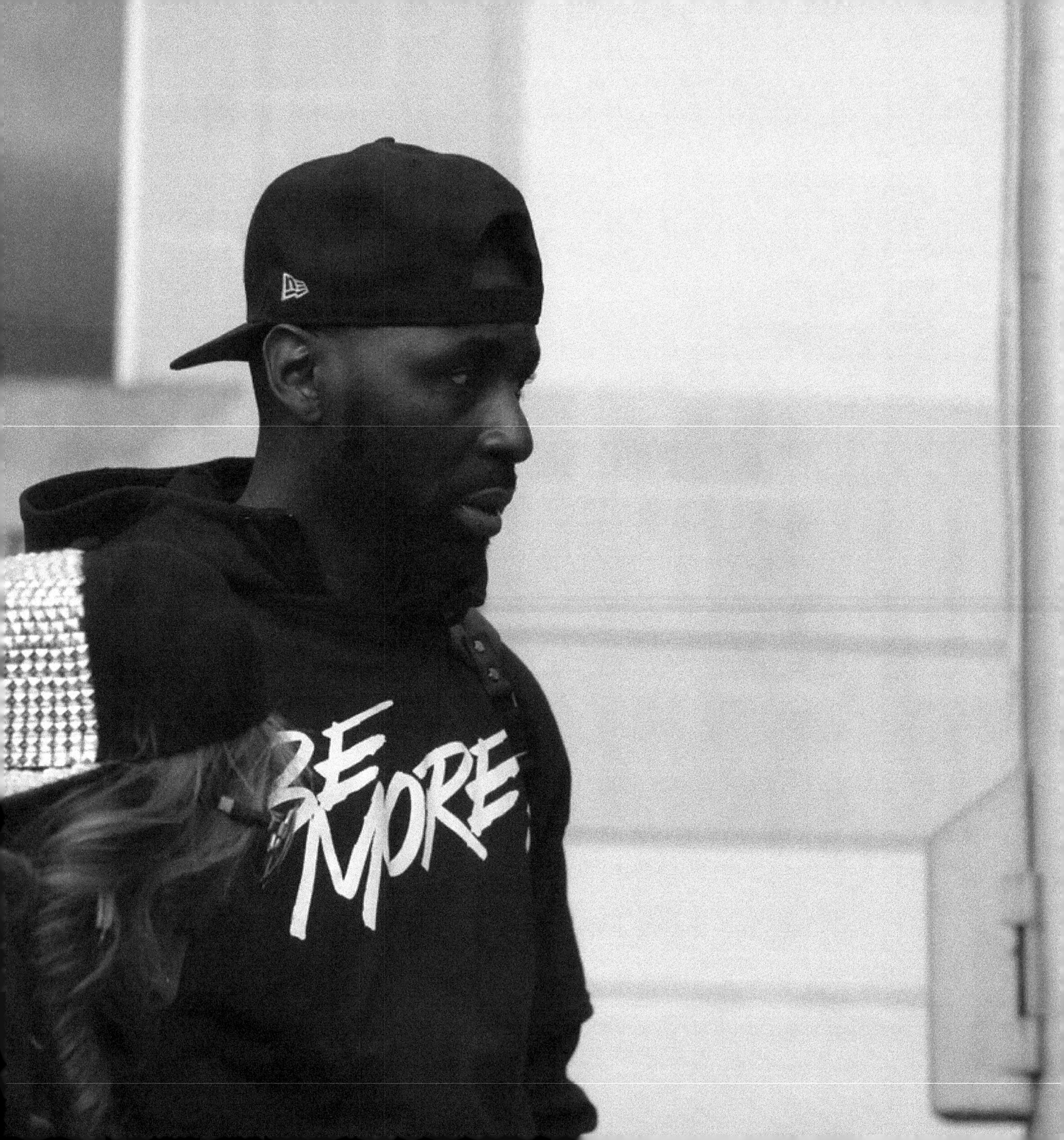
BE
MORE

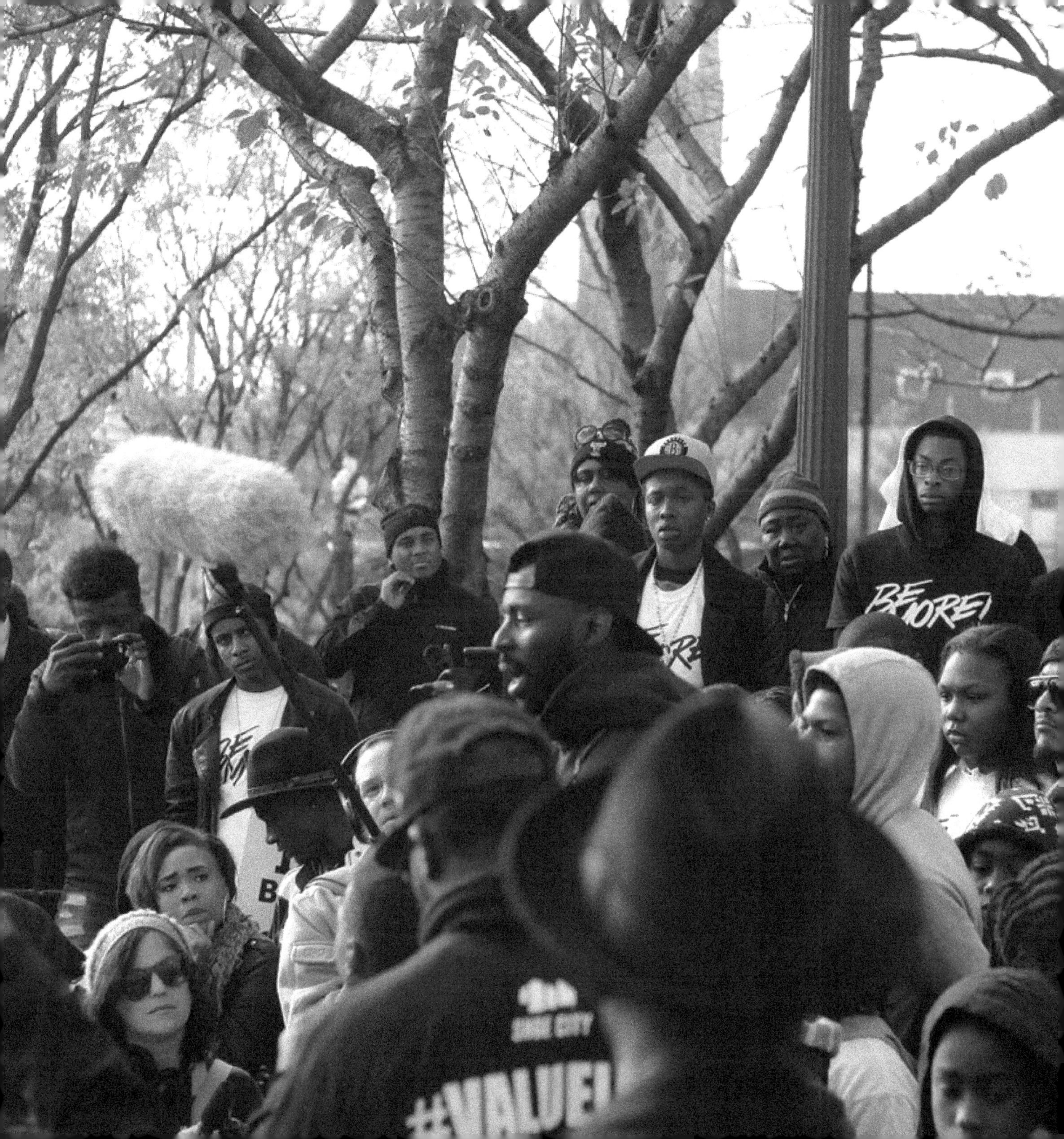
BE MORE

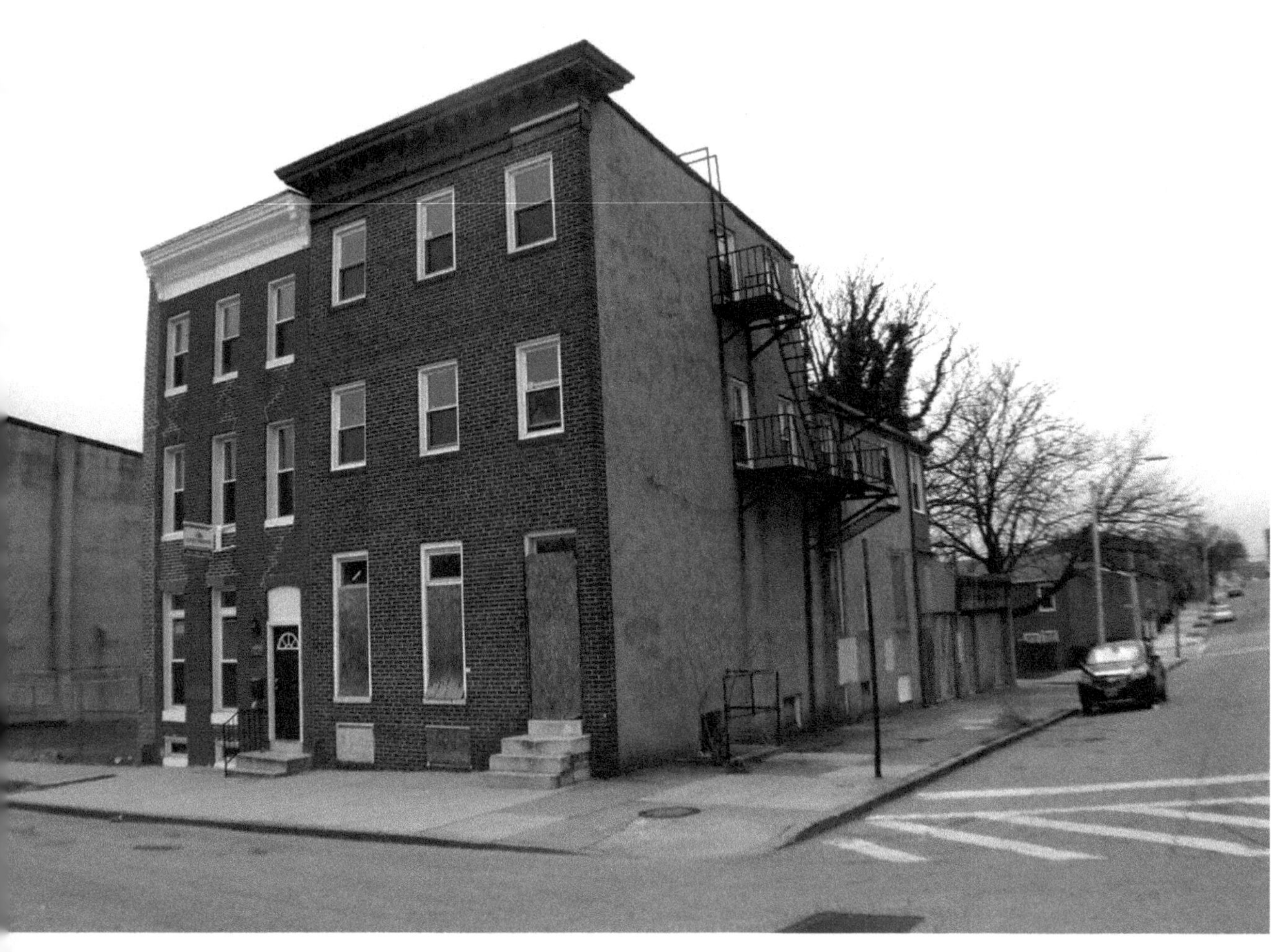

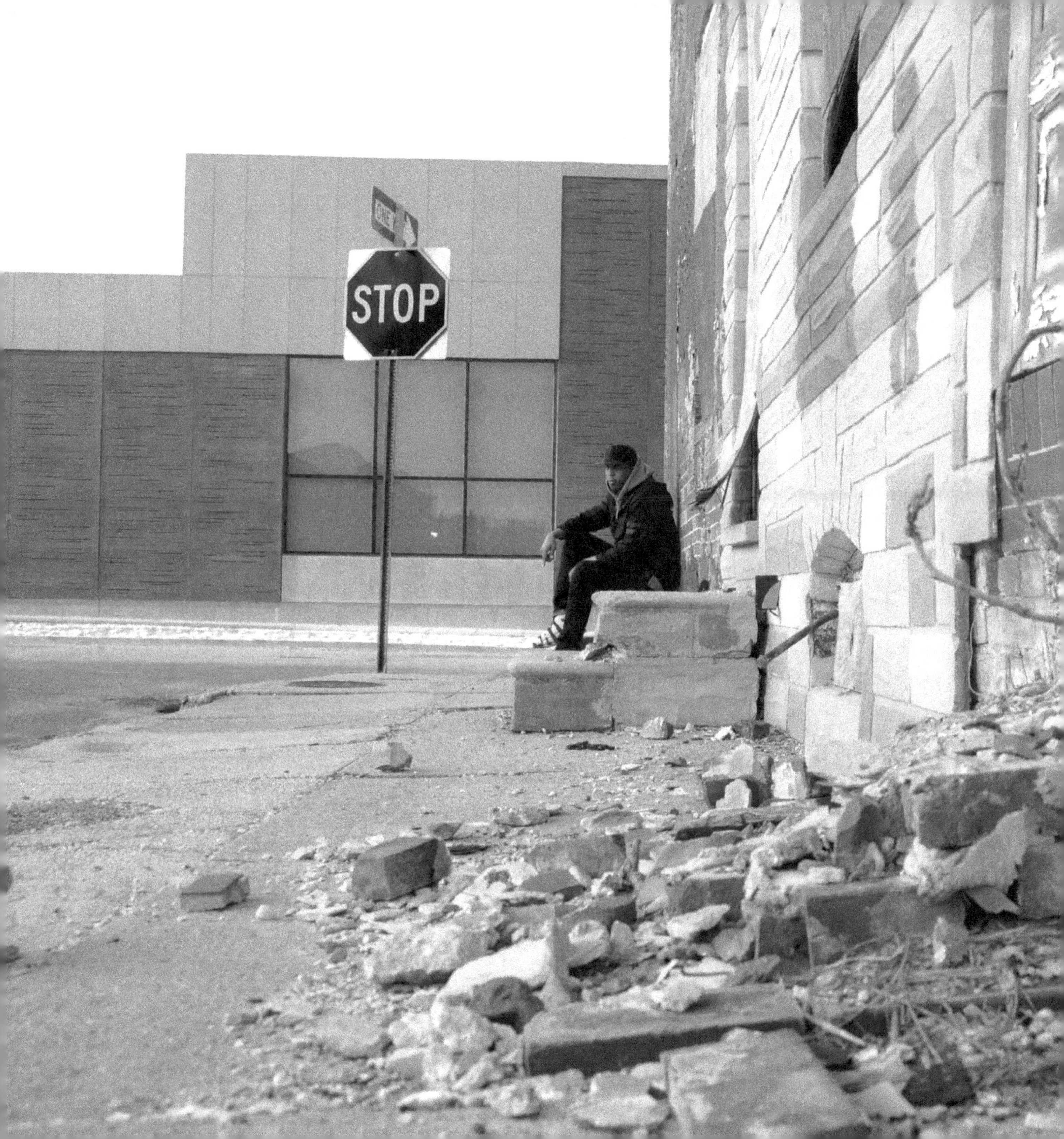
ONE
STOP

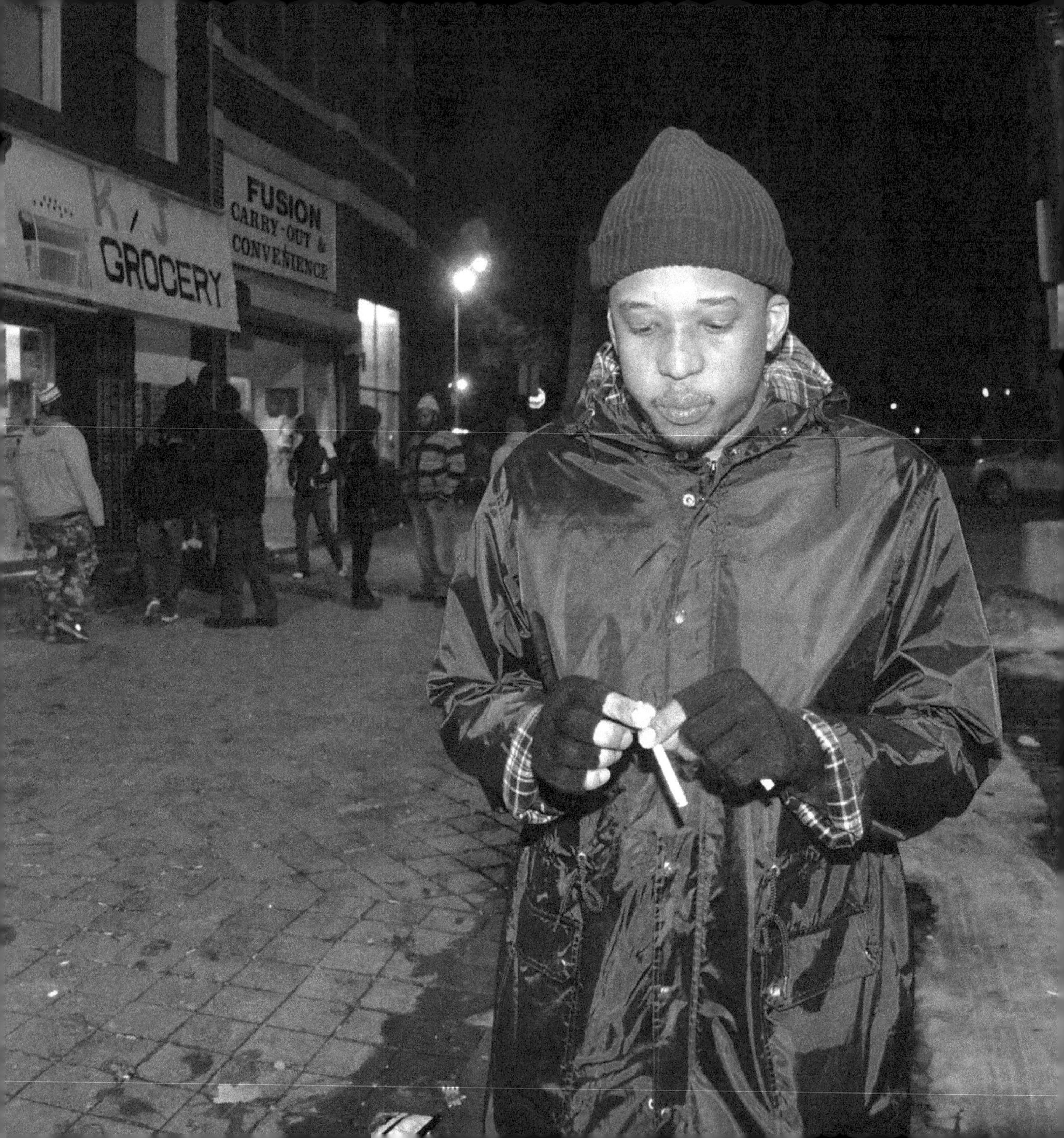
K / J
GROCERY
FUSION
CARRY-OUT &
CONVENIENCE

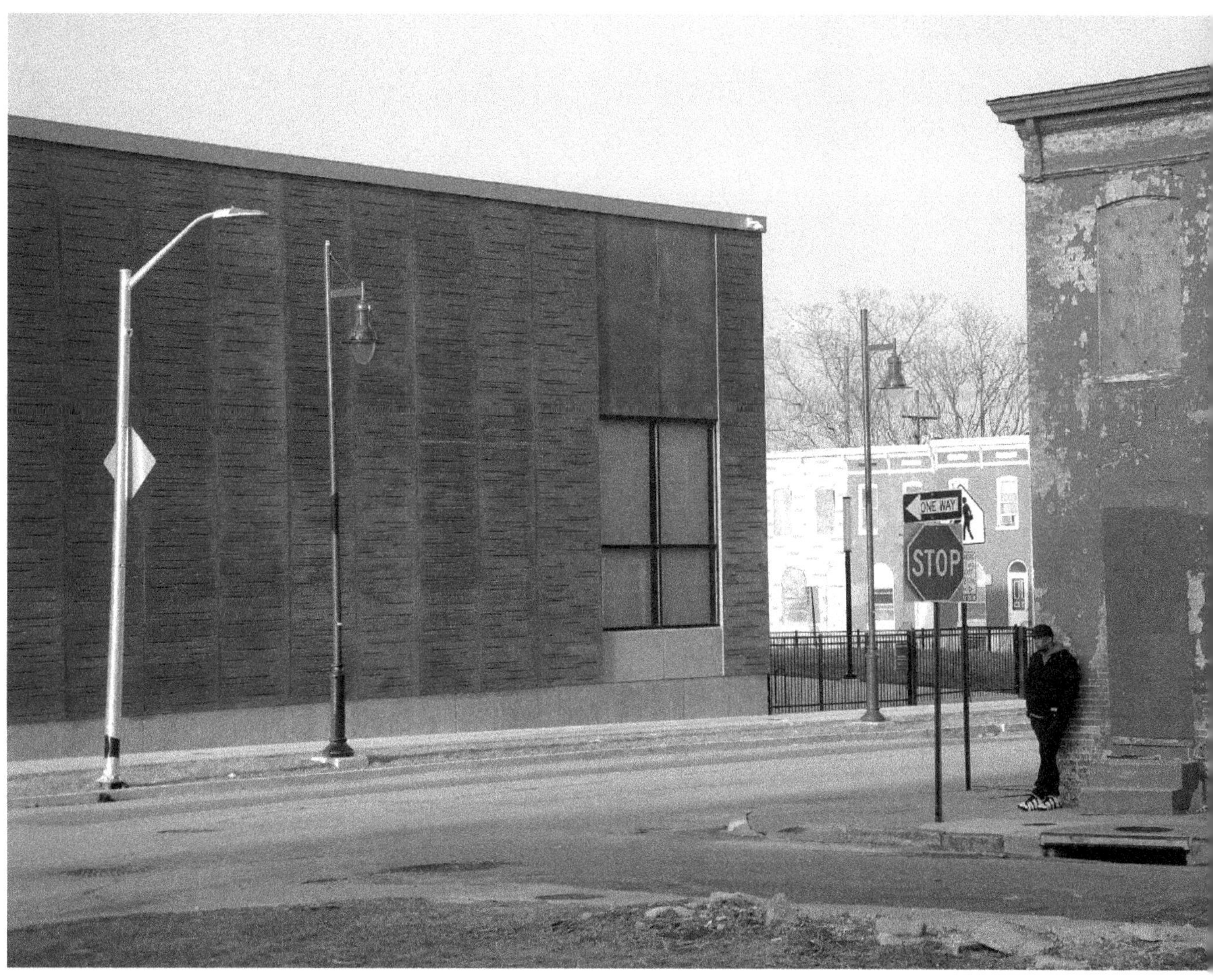
ONE WAY
STOP

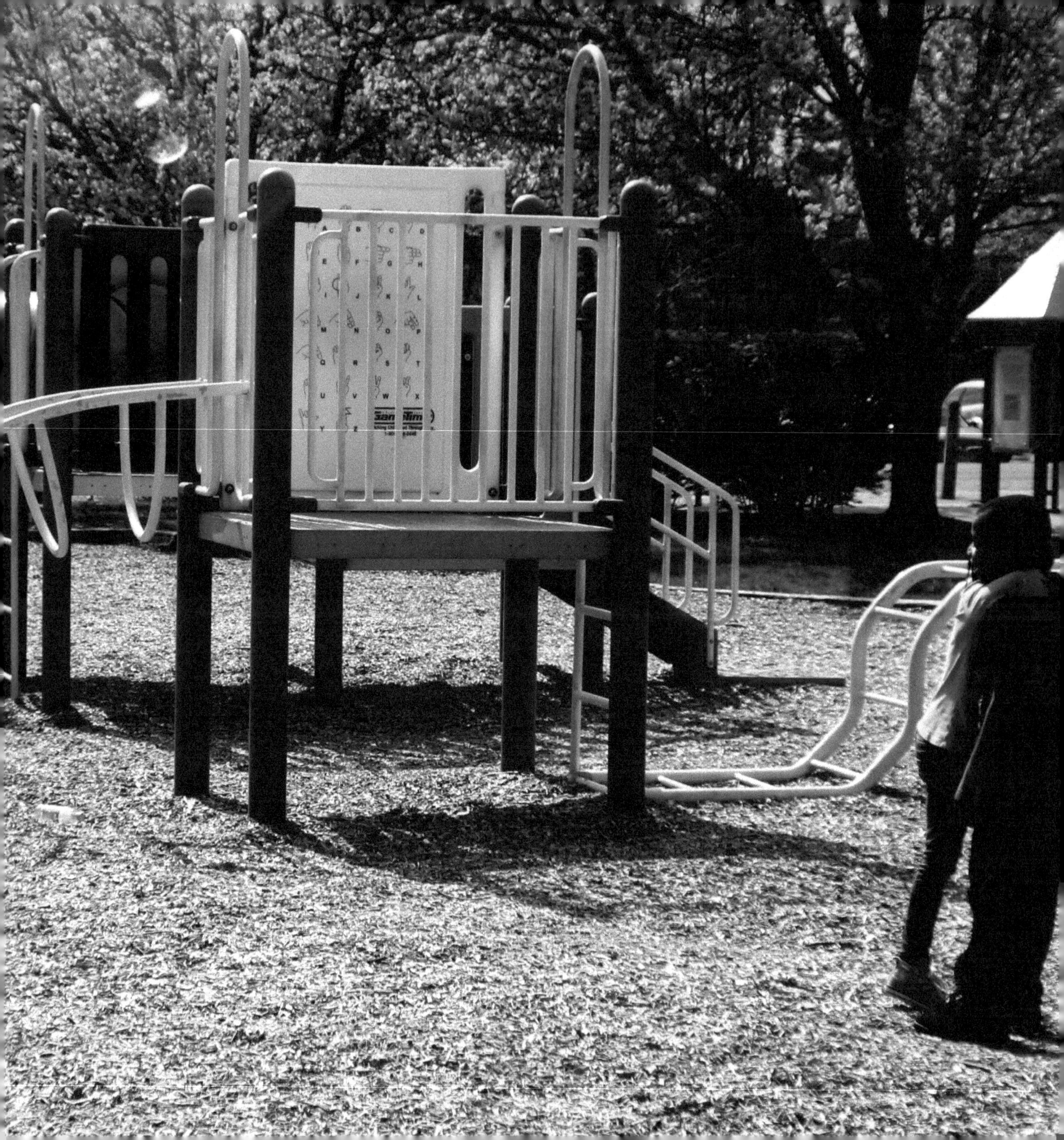

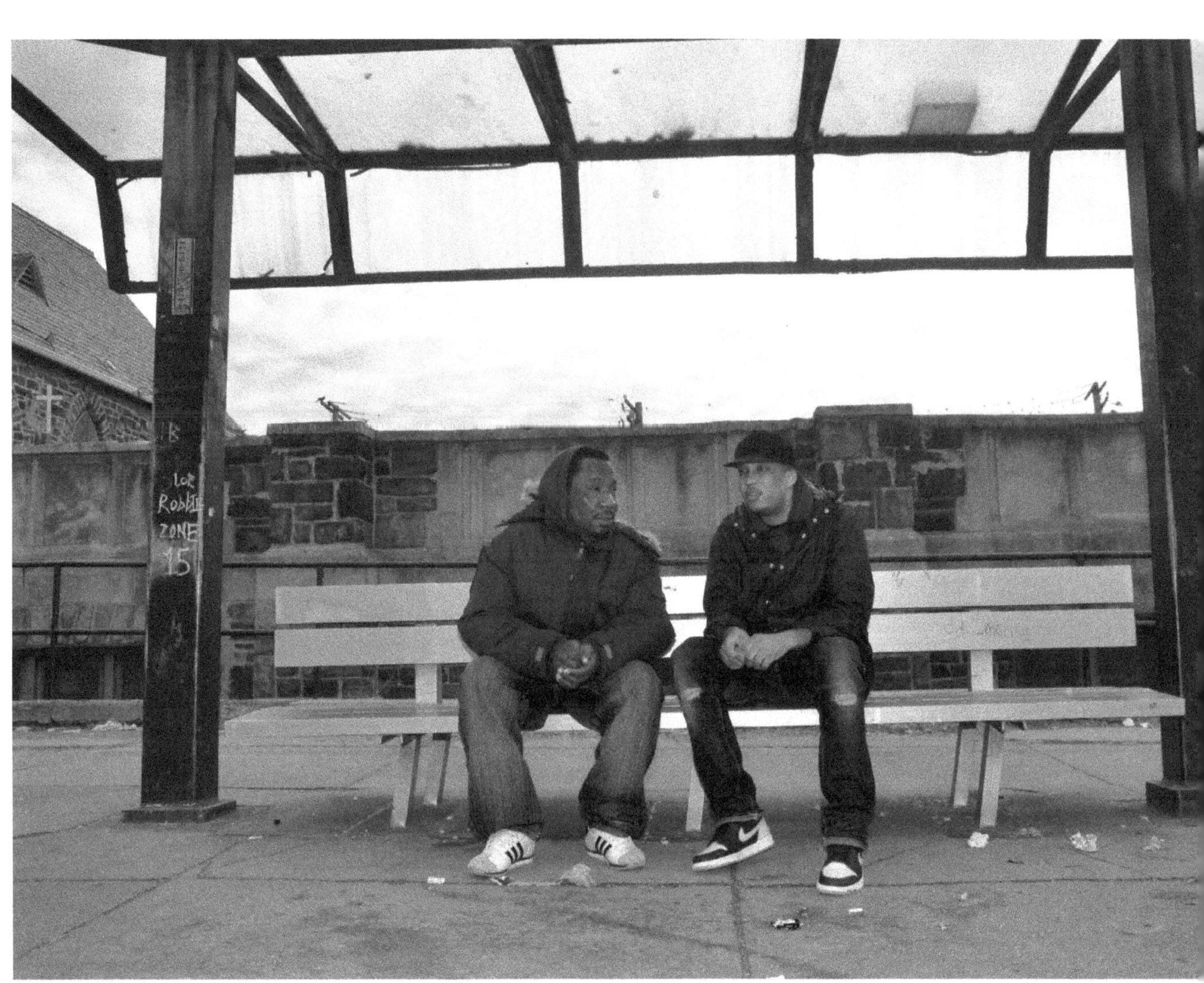
ZONE
15

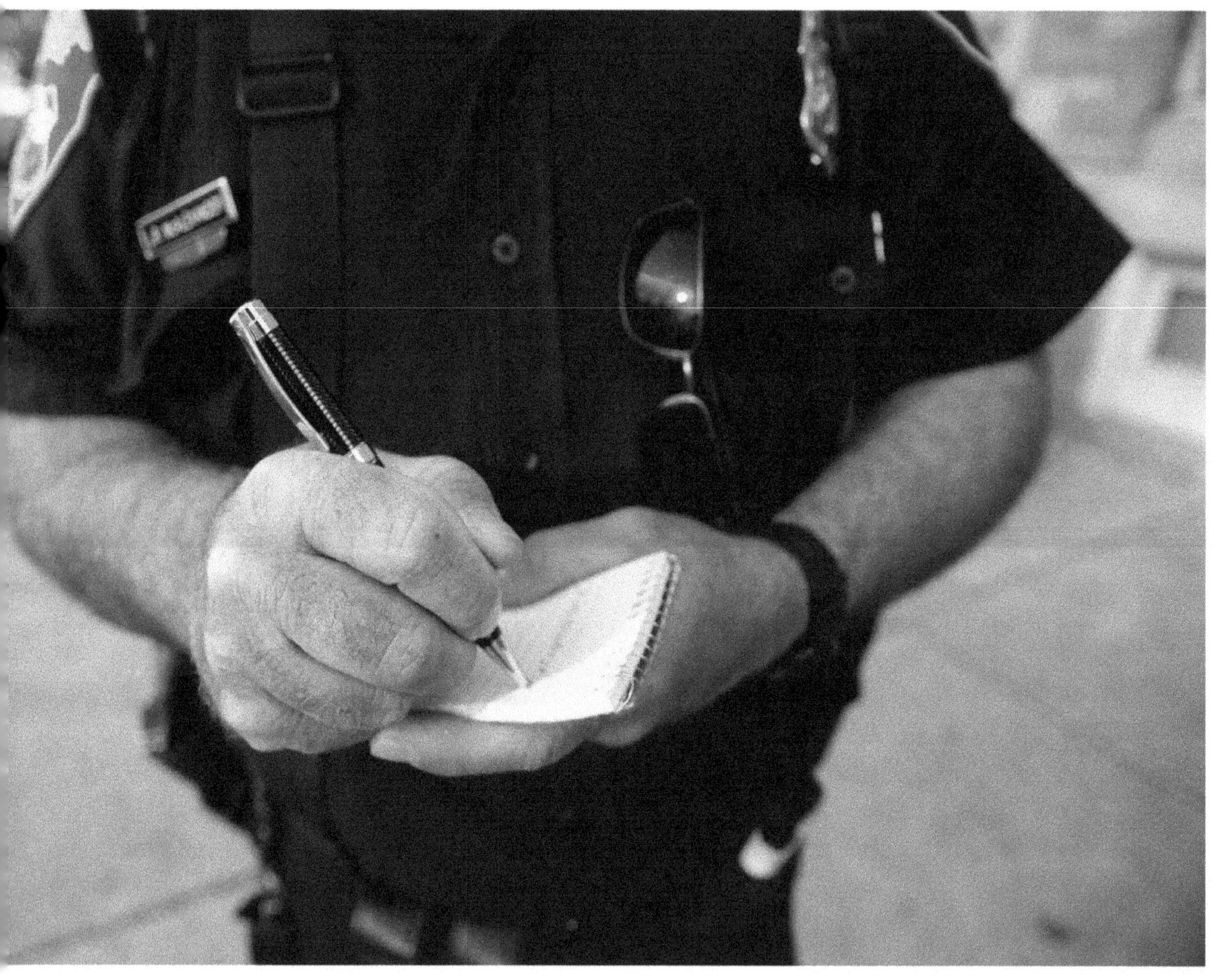

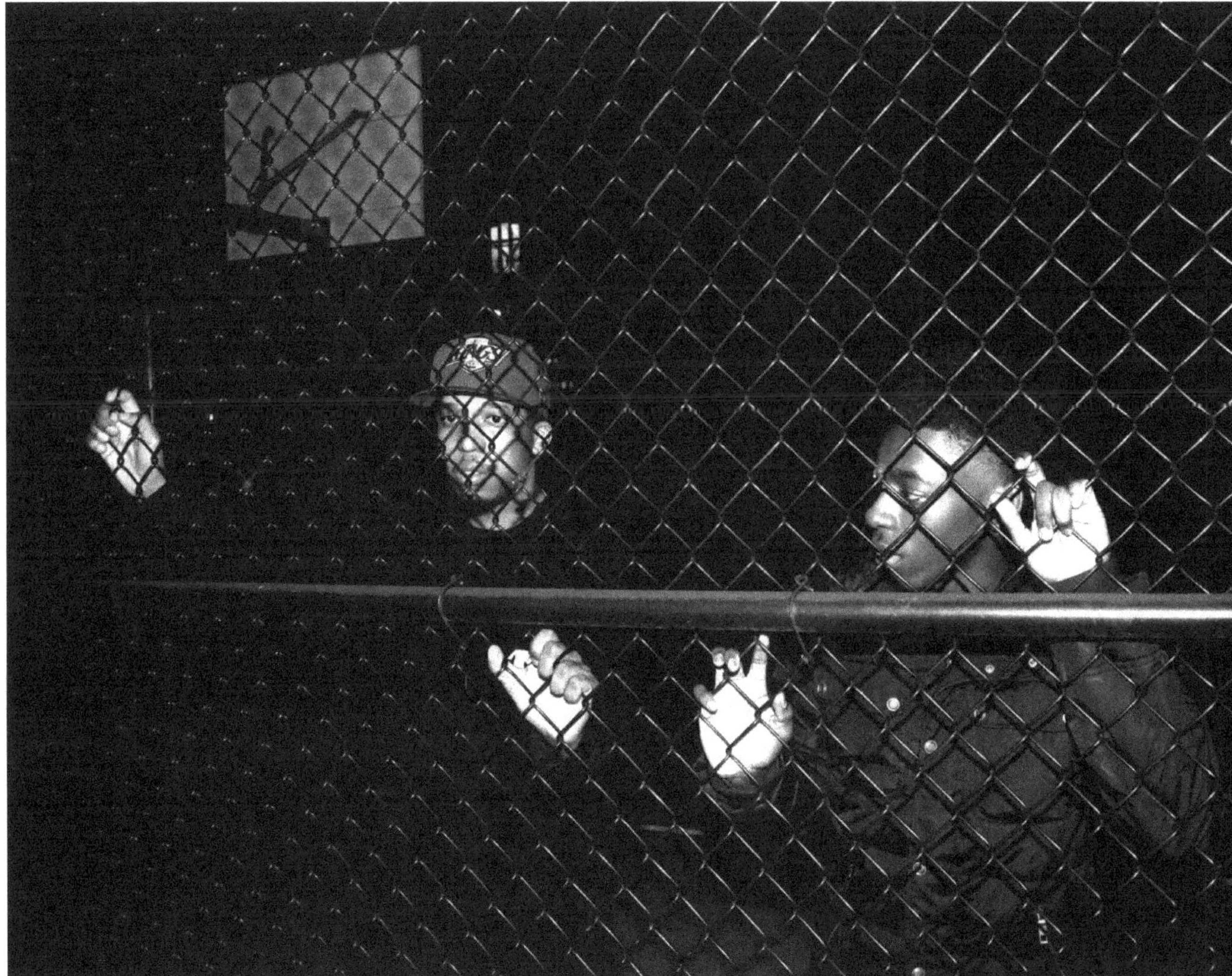

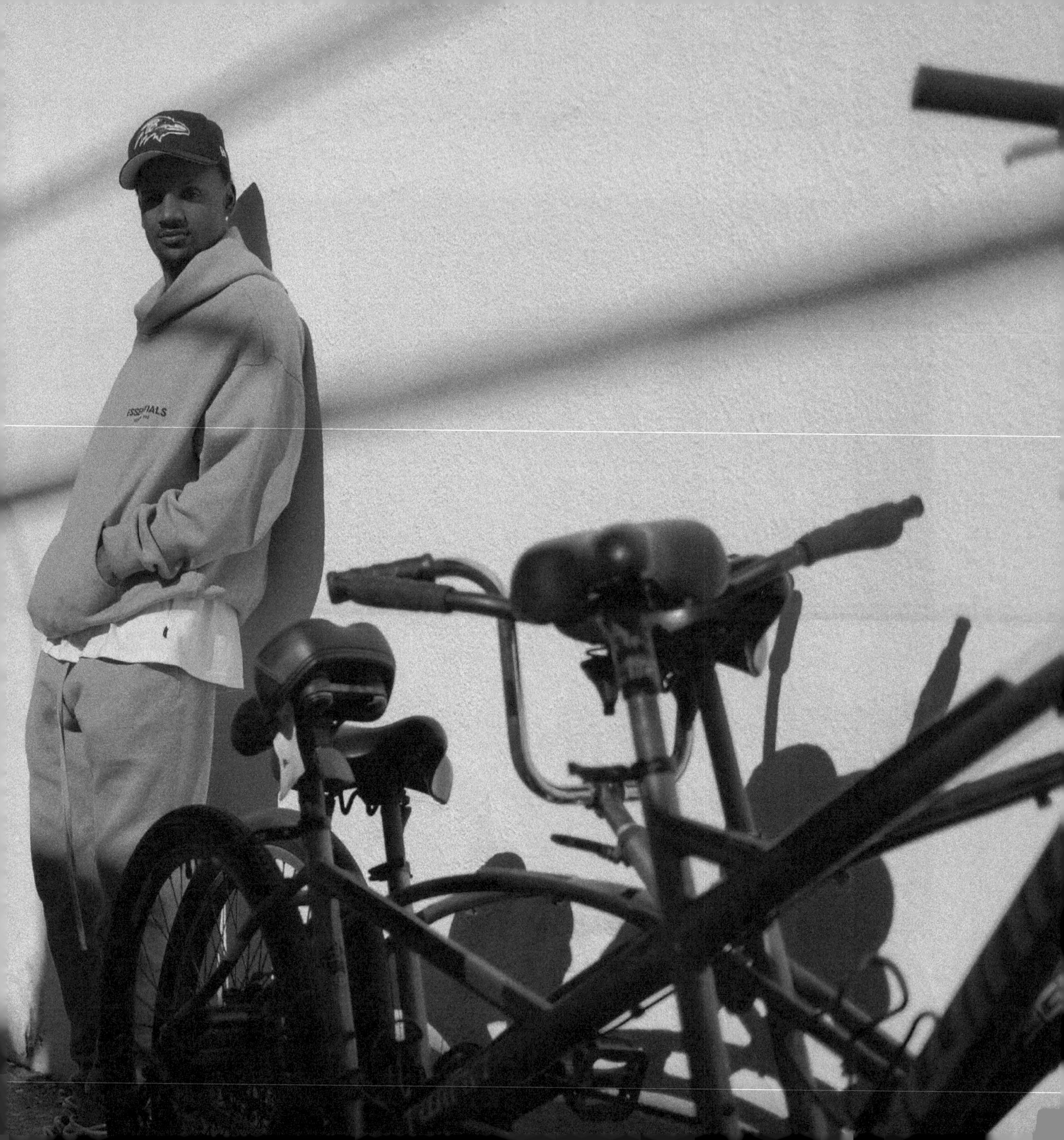

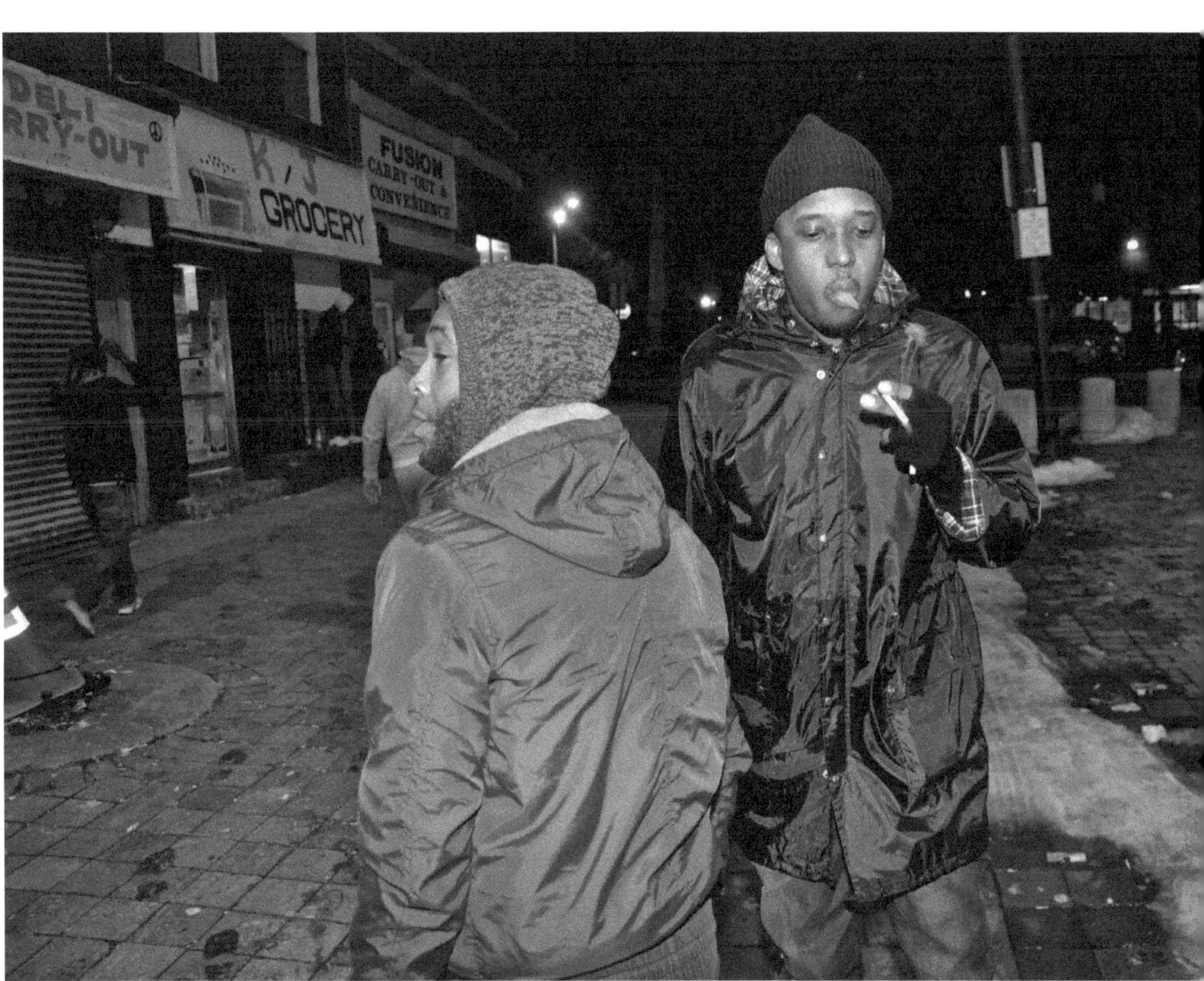
DELI
RRY-OUT
GROCERY
FUSION
CARRY-OUT &
CONVENIENCE

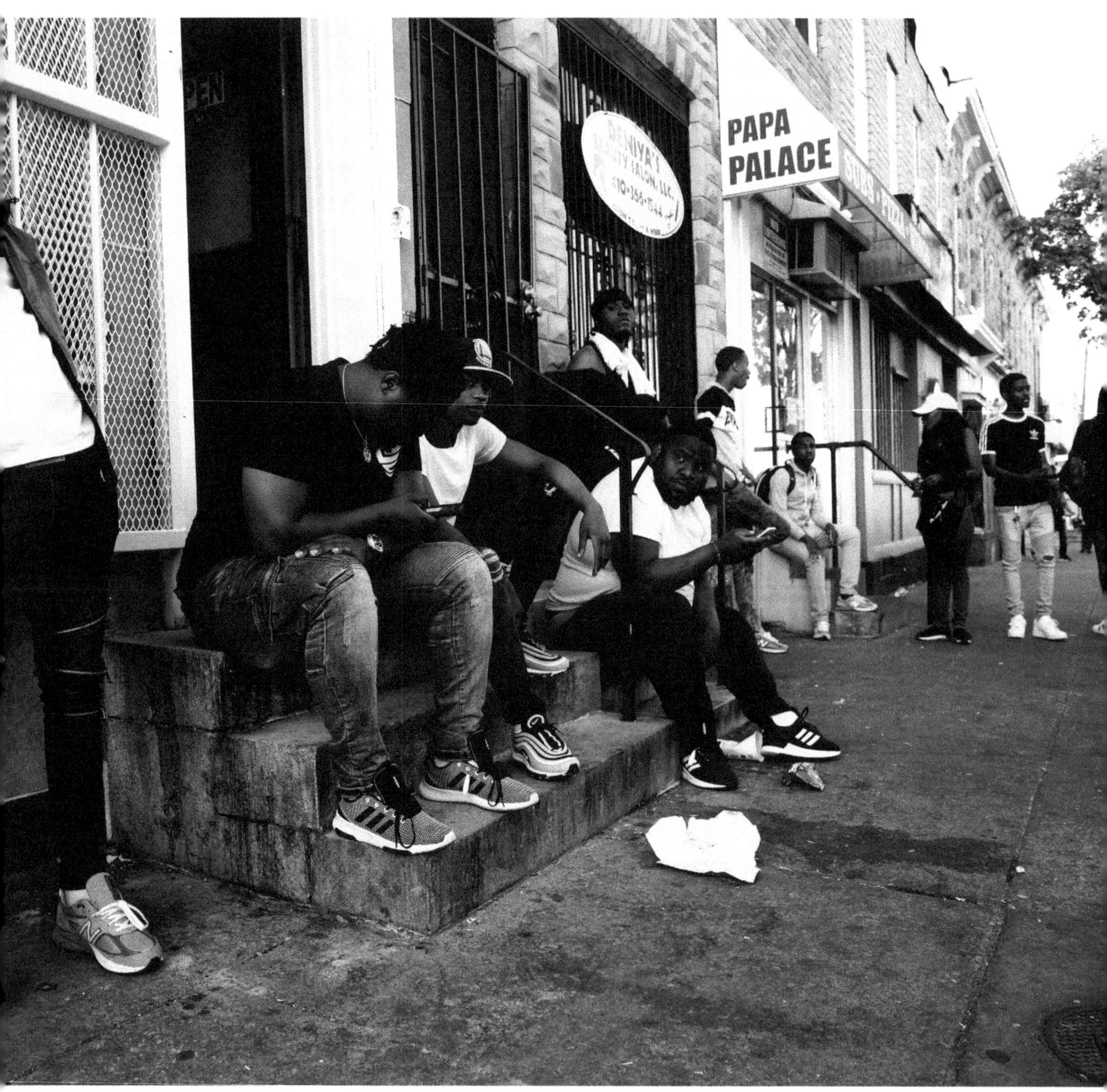
PAPA
PALACE

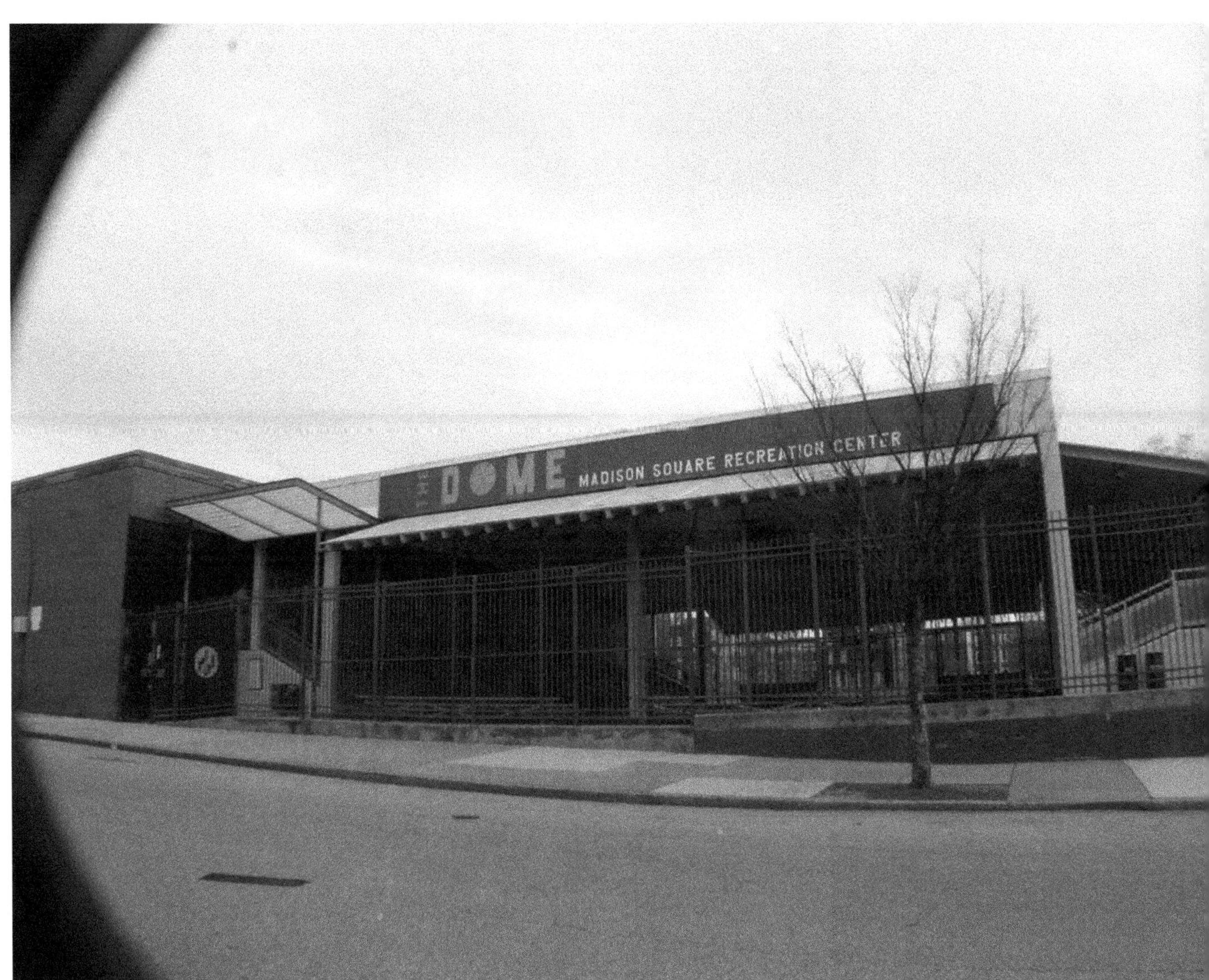
THE DOME
MADISON SQUARE RECREATION CENTER

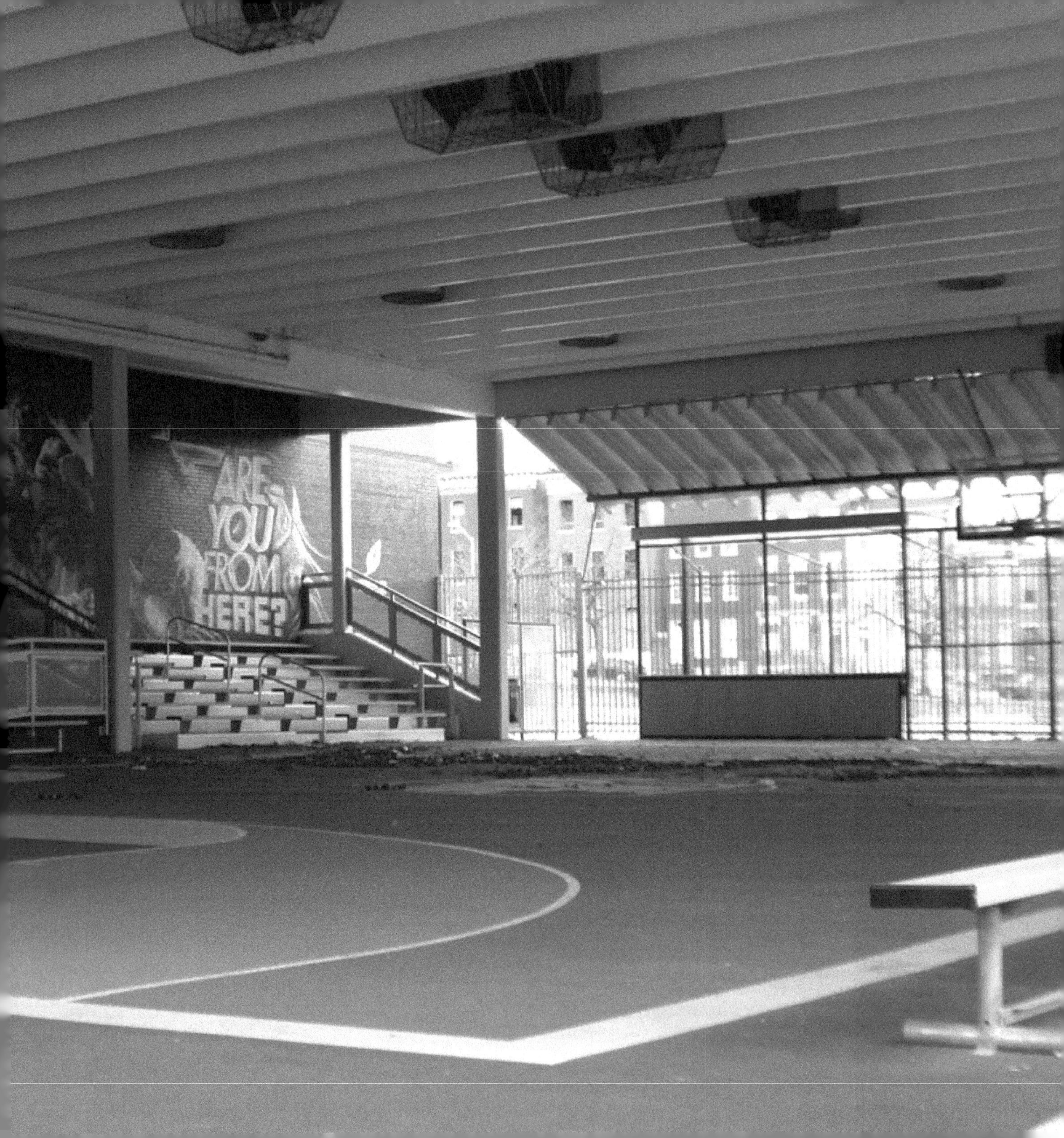
ARE YOU FROM HERE?

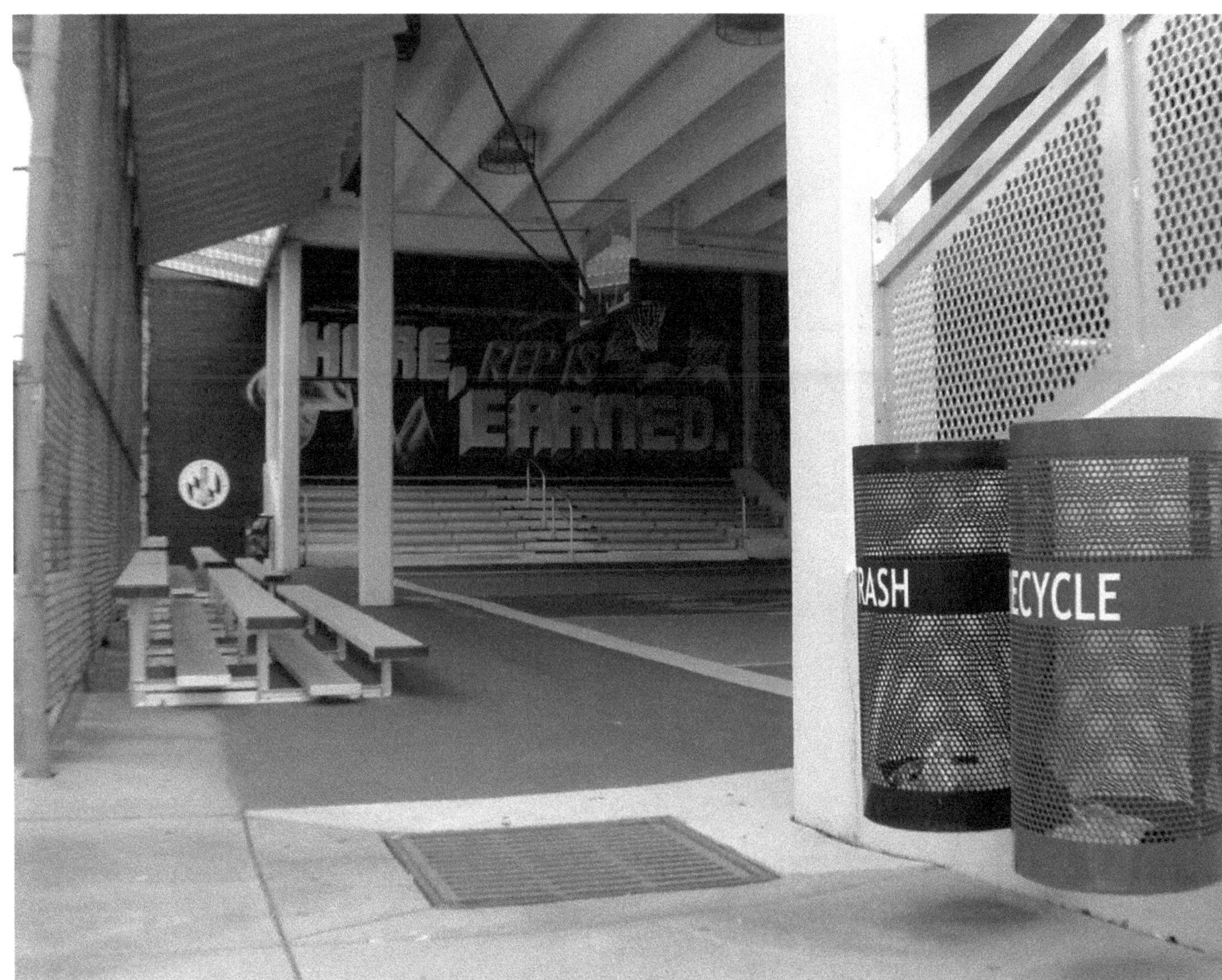
EARNED.
RASH
ECYCLE

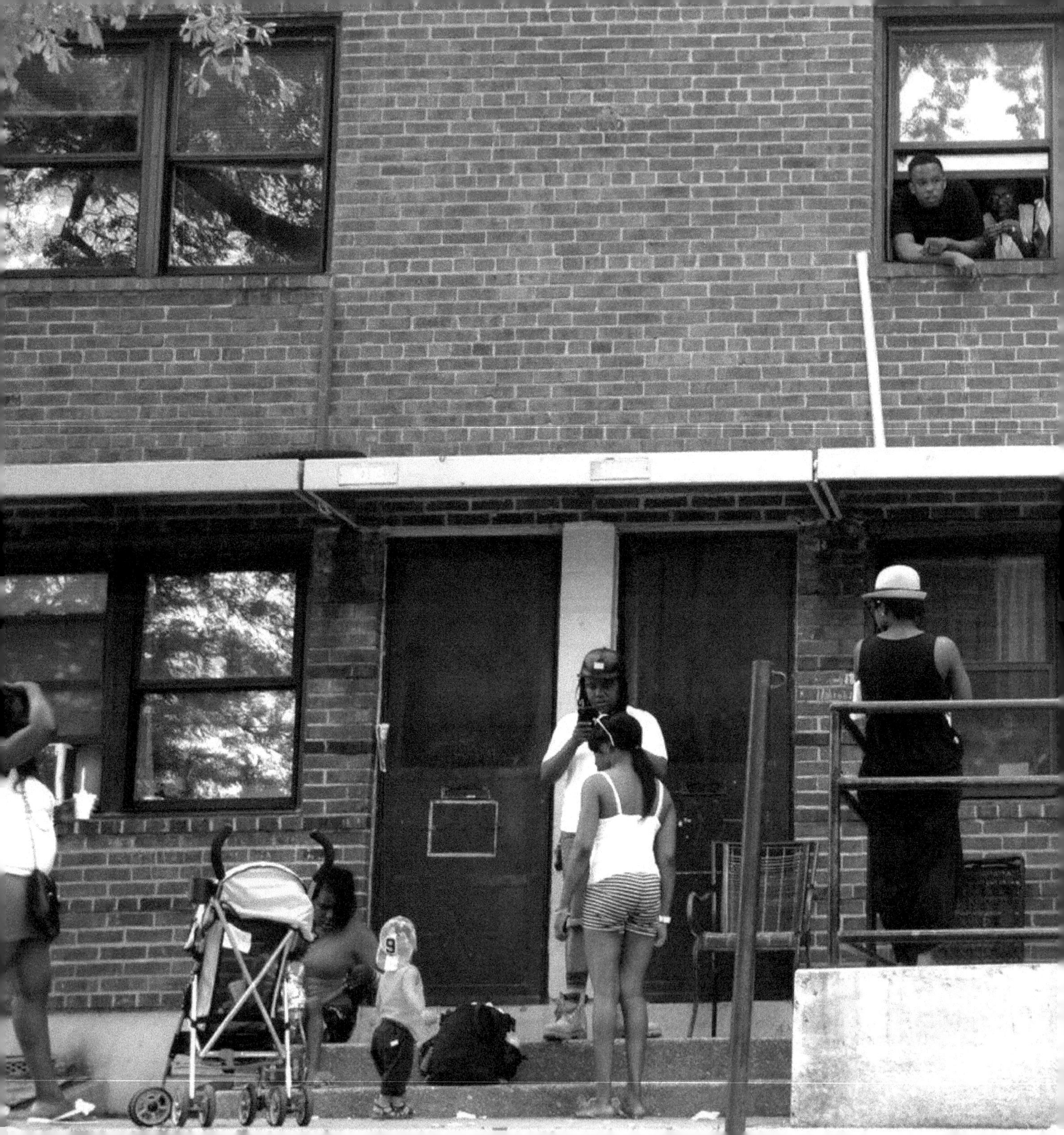

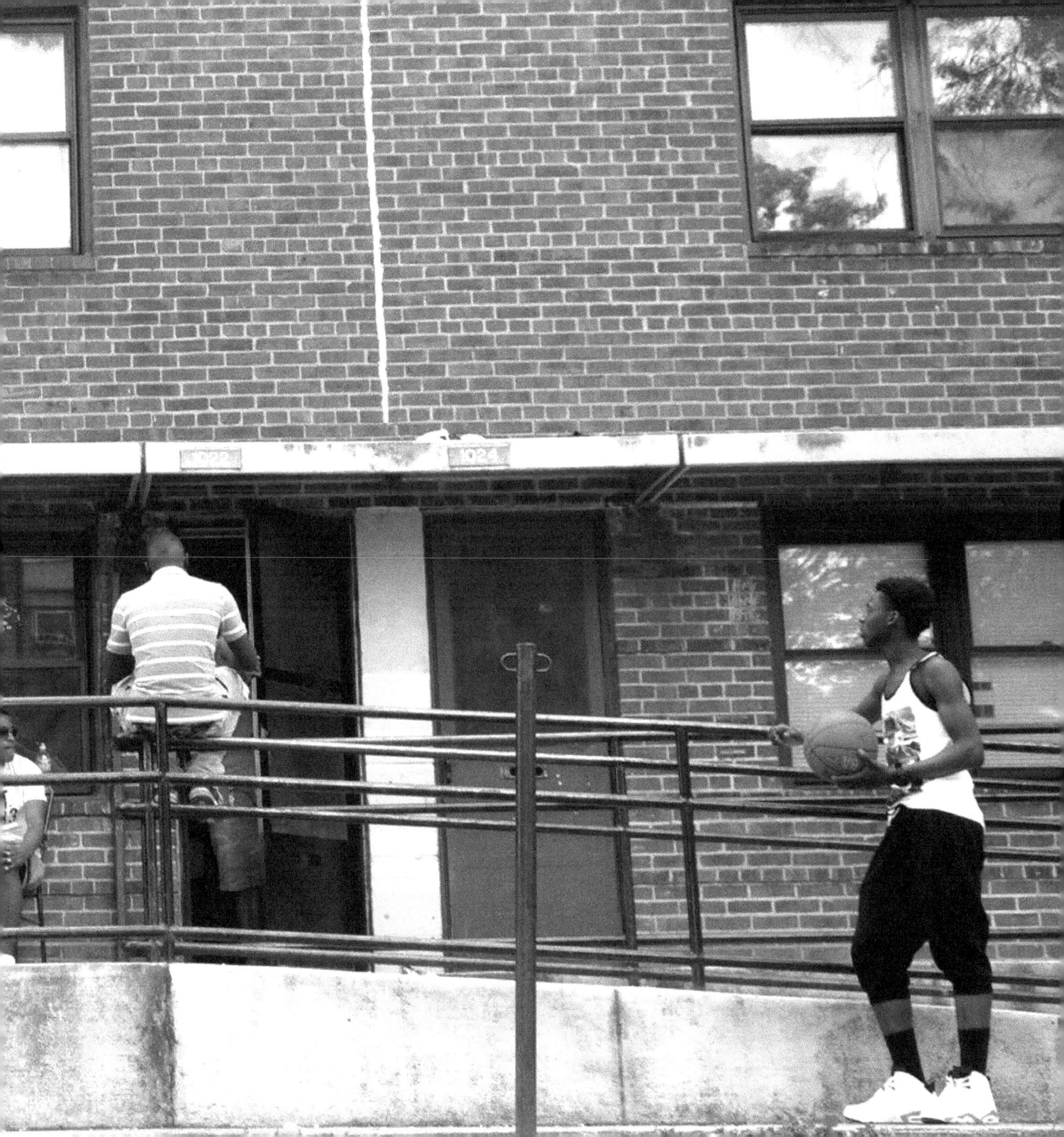
1024

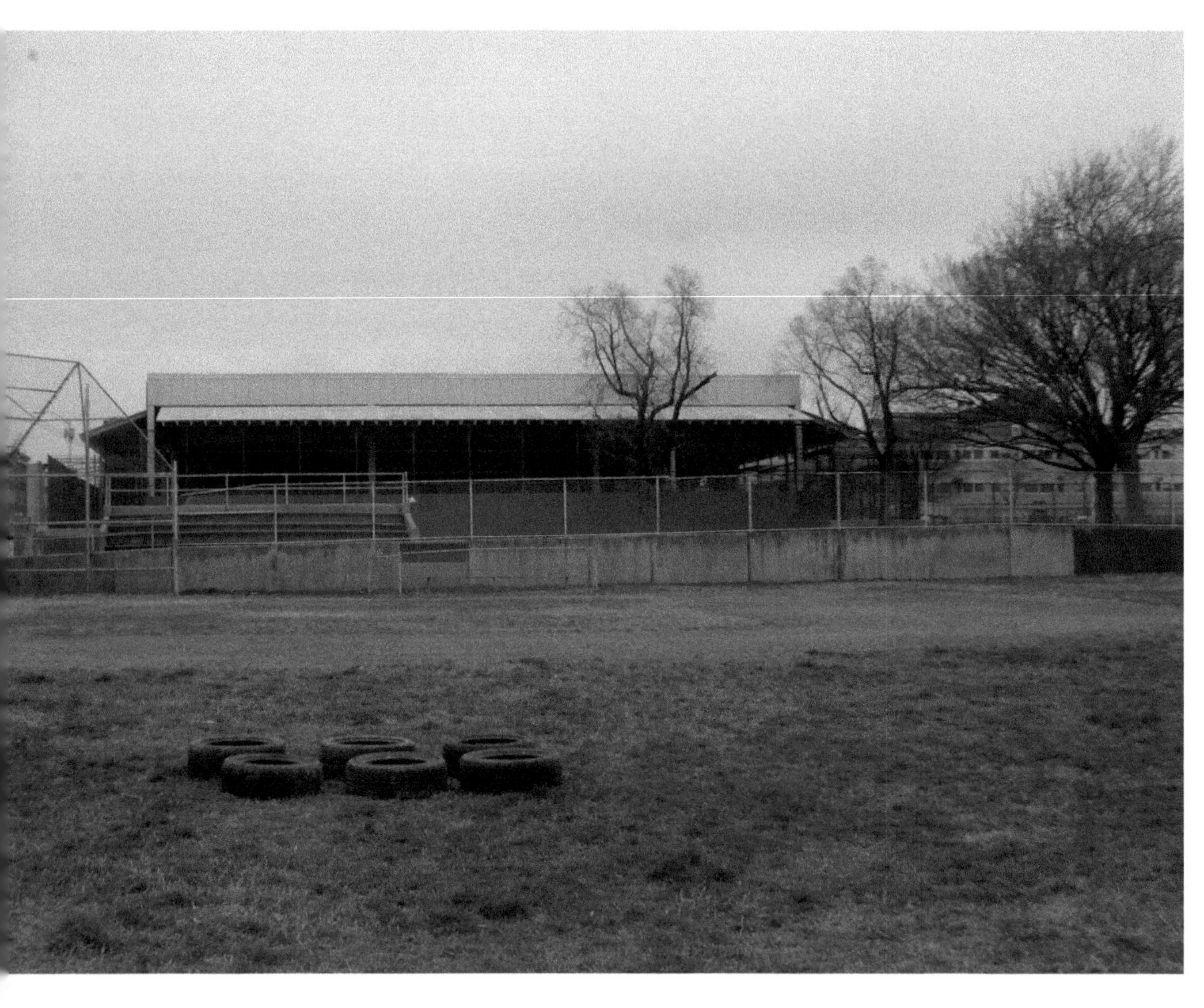

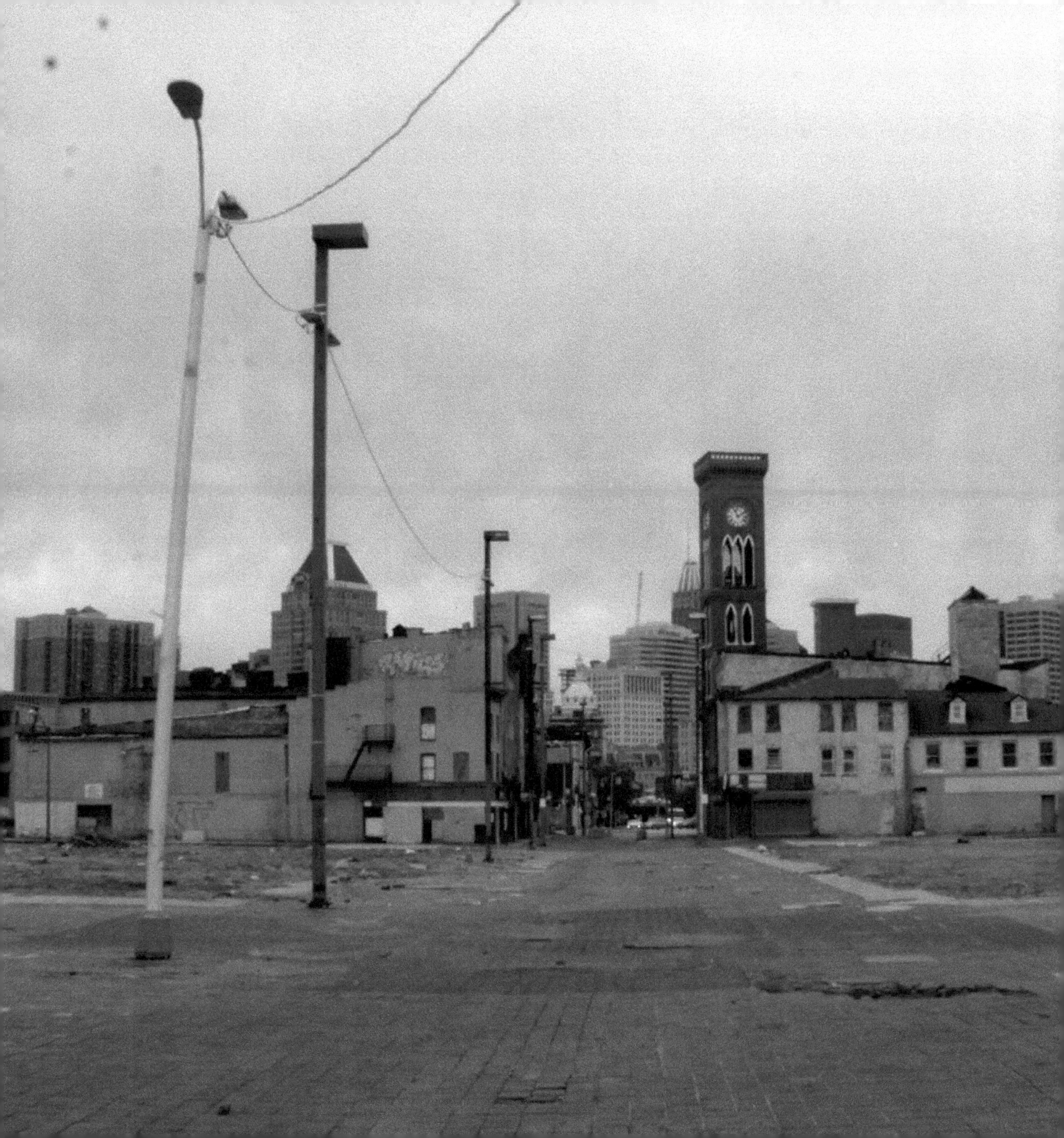

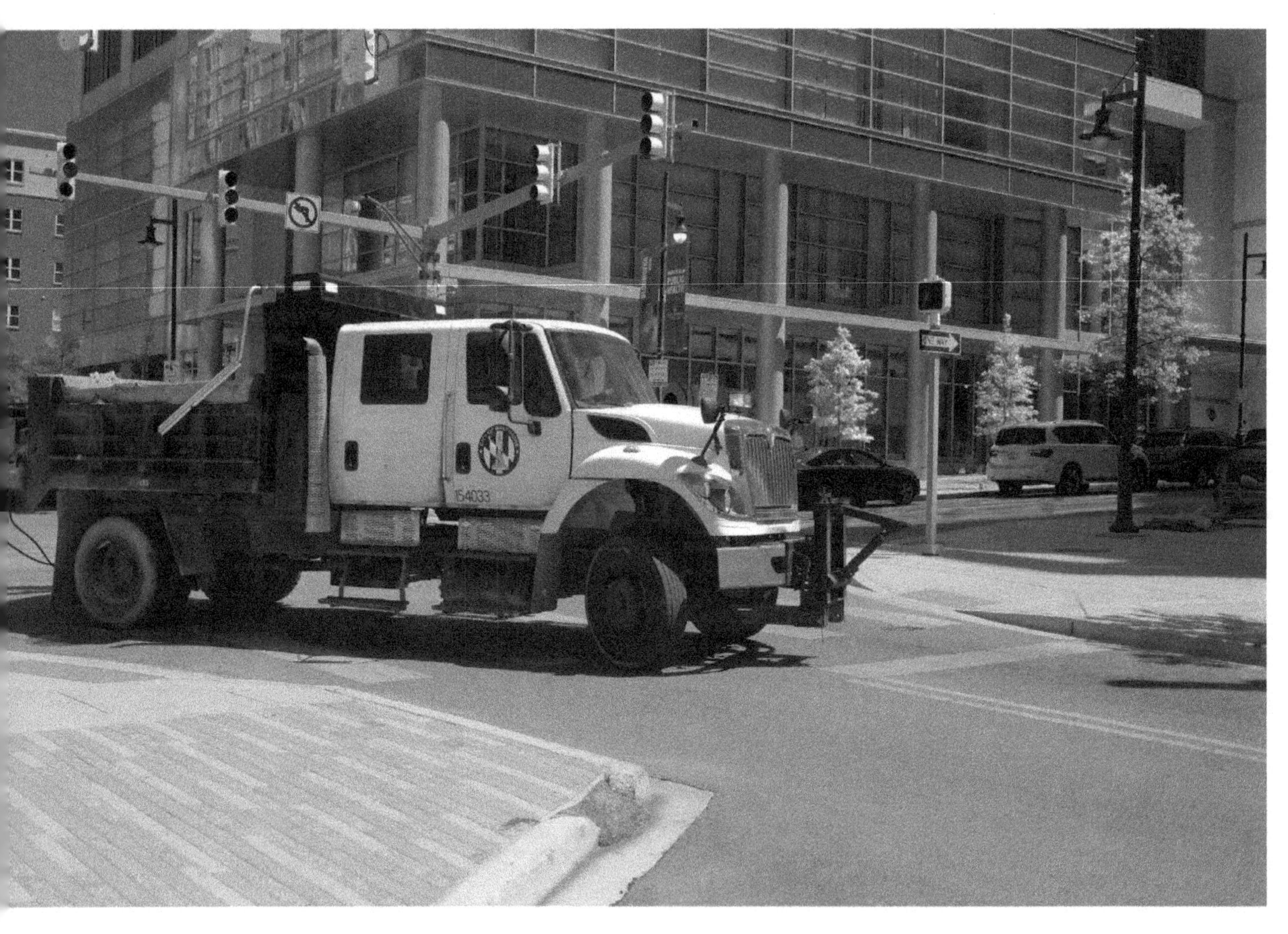
154033

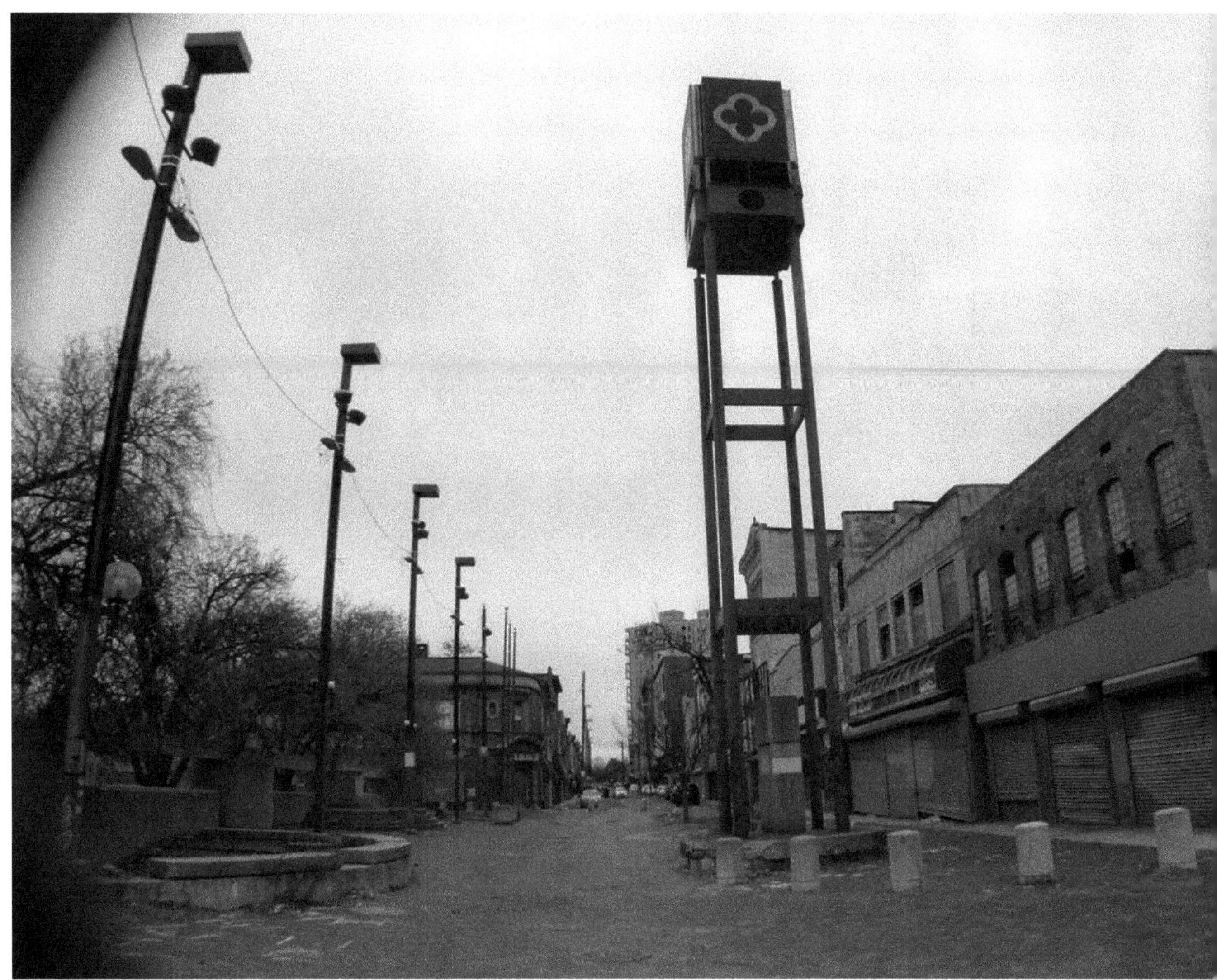

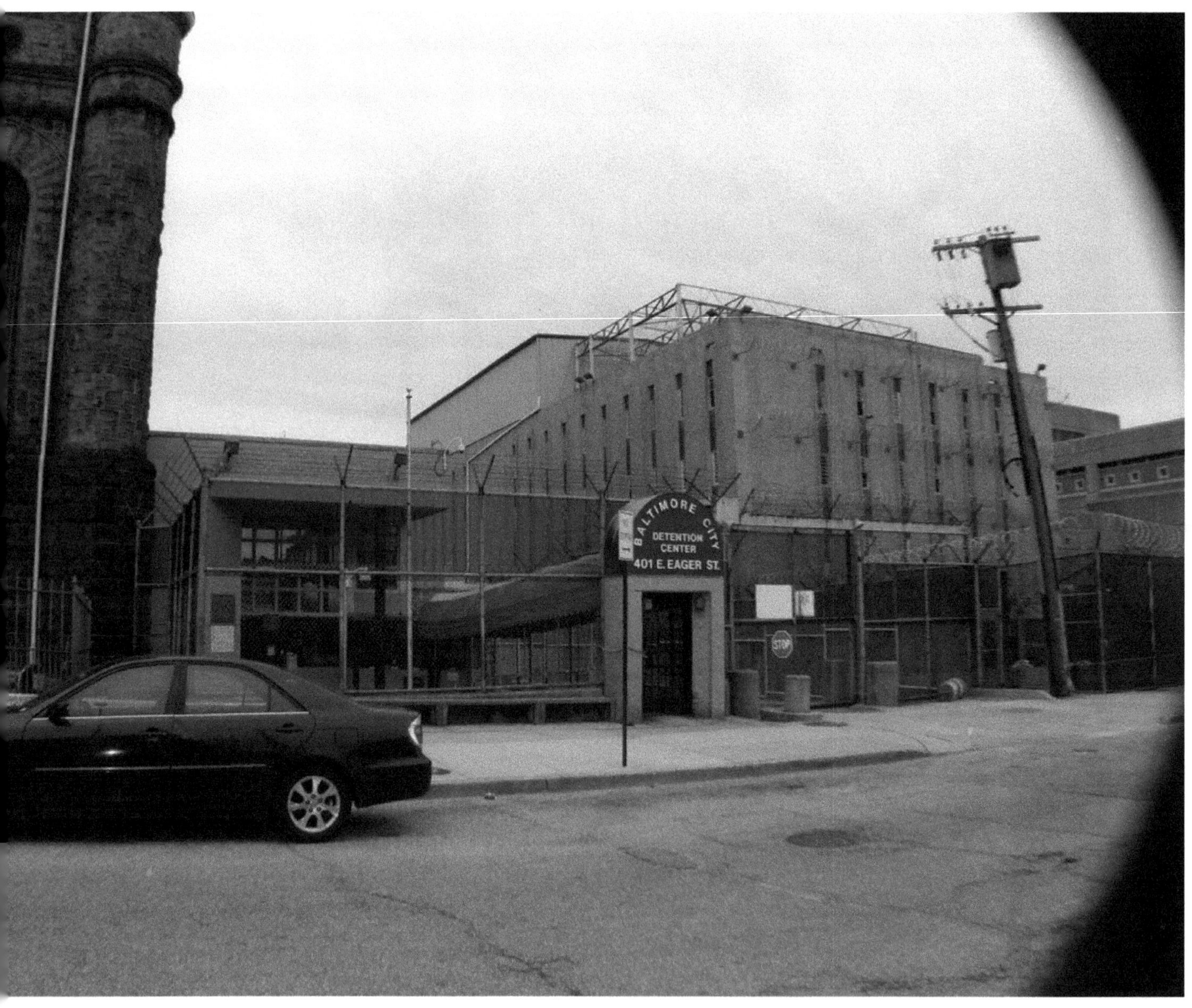
BALTIMORE CITY
DETENTION CENTER
401 E. EAGER ST.
STOP

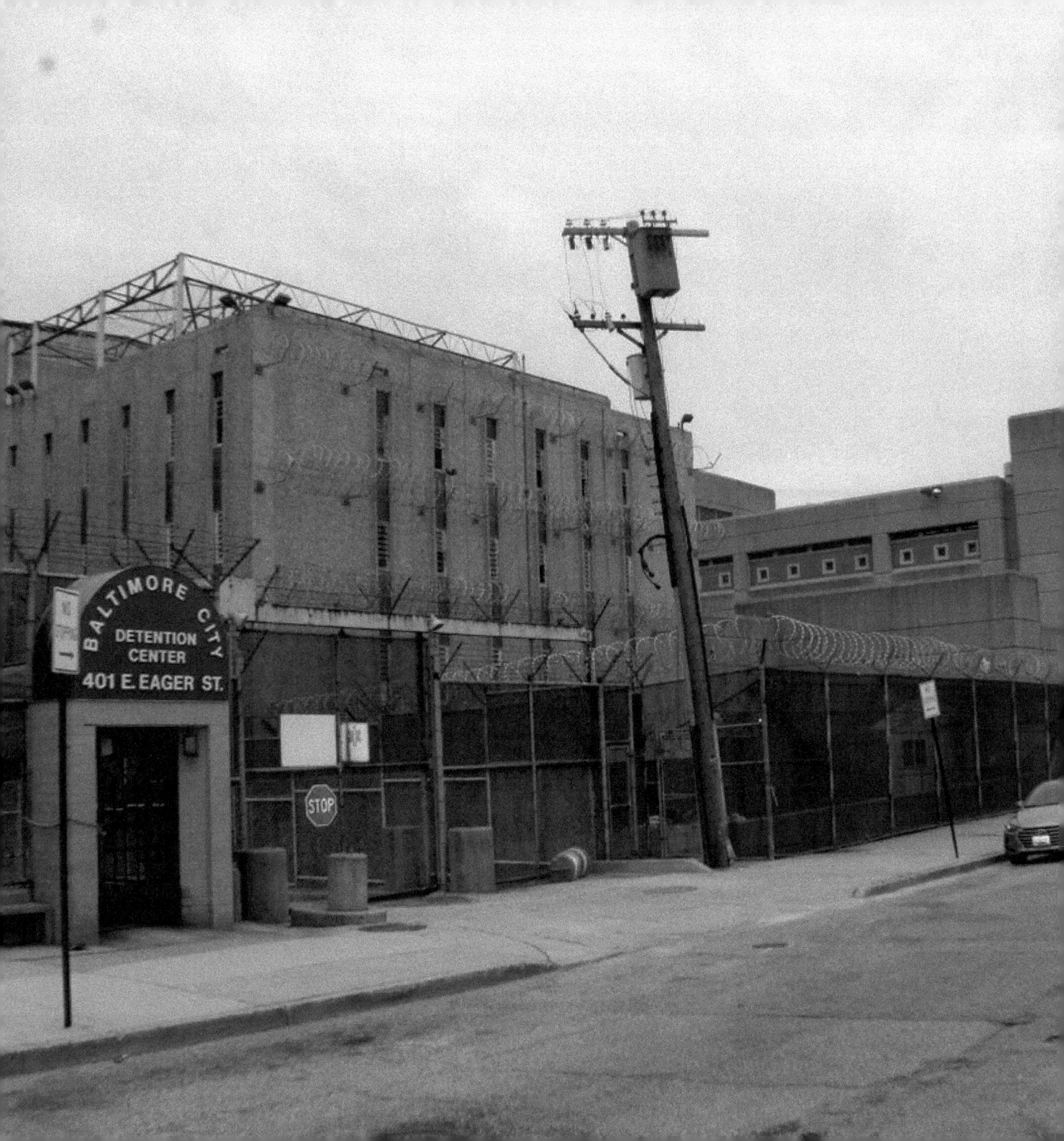
BALTIMORE CITY
DETENTION CENTER
401 E. EAGER ST.
STOP

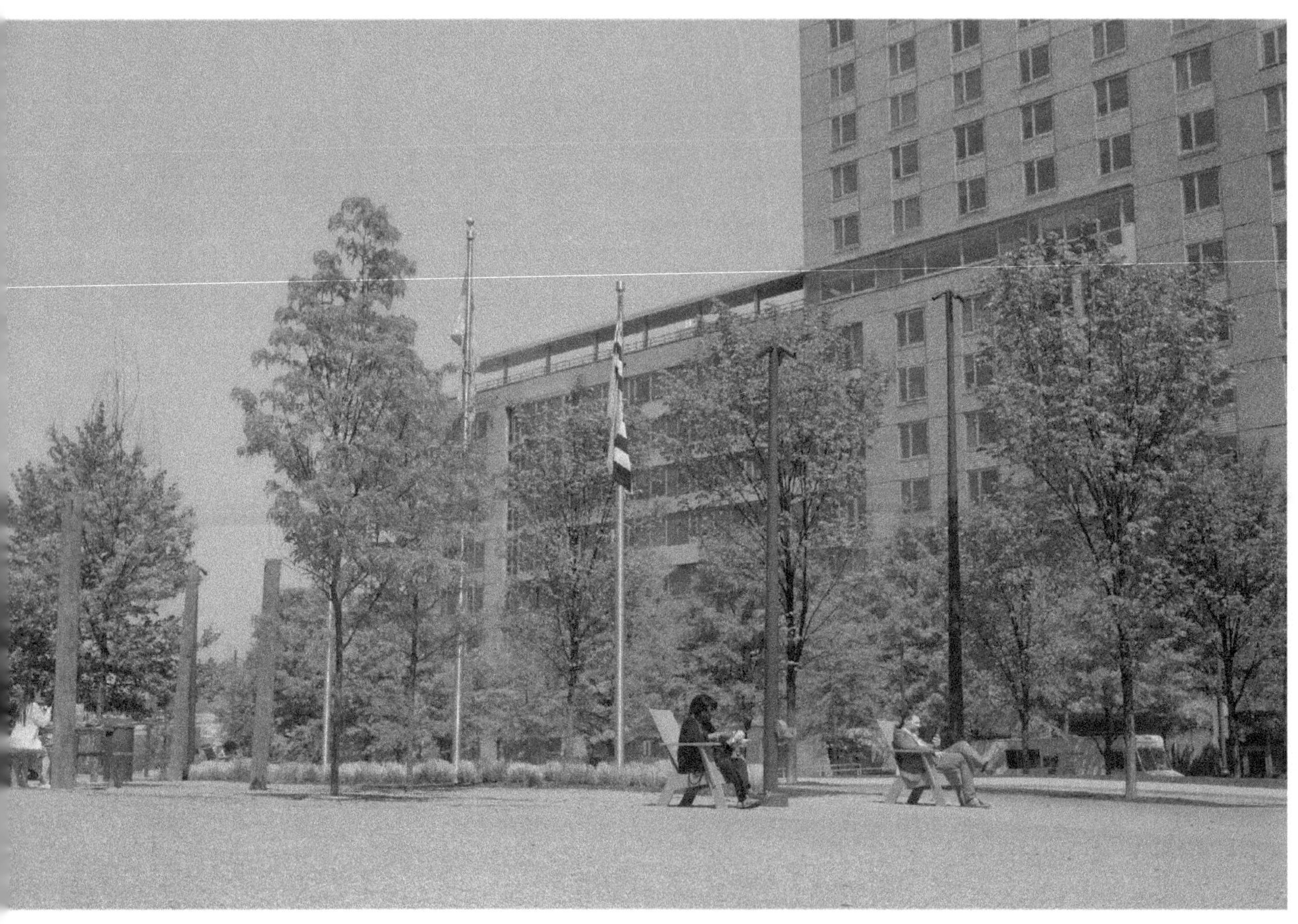

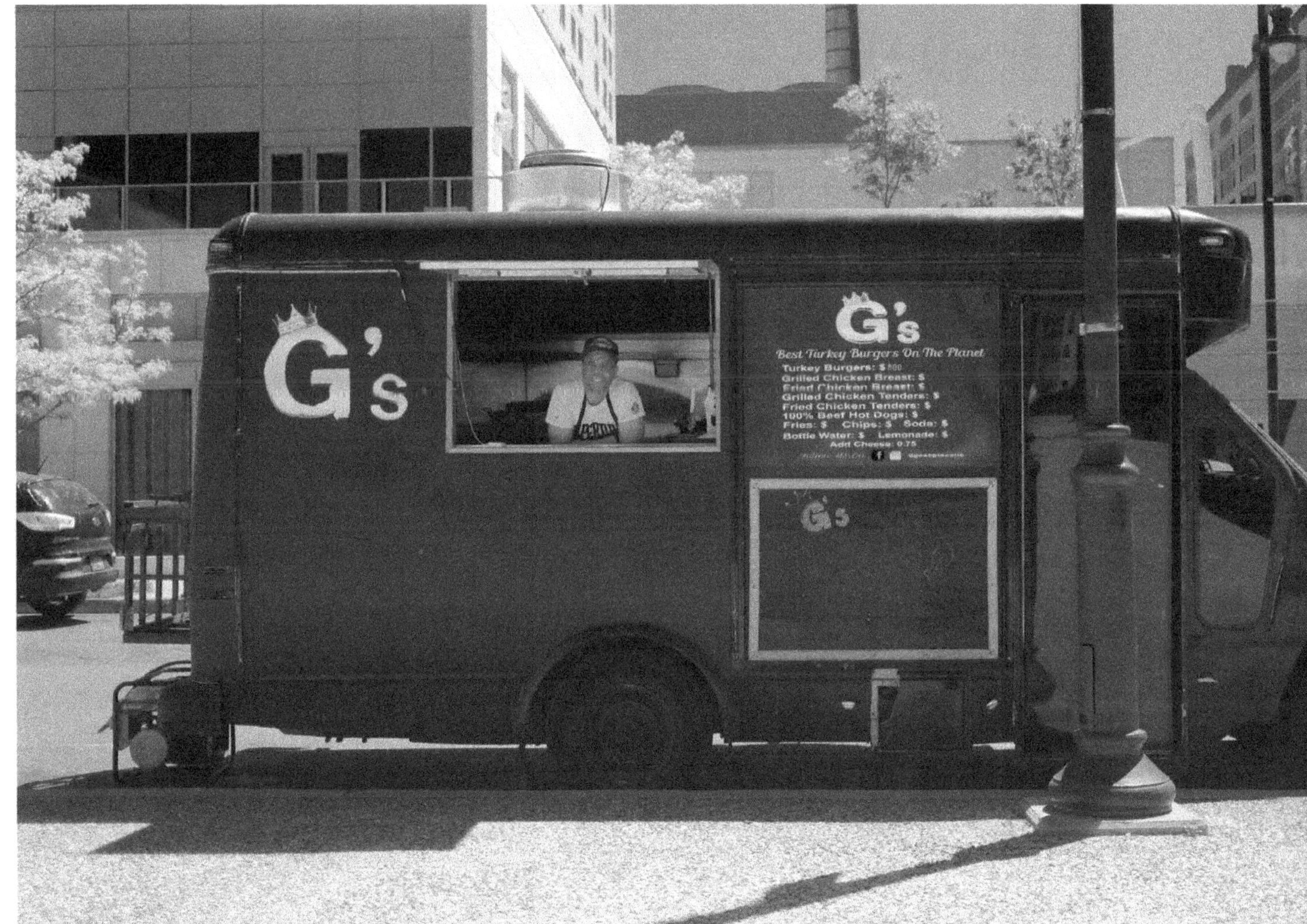
G's
G's
Best Turkey Burgers On The Planet
Turkey Burgers: $
Grilled Chicken Breast: $
Fried Chicken Breast: $
Grilled Chicken Tenders: $
Fried Chicken Tenders: $
100% Beef Hot Dogs: $
Fries: $ Chips: $ Soda: $
Bottle Water: $ Lemonade: $
Add Cheese: 0.75
G's

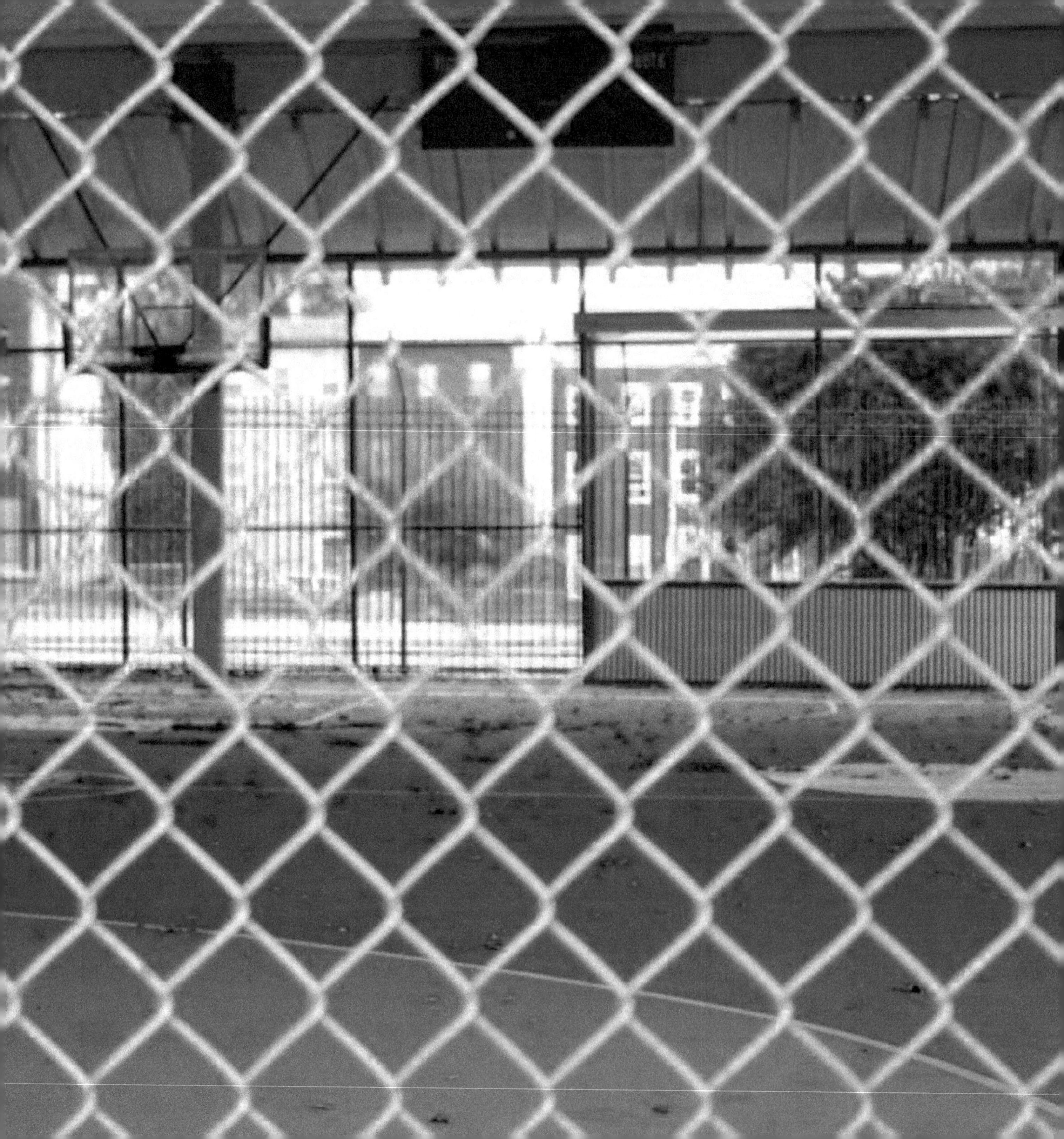

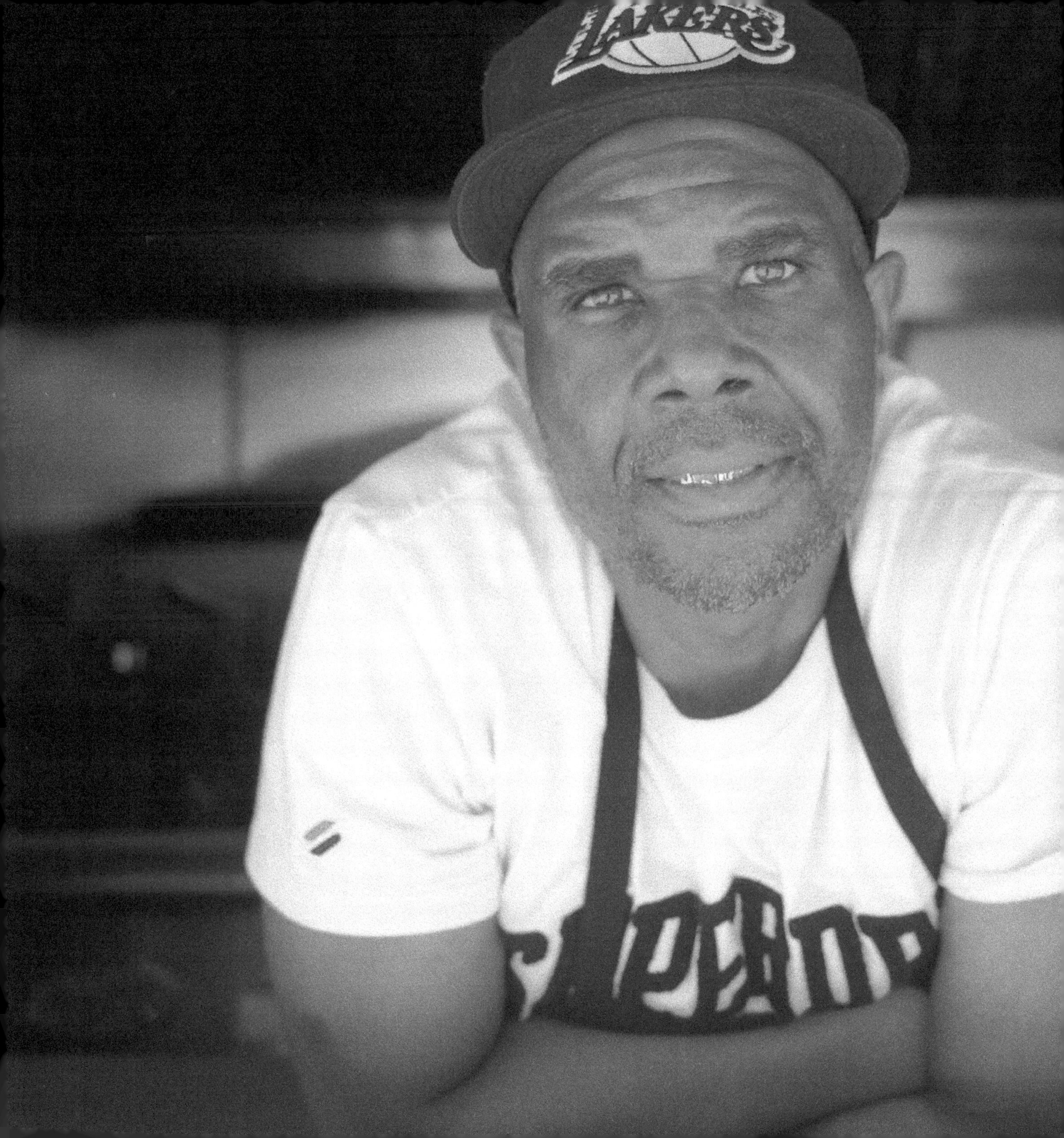
LAKERS

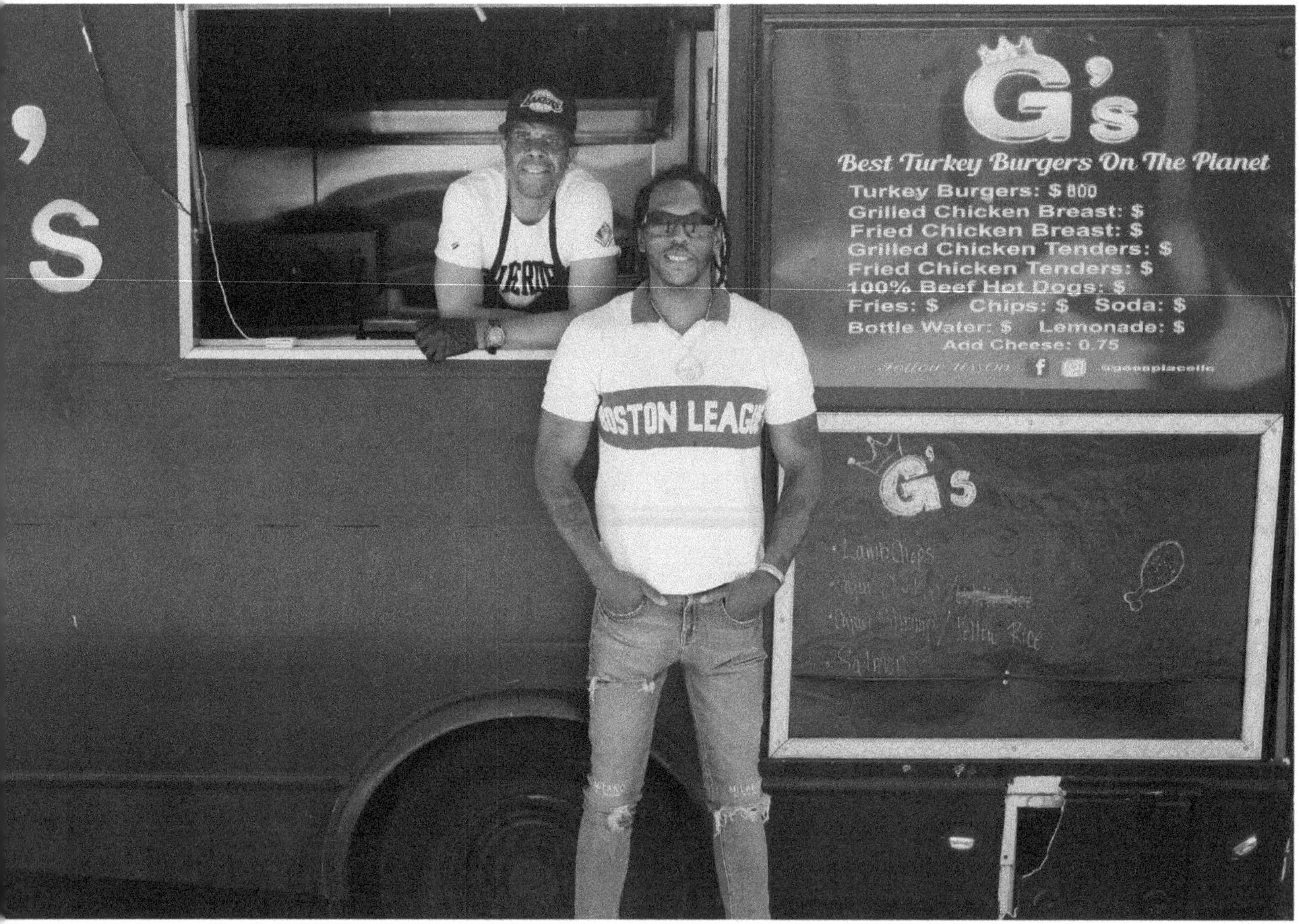

'S
G's
Best Turkey Burgers On The Planet
Turkey Burgers: $ 800
Grilled Chicken Breast: $
Fried Chicken Breast: $
Grilled Chicken Tenders: $
Fried Chicken Tenders: $
100% Beef Hot Dogs: $
Fries: $ Chips: $ Soda: $
Bottle Water: $ Lemonade: $
Add Cheese: 0.75
BOSTON LEAGUE
G's
Lamb Chops
Salmon

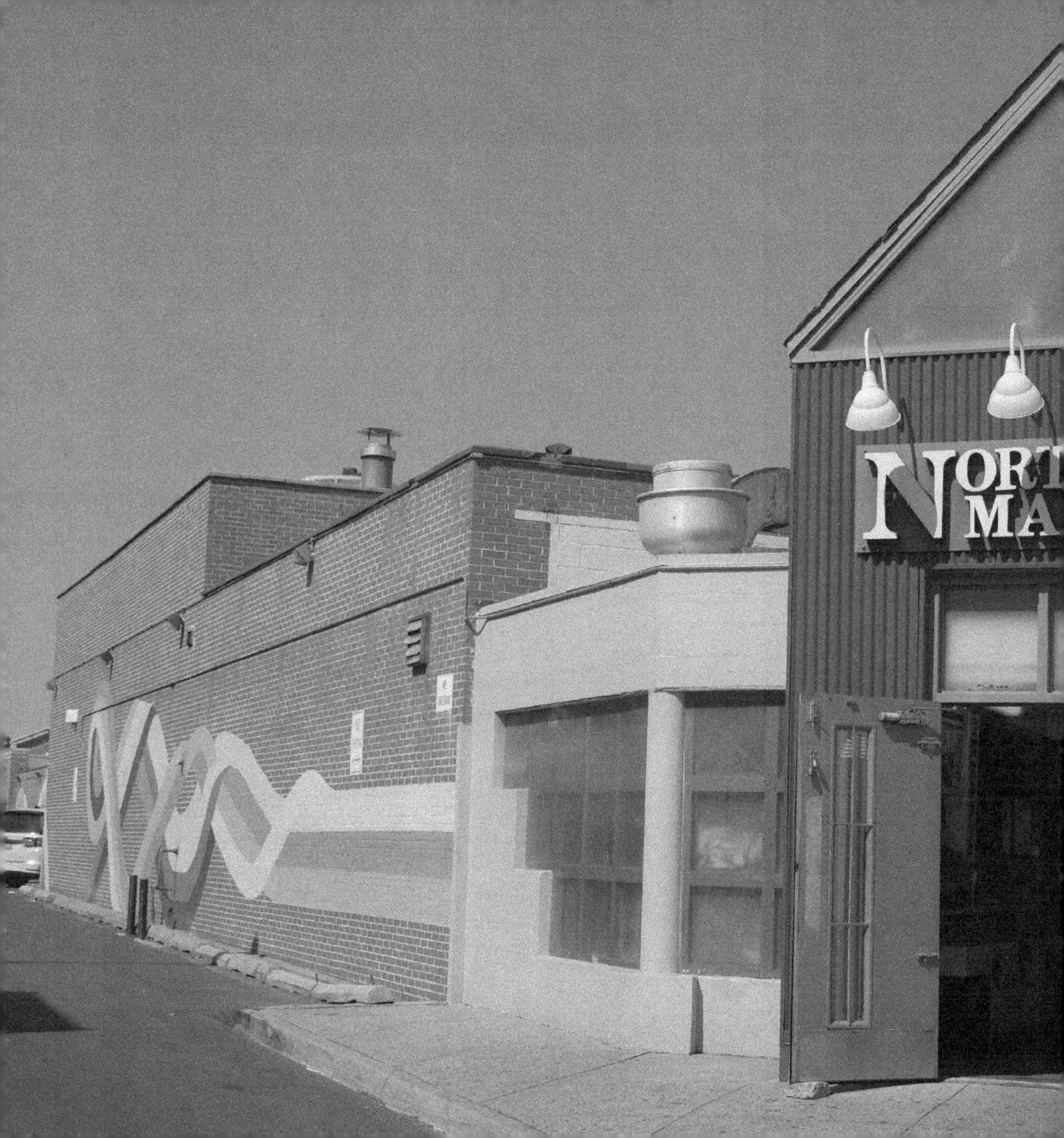
NORT
MA

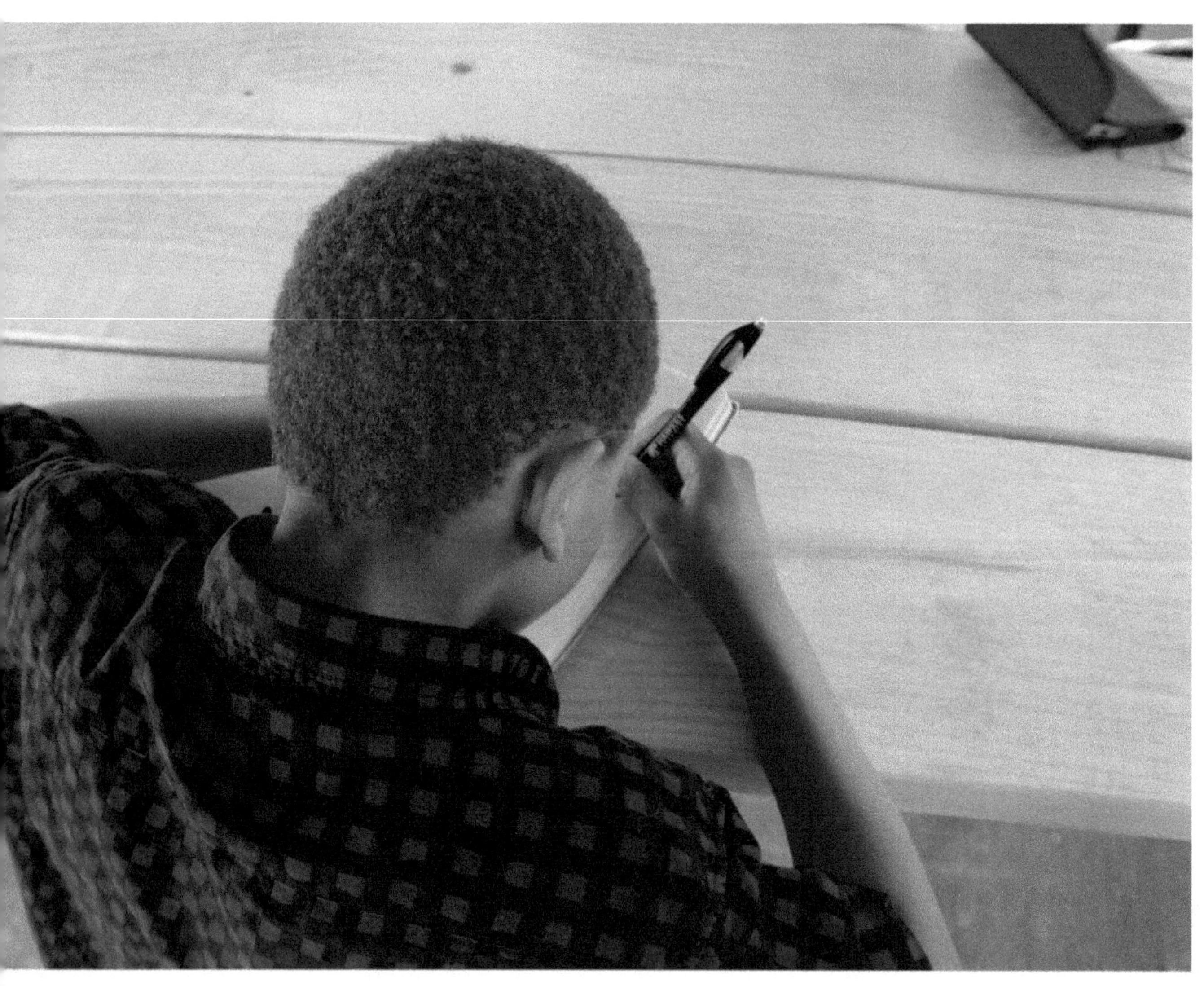

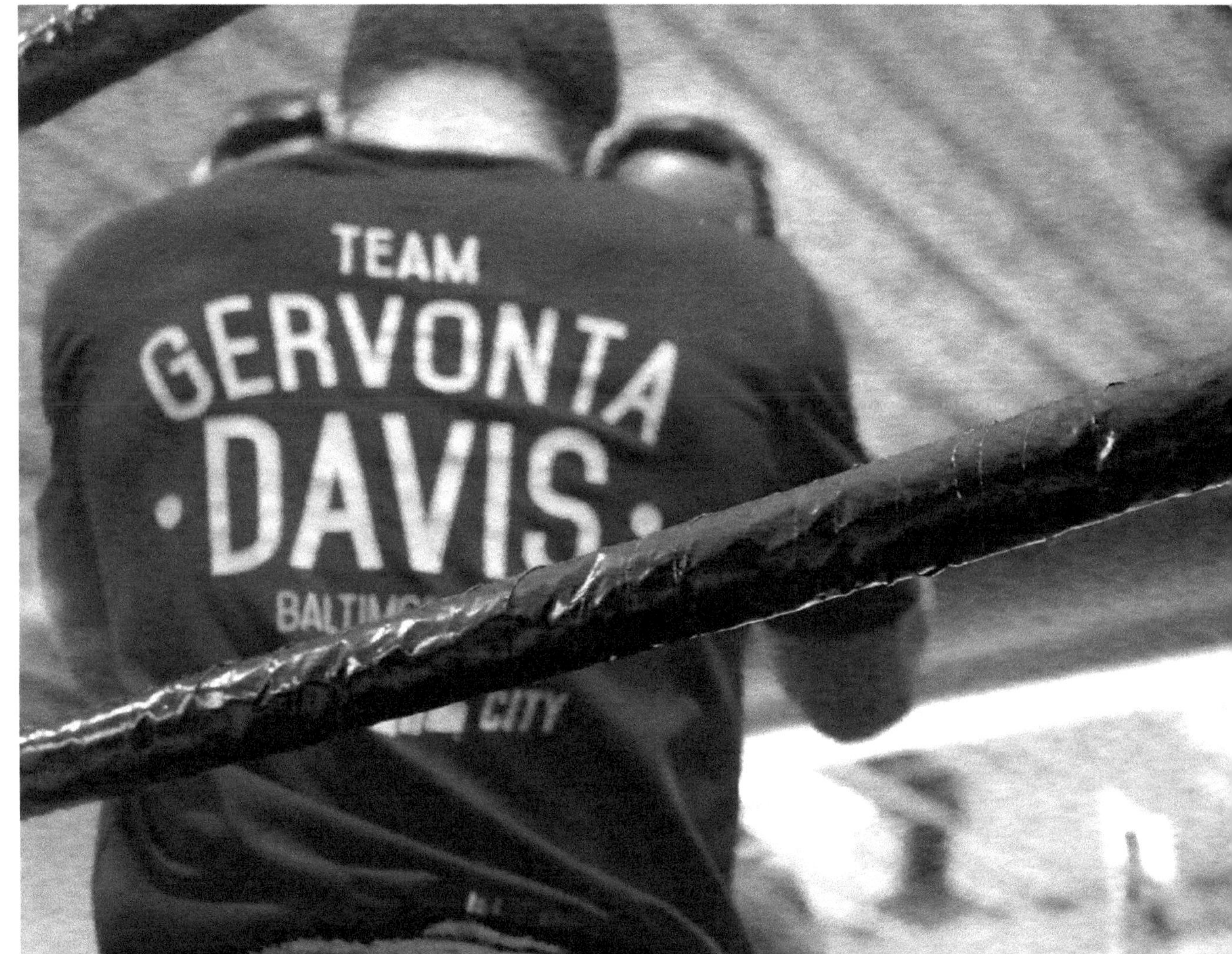
TEAM
GERVONTA
DAVIS
CITY

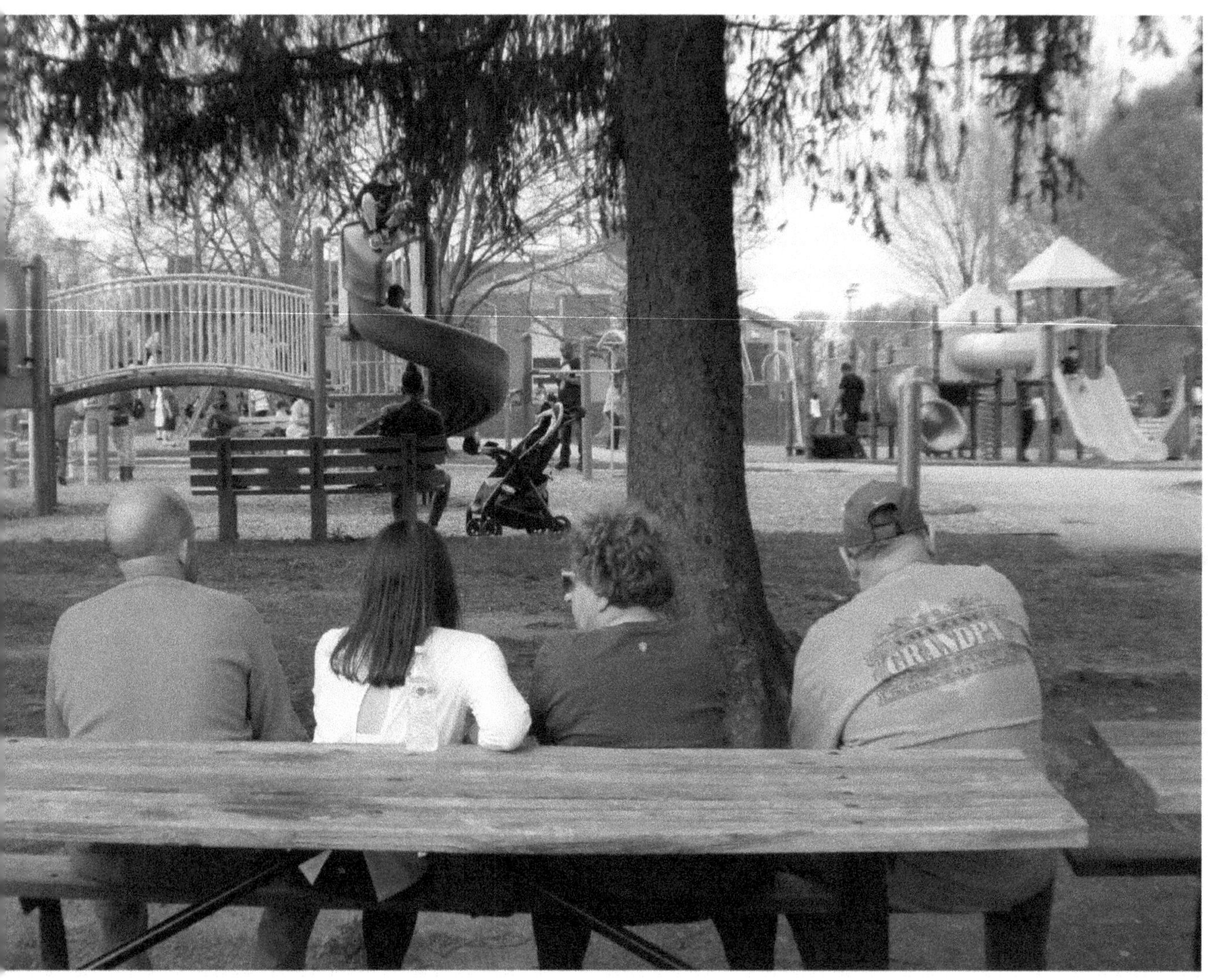
GRANDPA

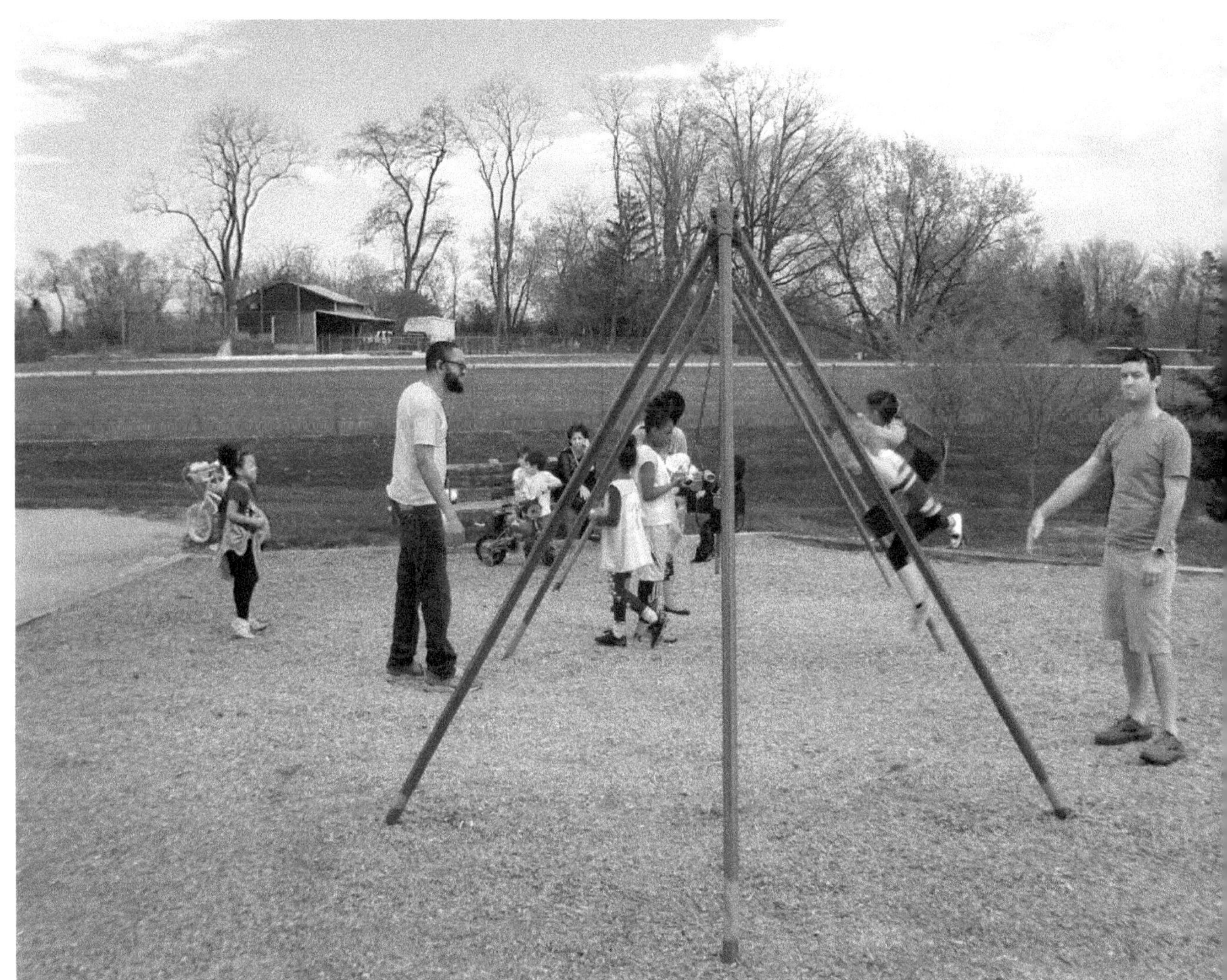

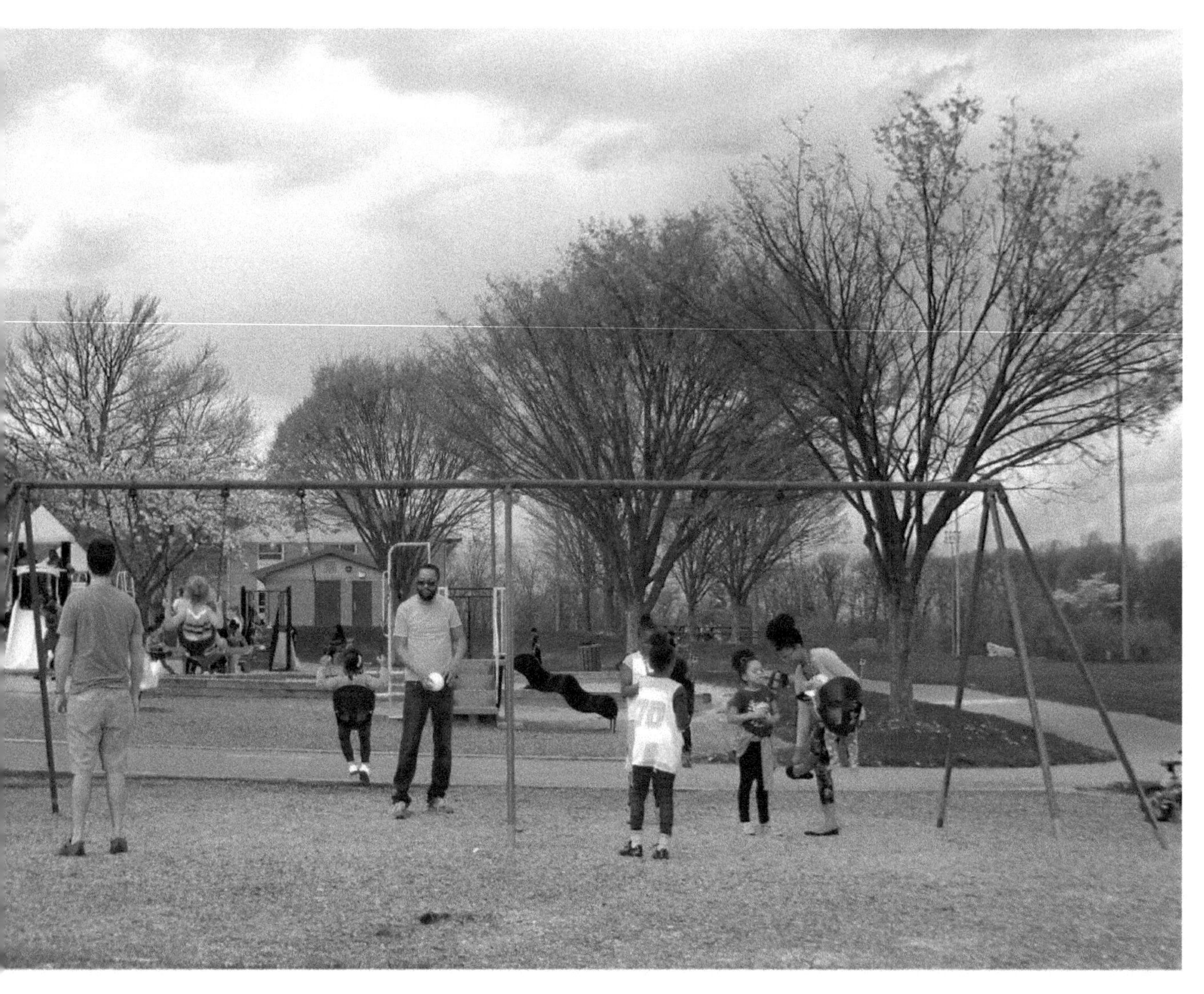

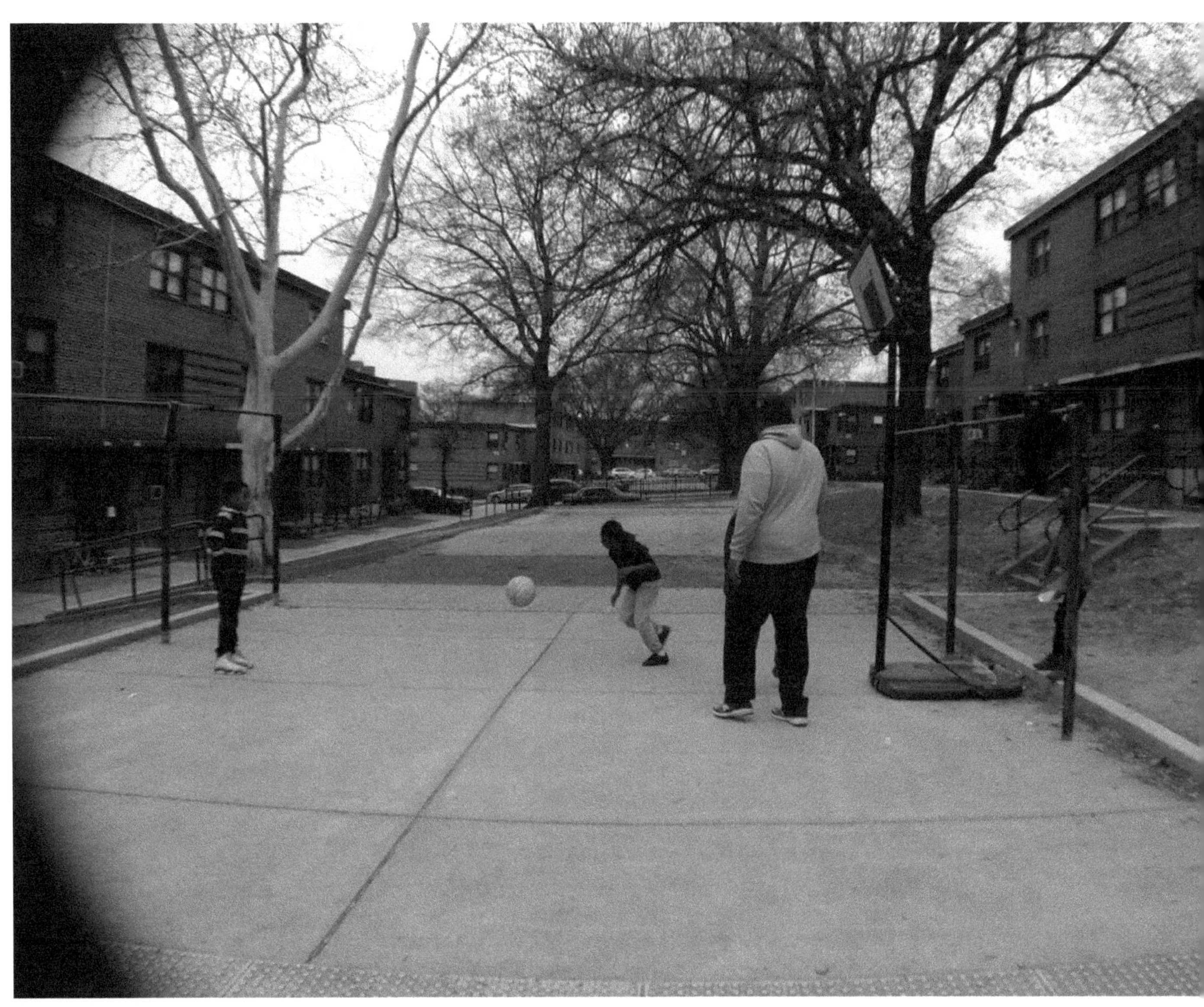

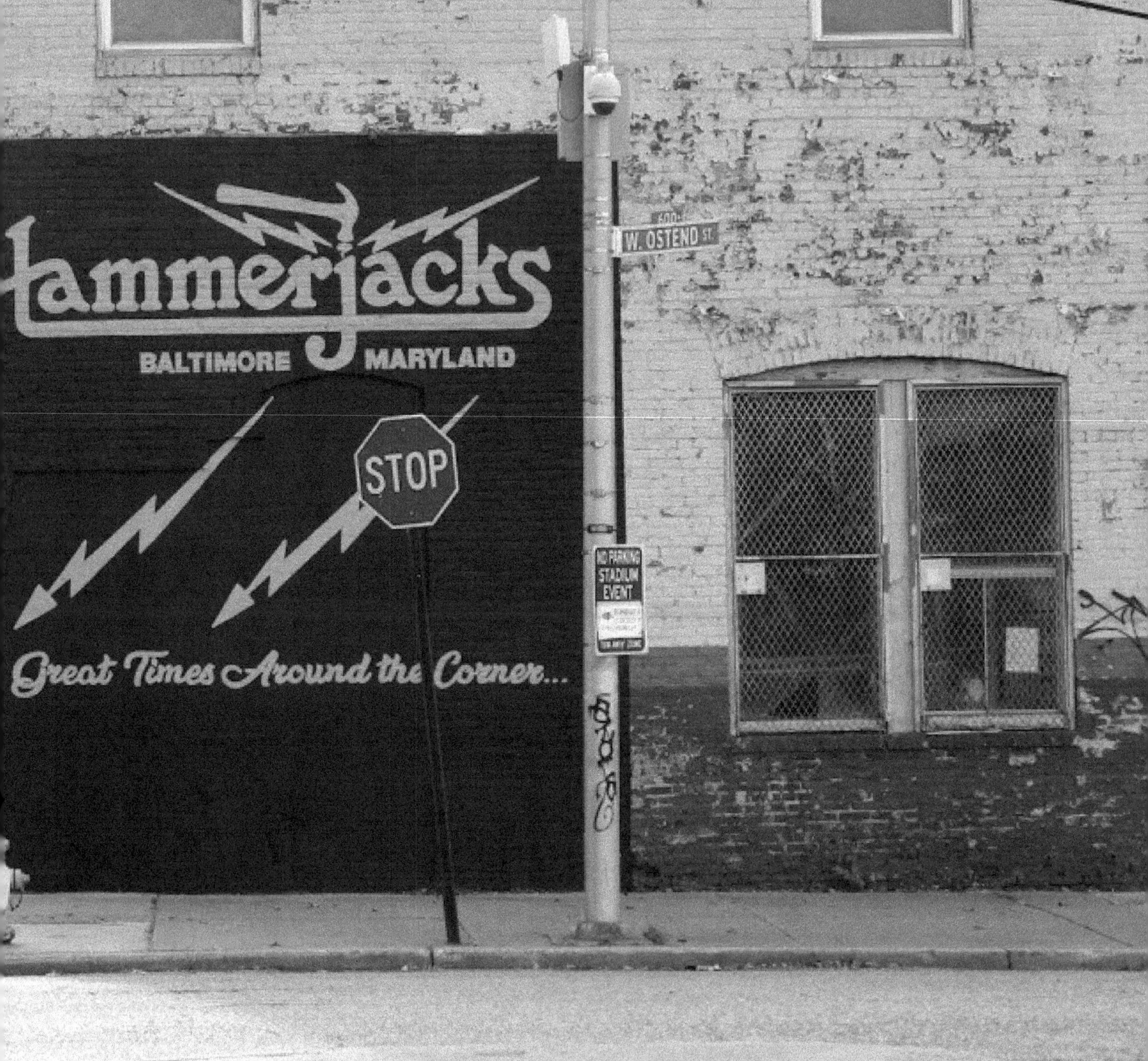
Hammerjacks
BALTIMORE MARYLAND
Great Times Around the Corner...
STOP
W. OSTEND ST.
NO PARKING
STADIUM
EVENT

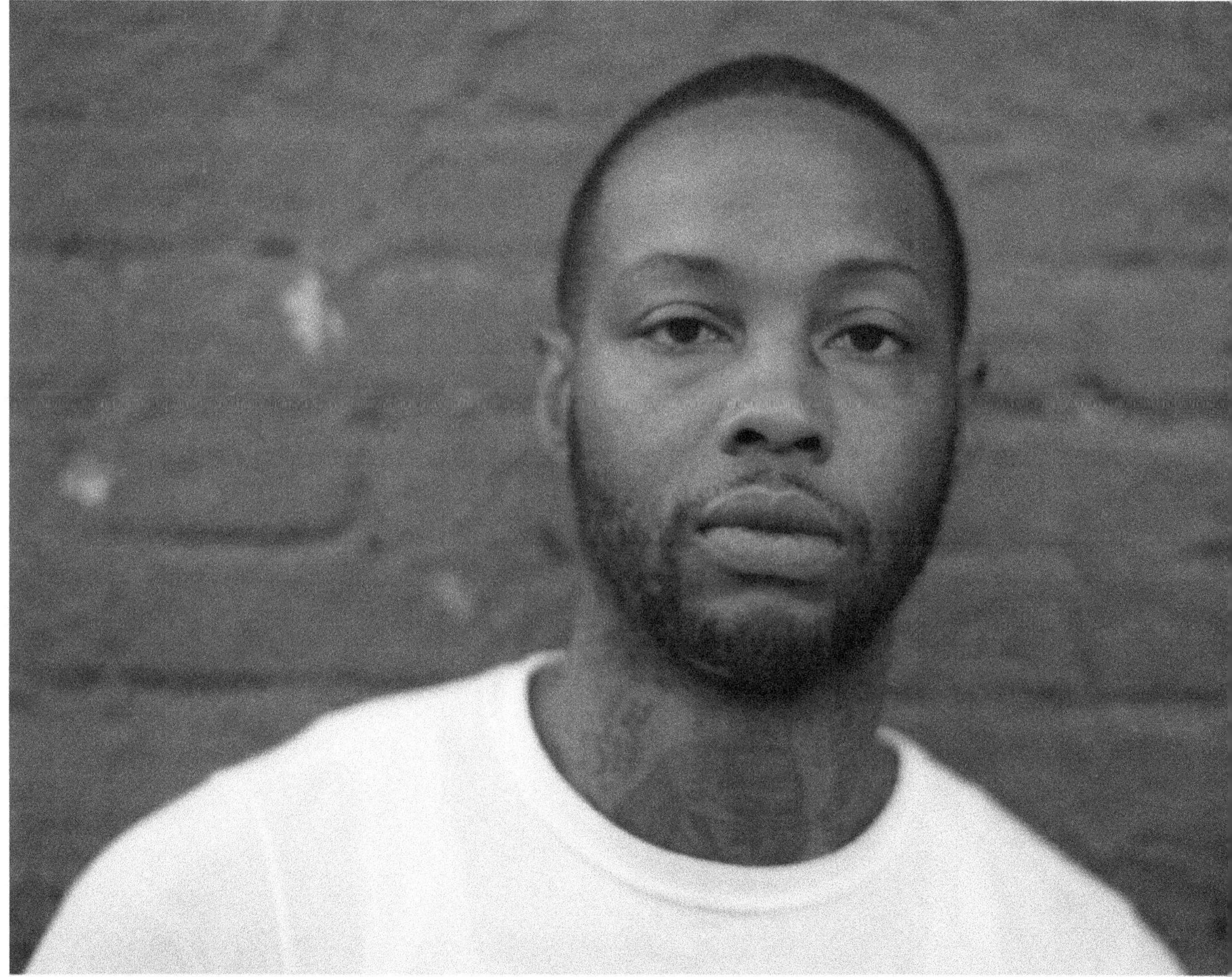

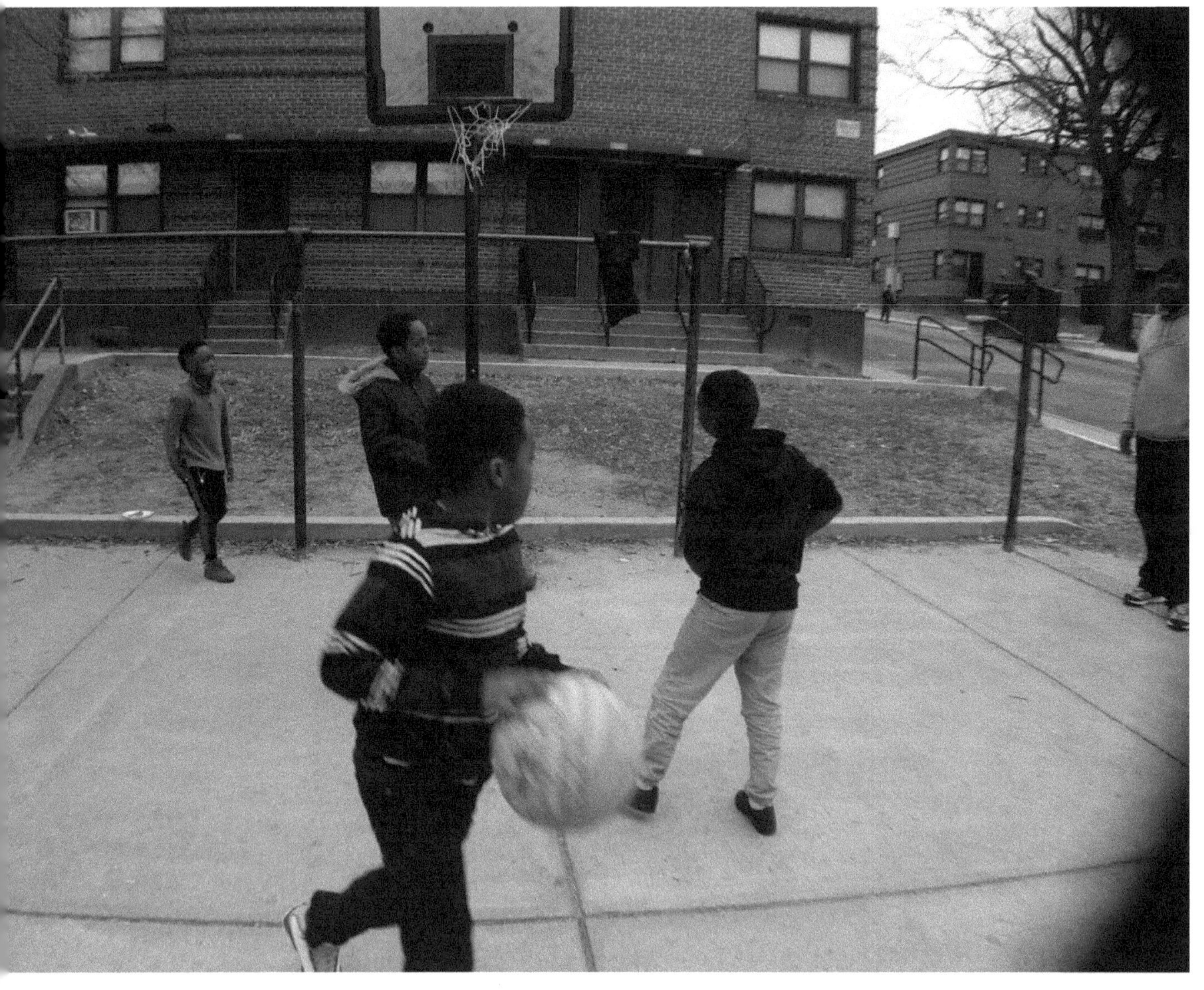

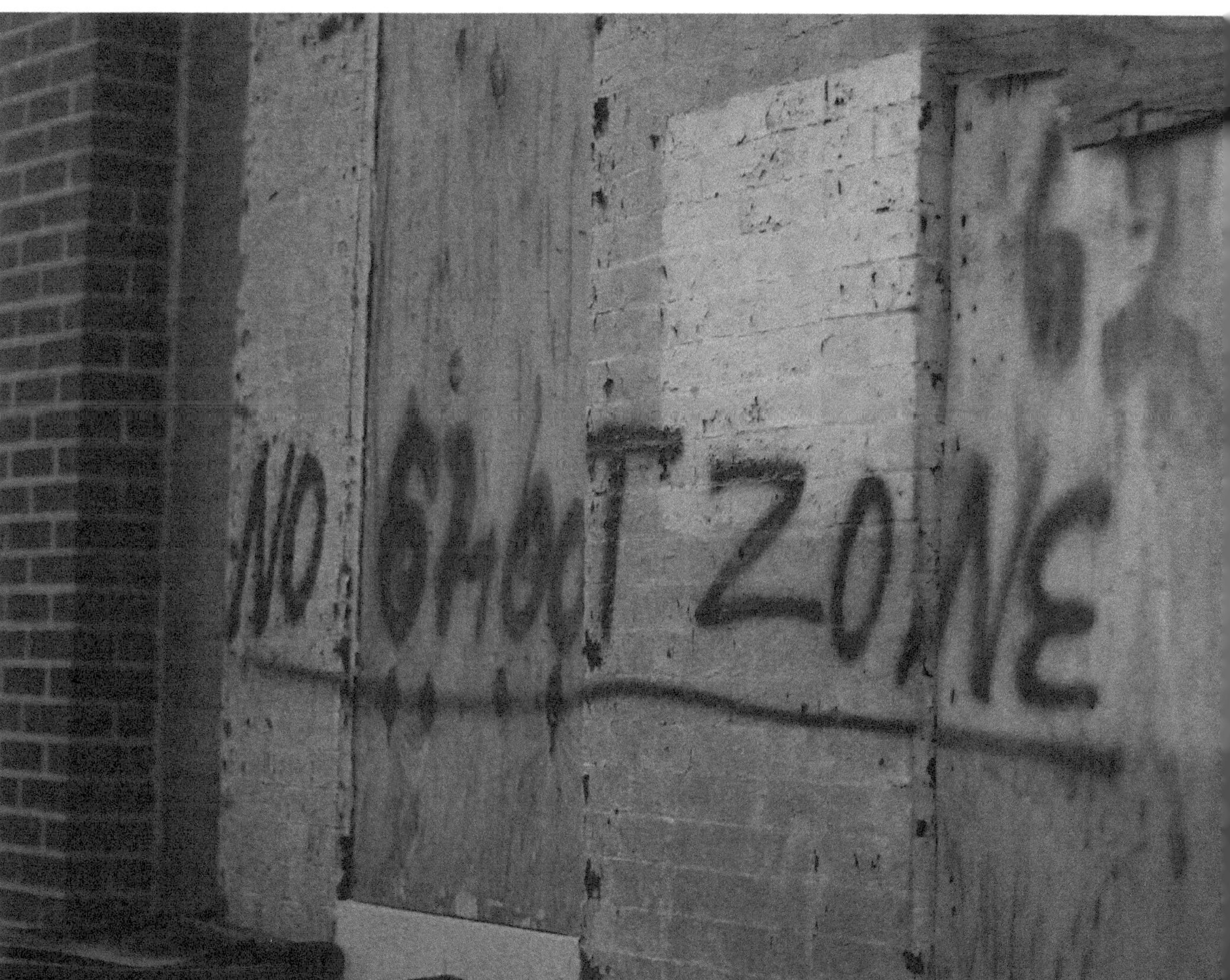
NO ShooT ZONE

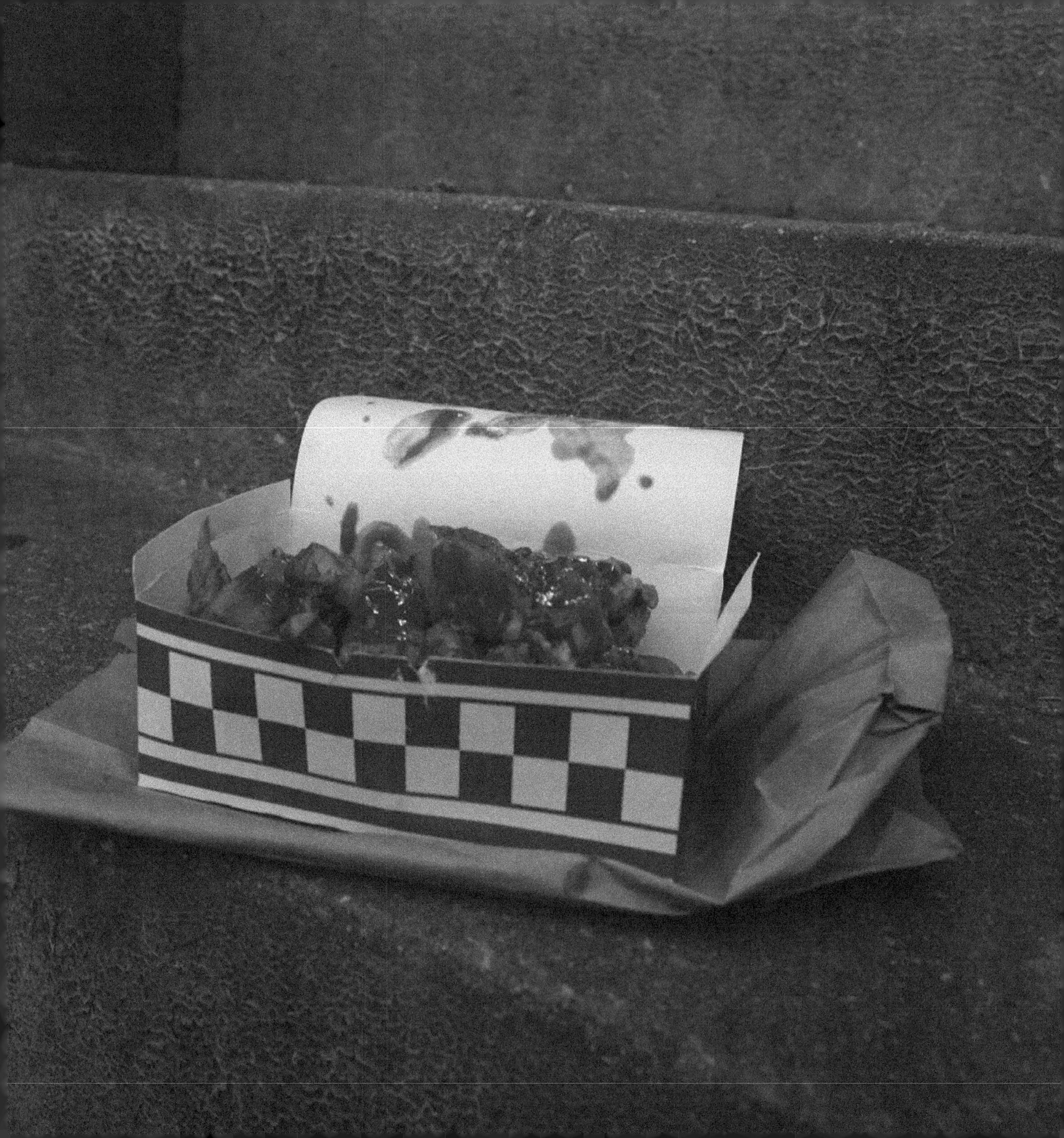

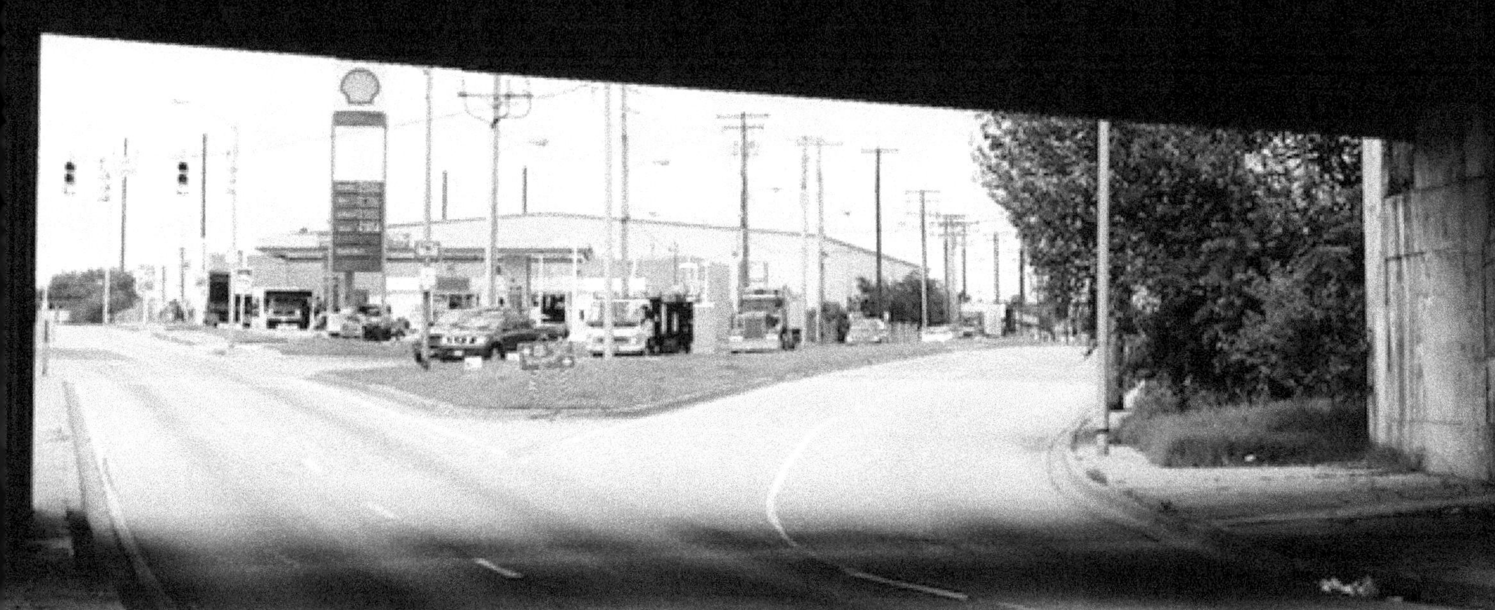
BALTIMOR

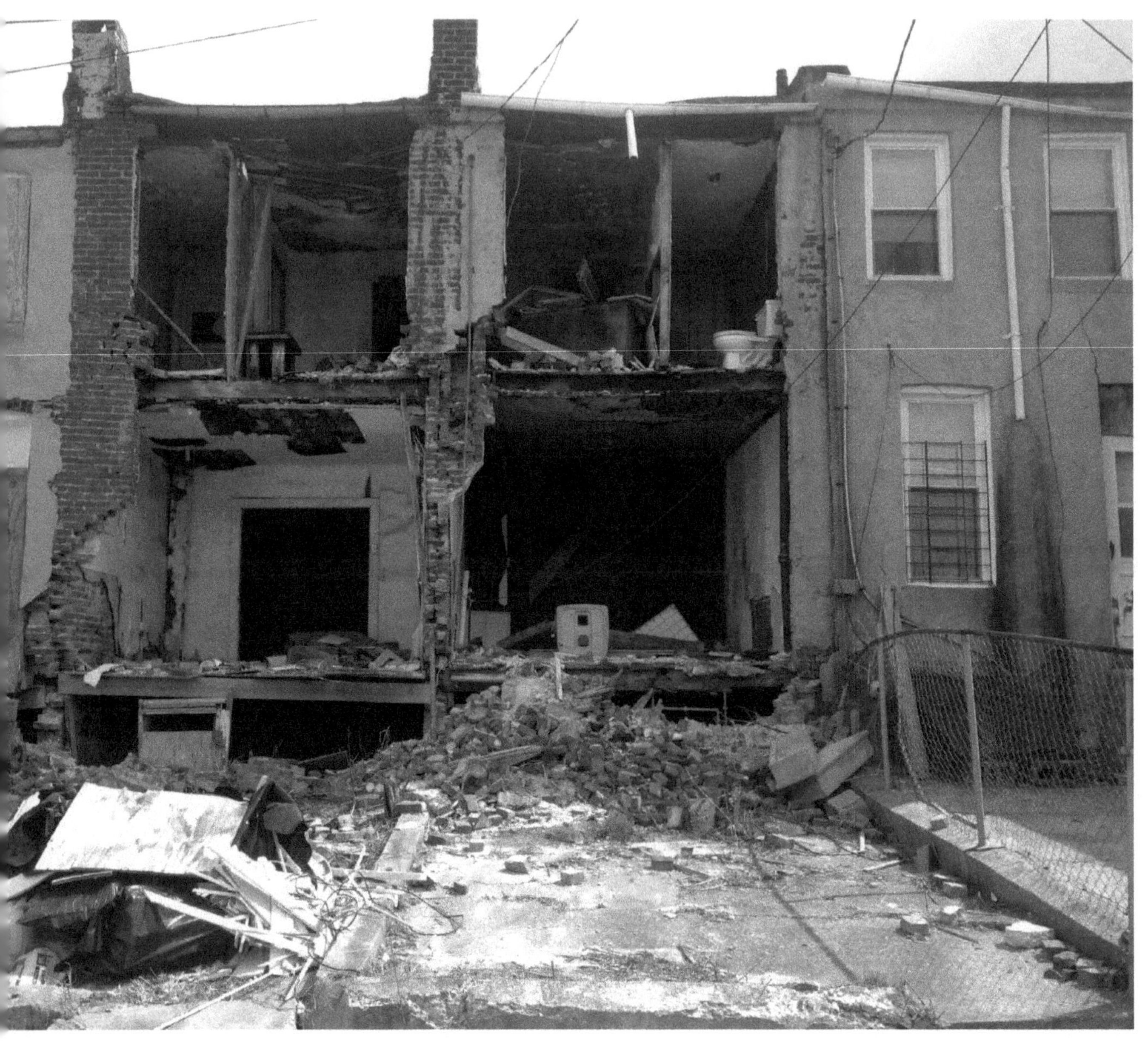

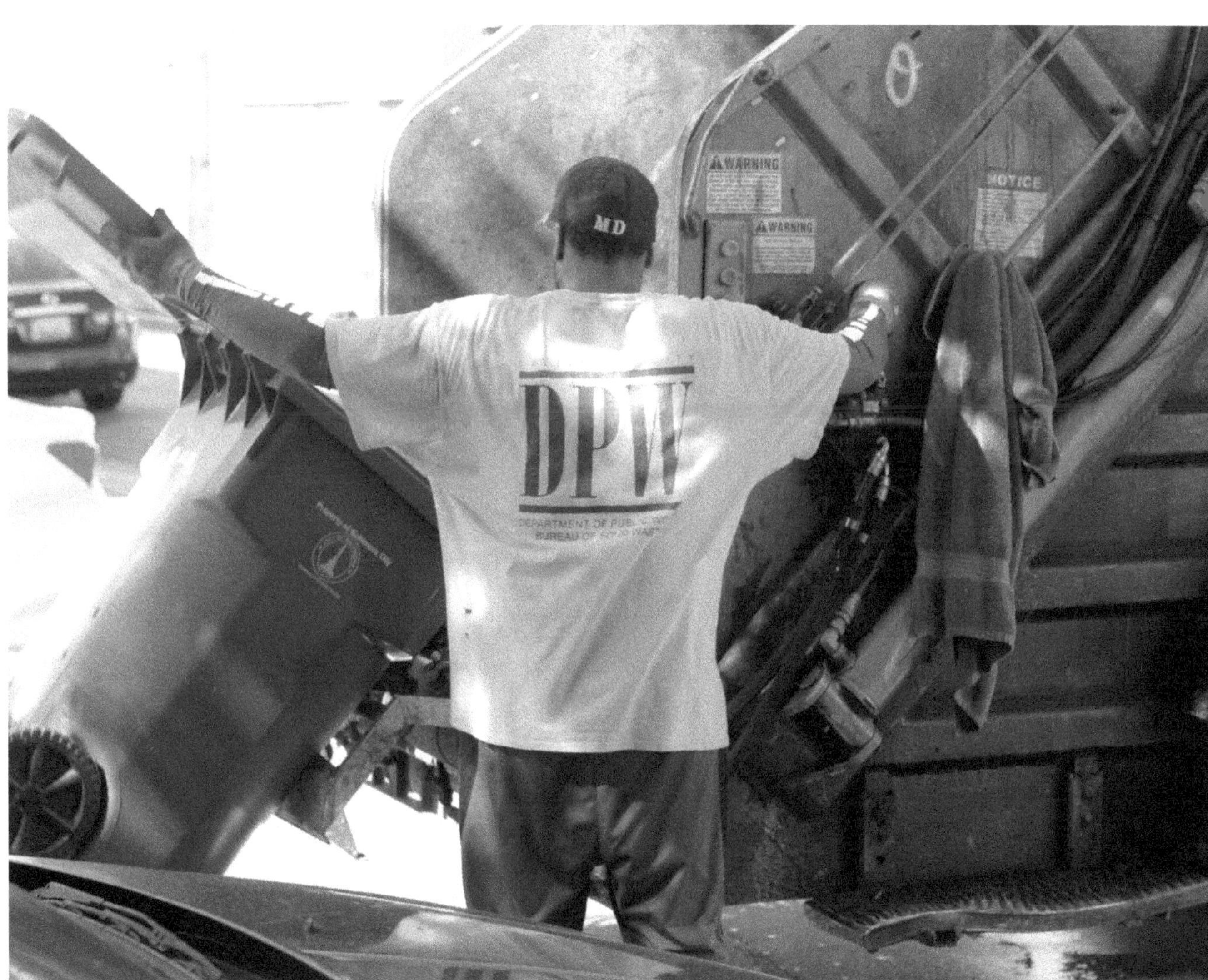
MD
WARNING
WARNING
NOTICE
DPW

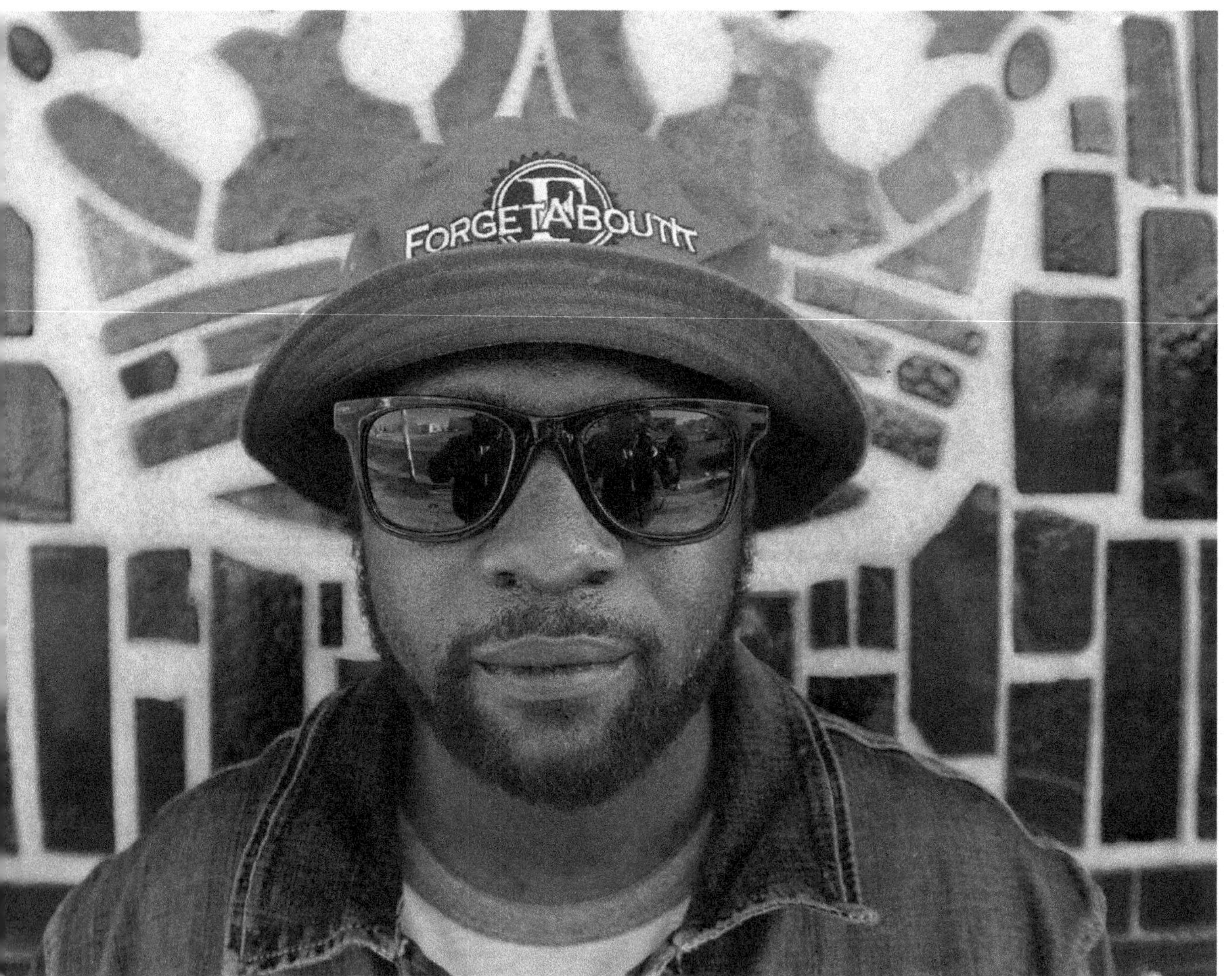
FORGETABOUTIT

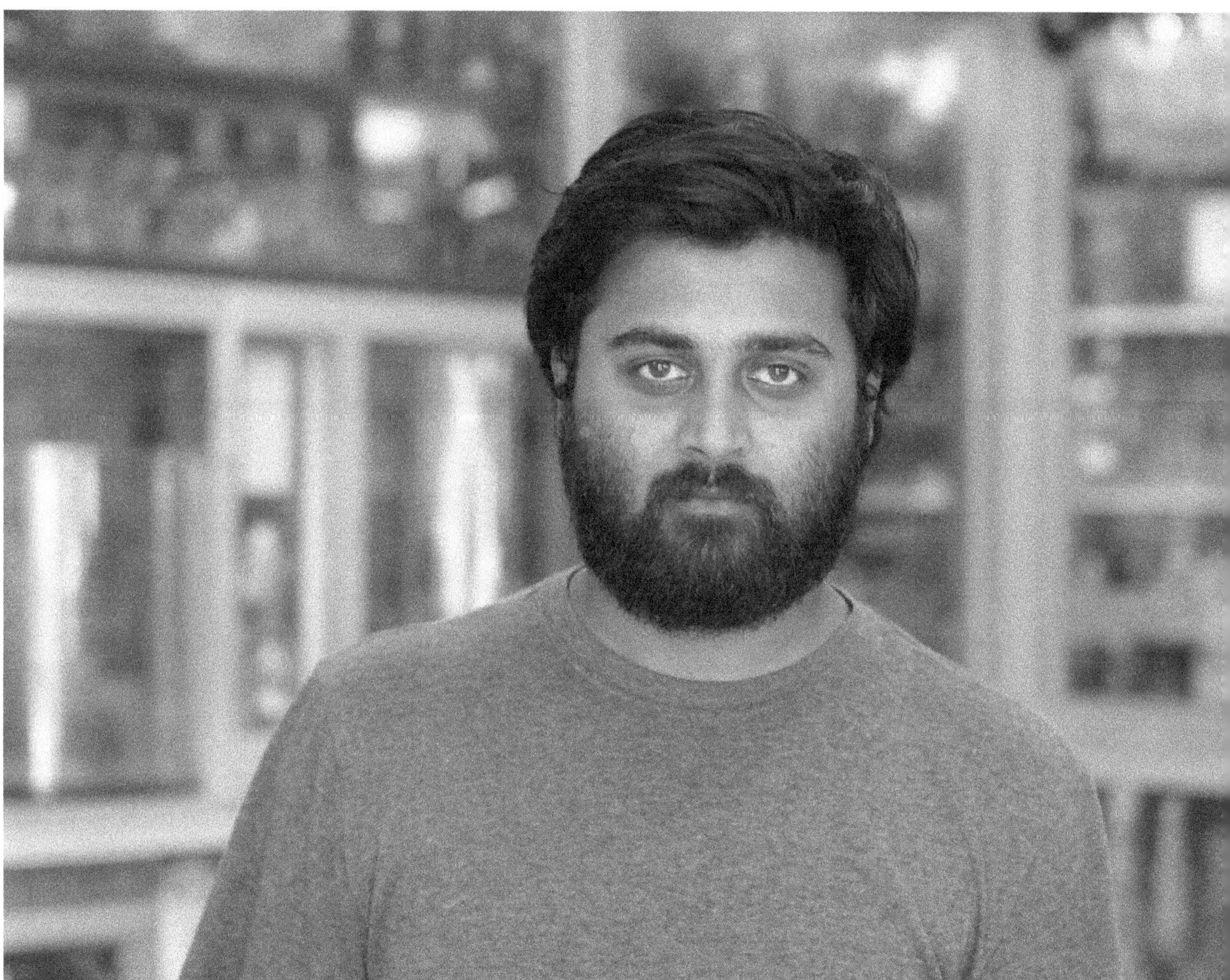

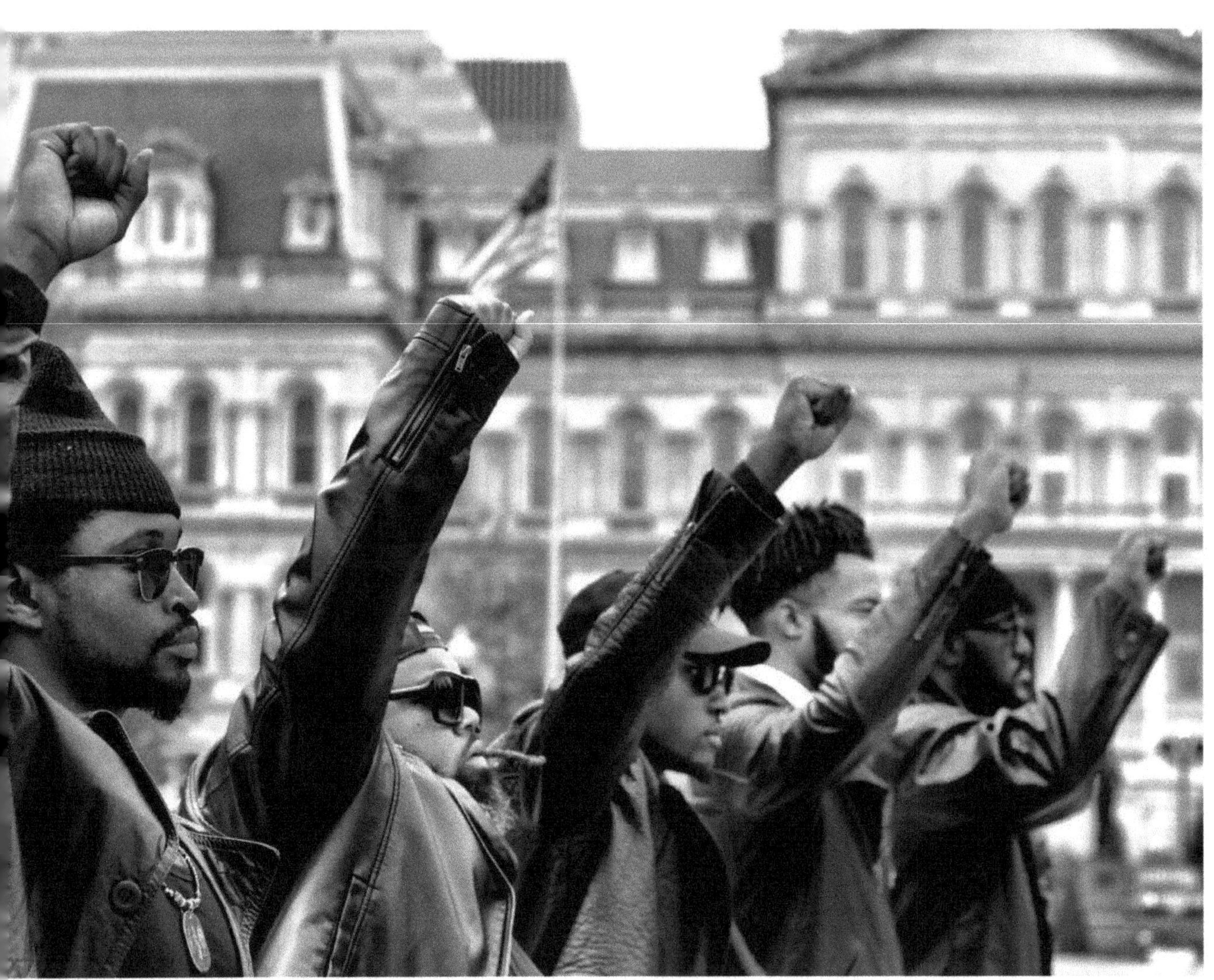

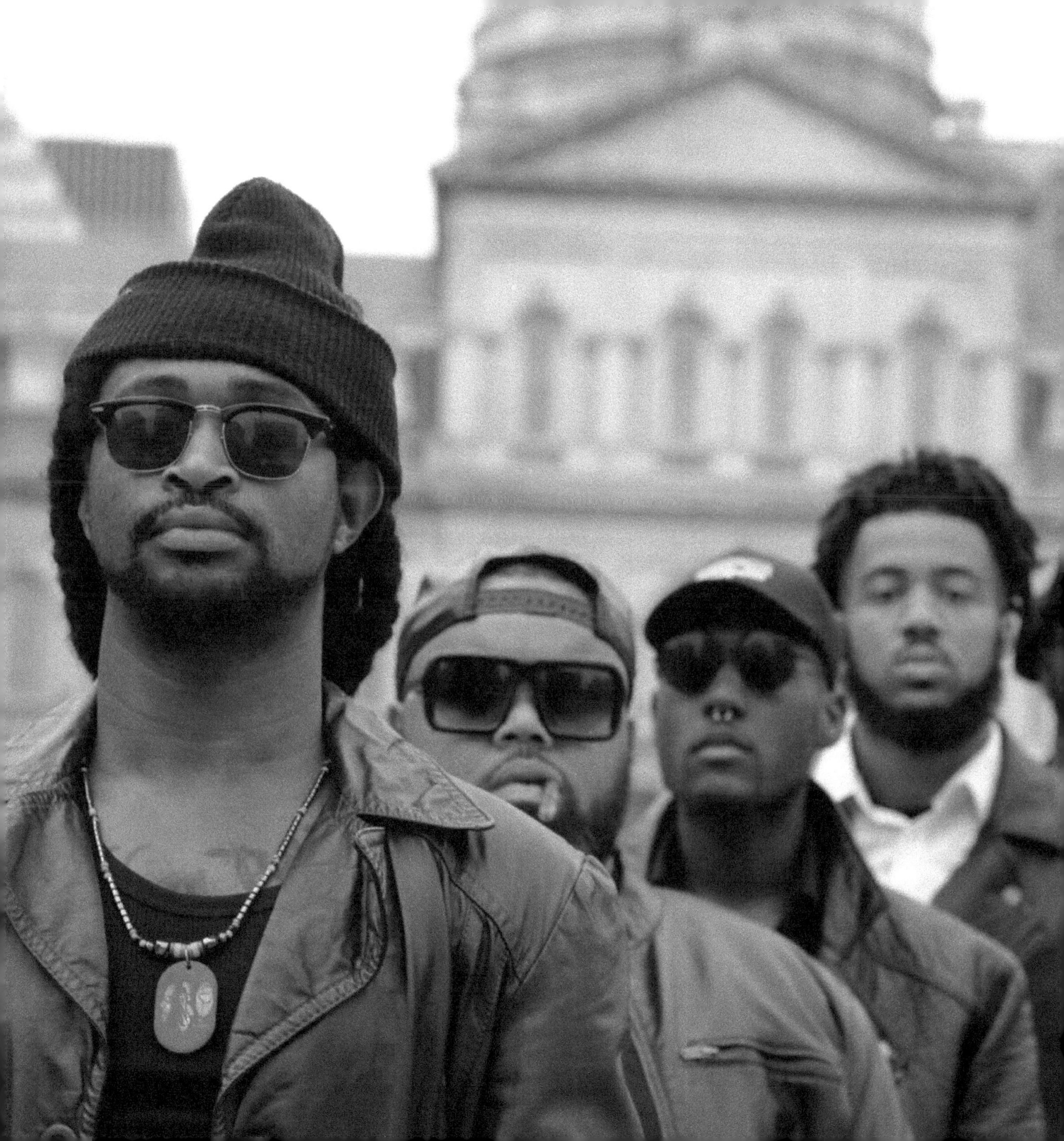

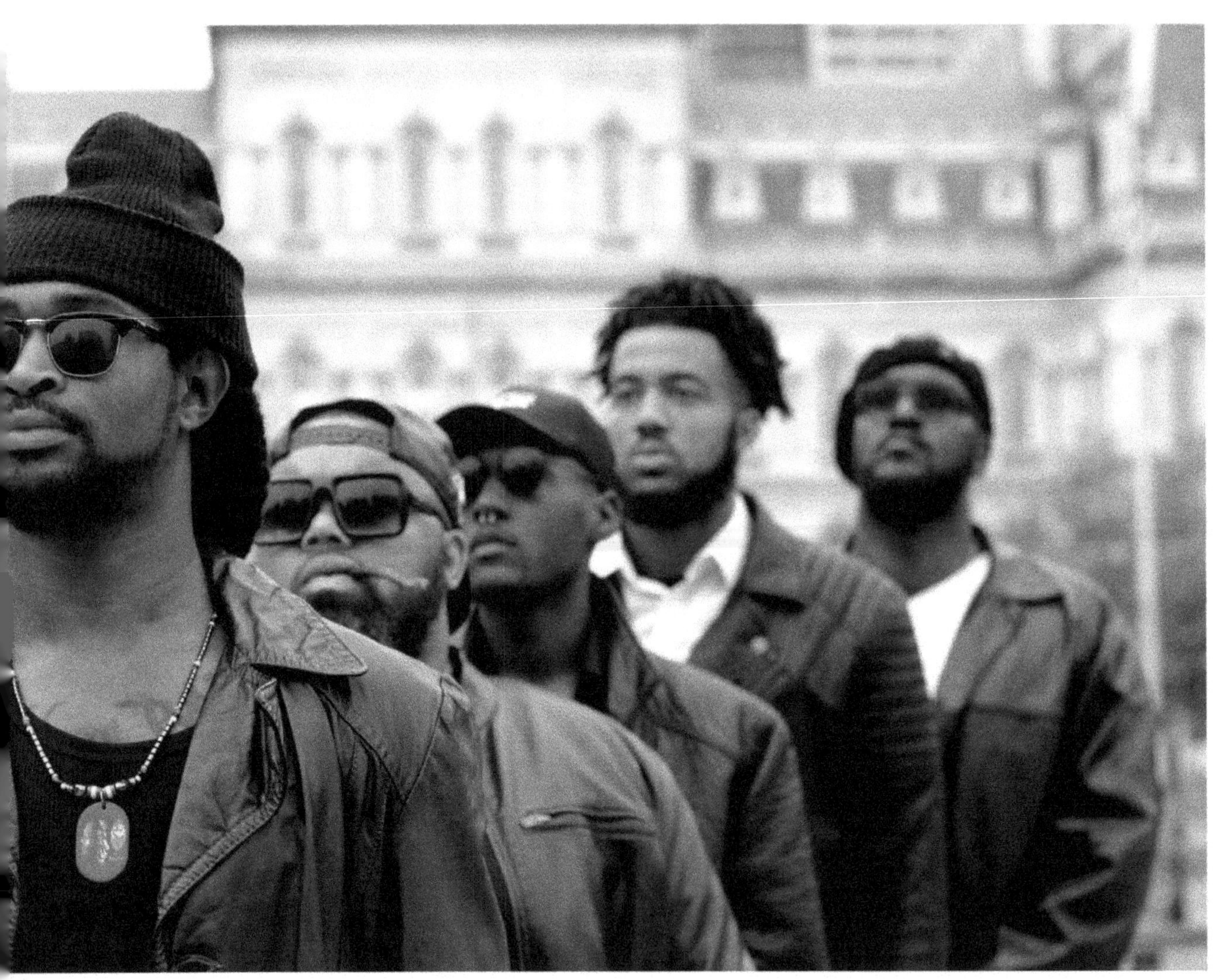

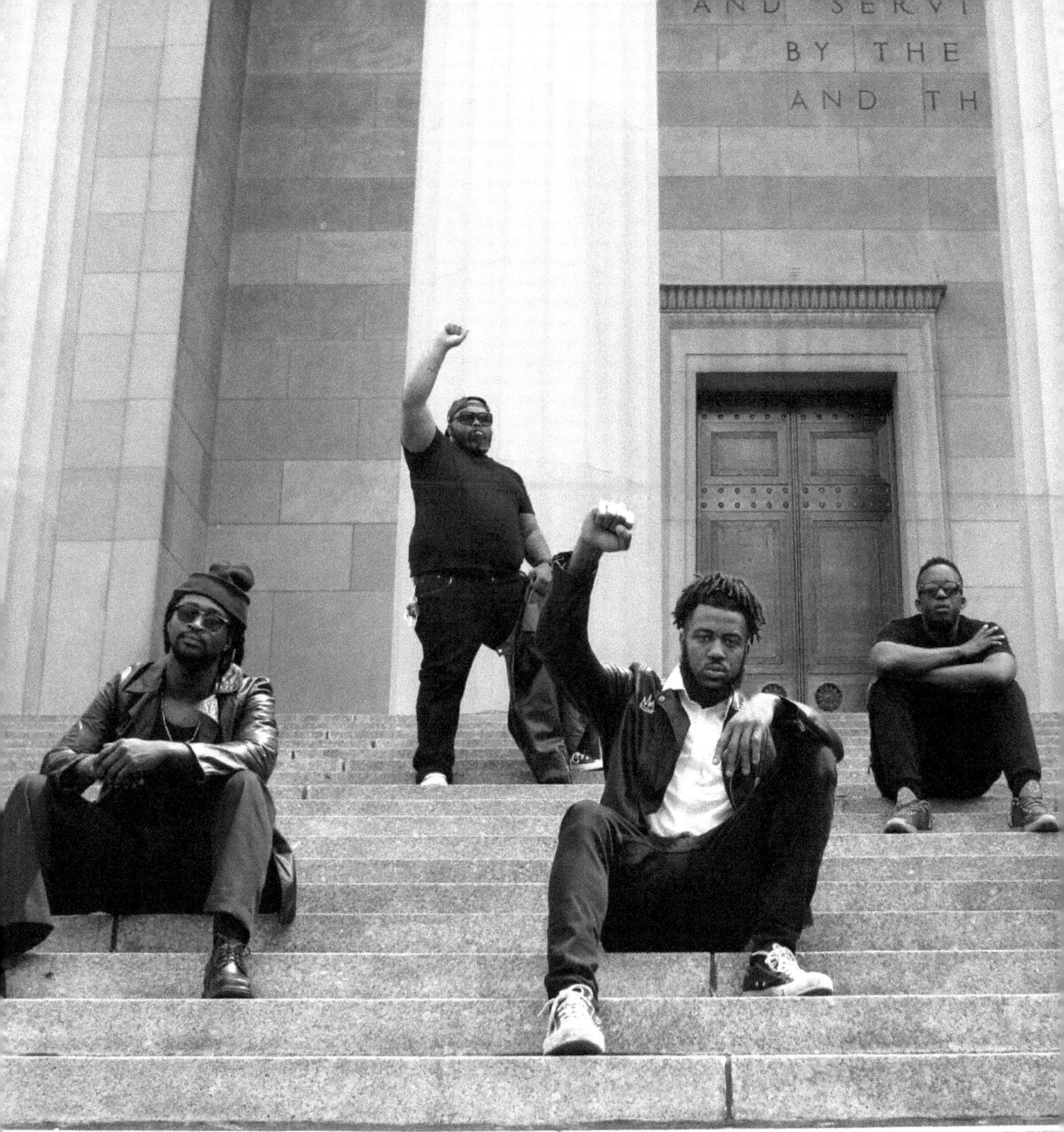
AND SERVI
BY THE
AND TH

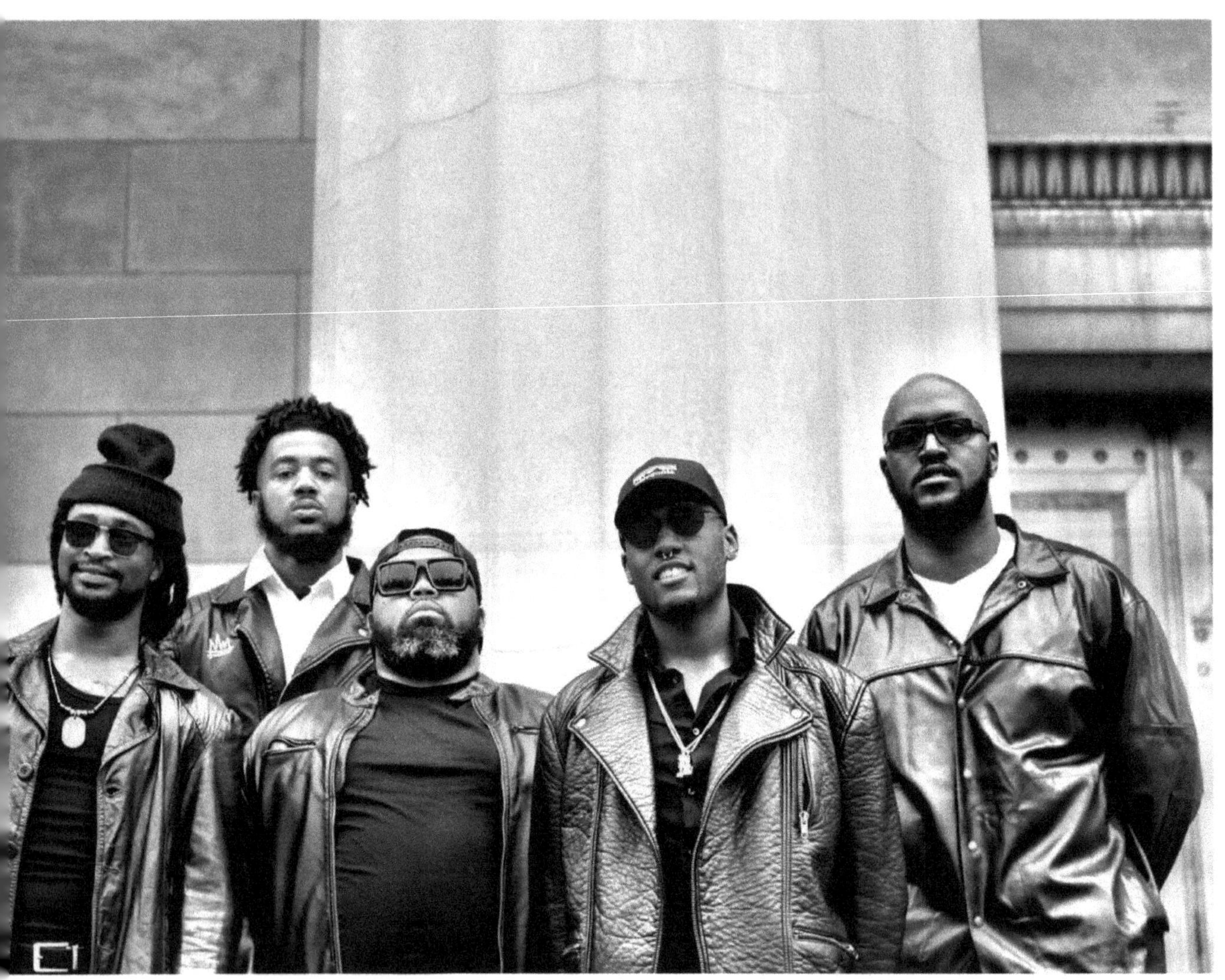

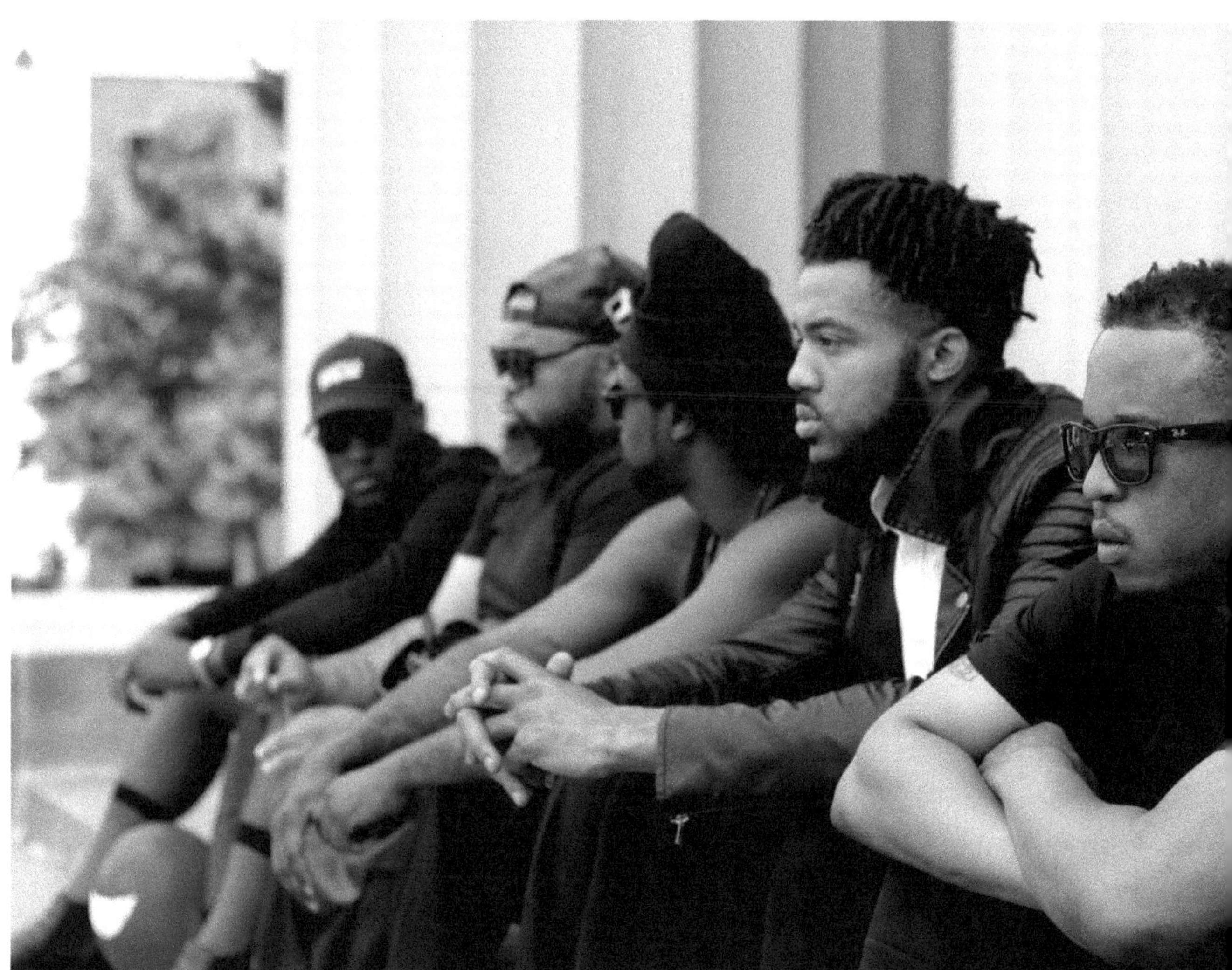

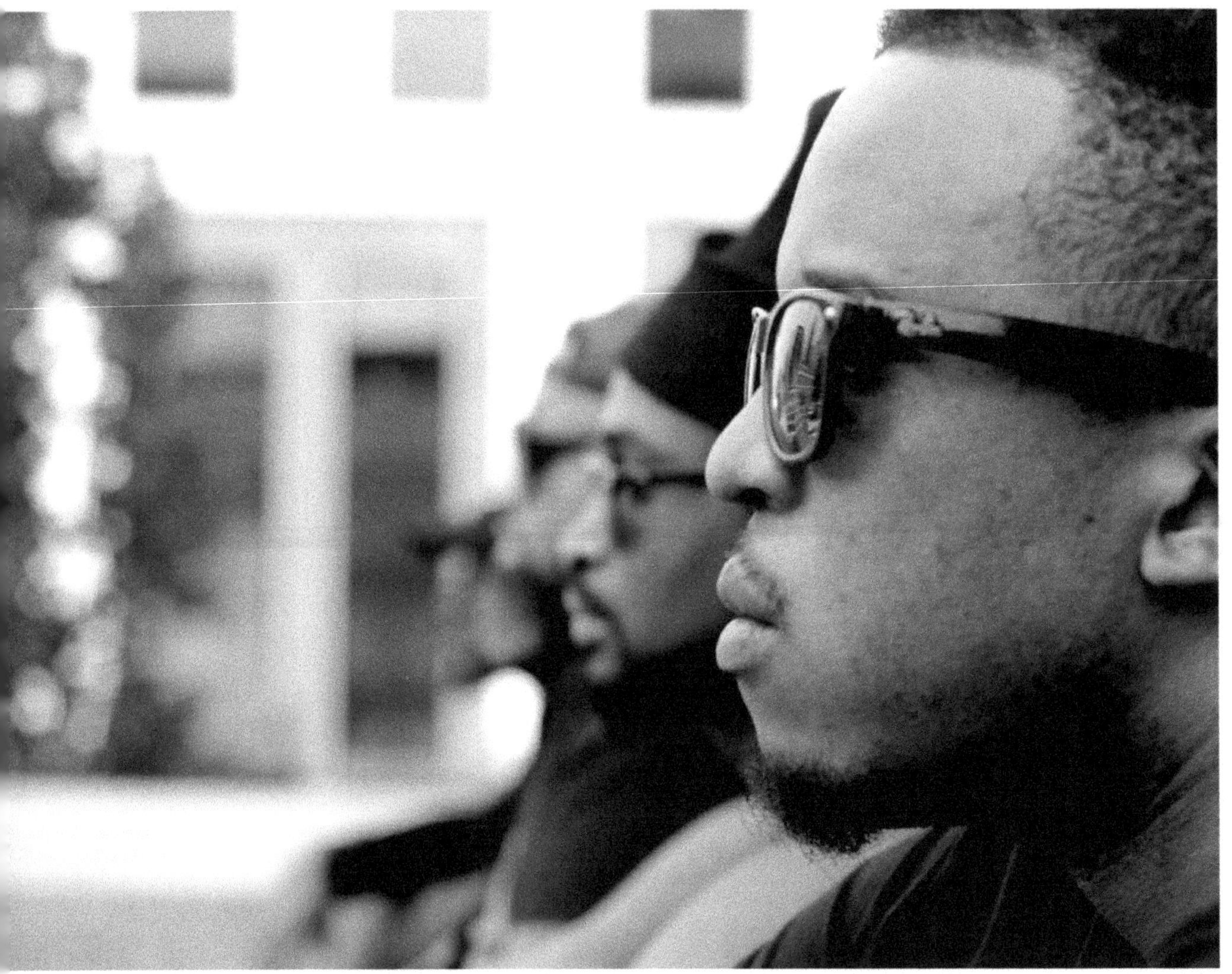

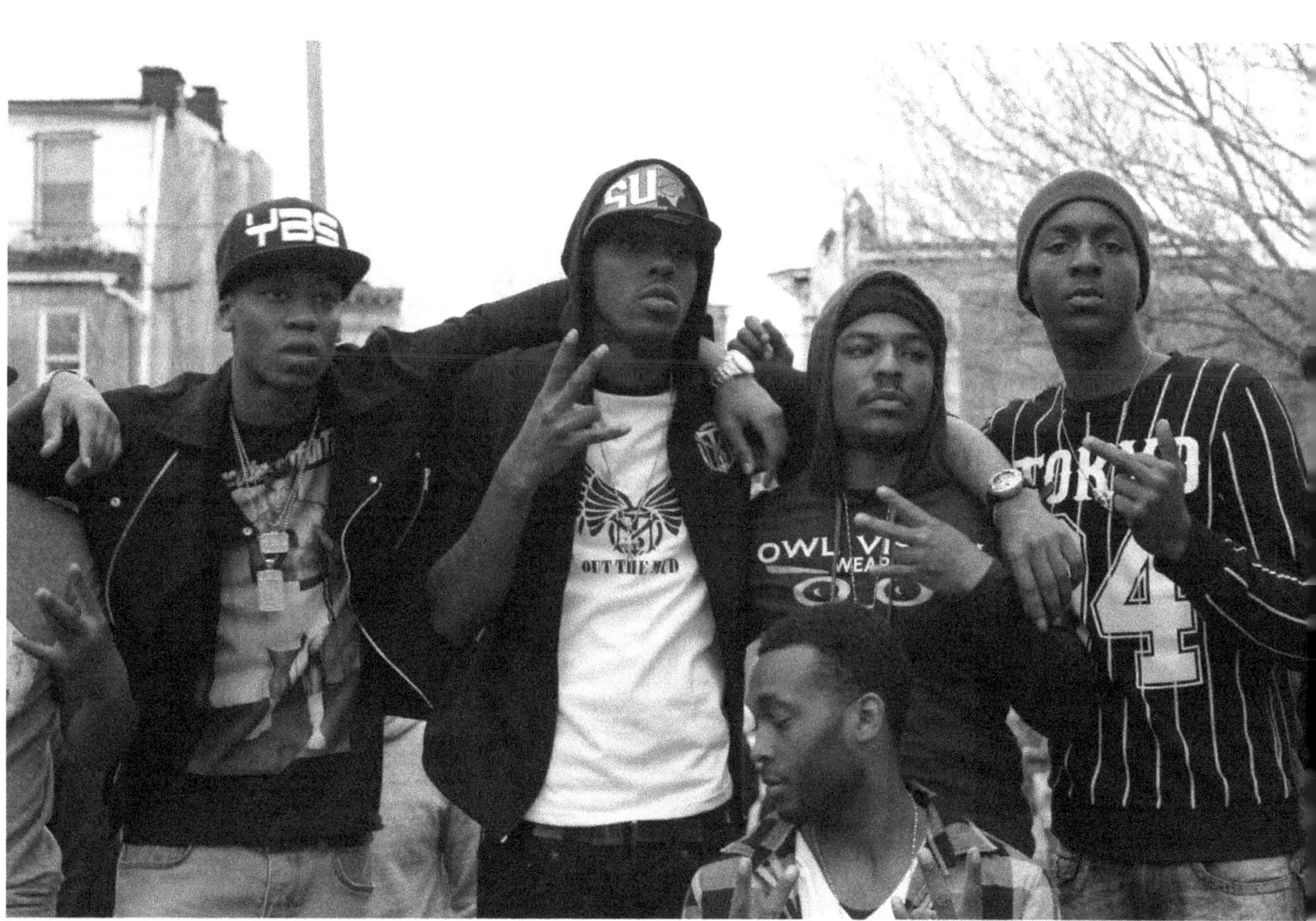
YBS
SU

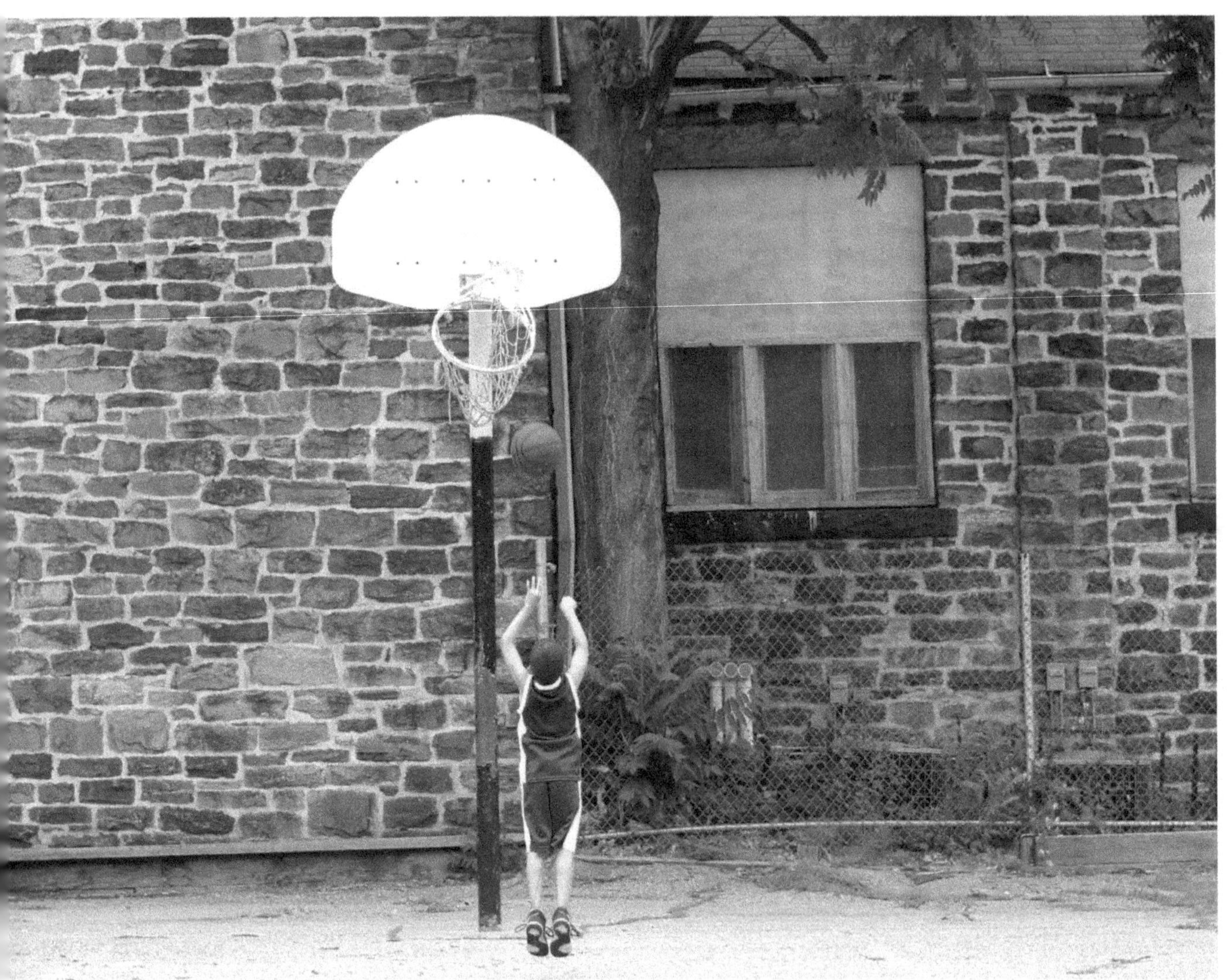

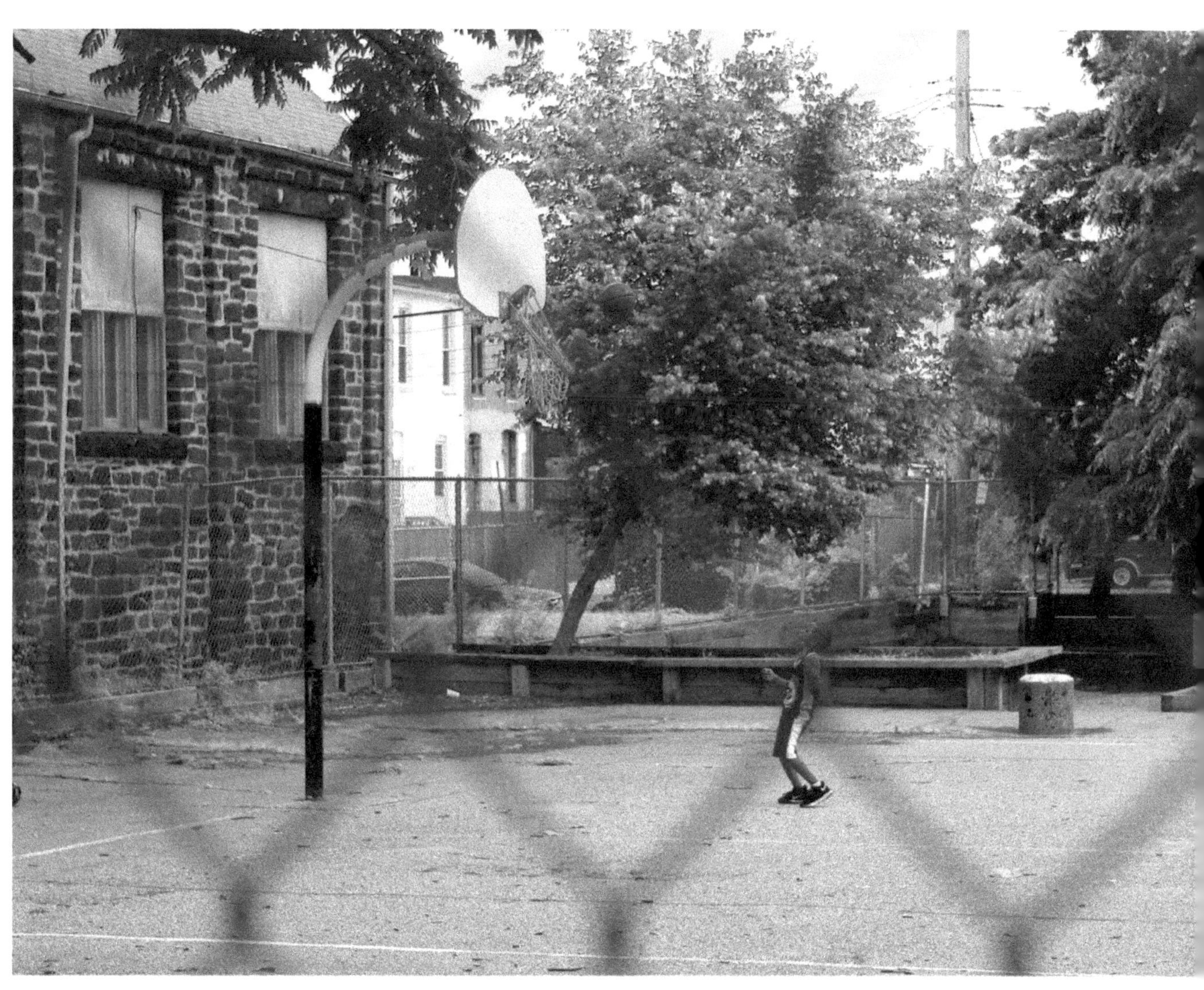

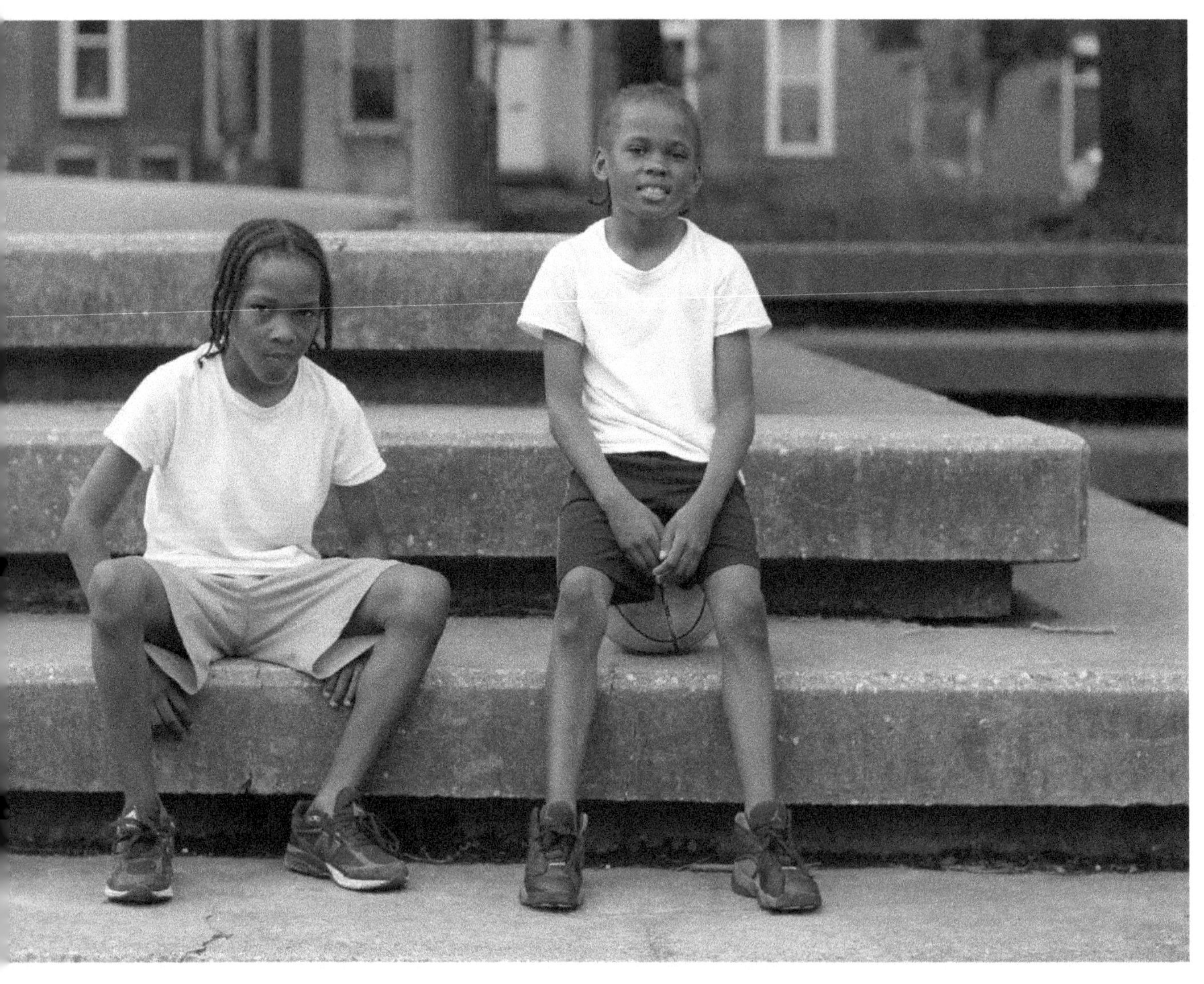

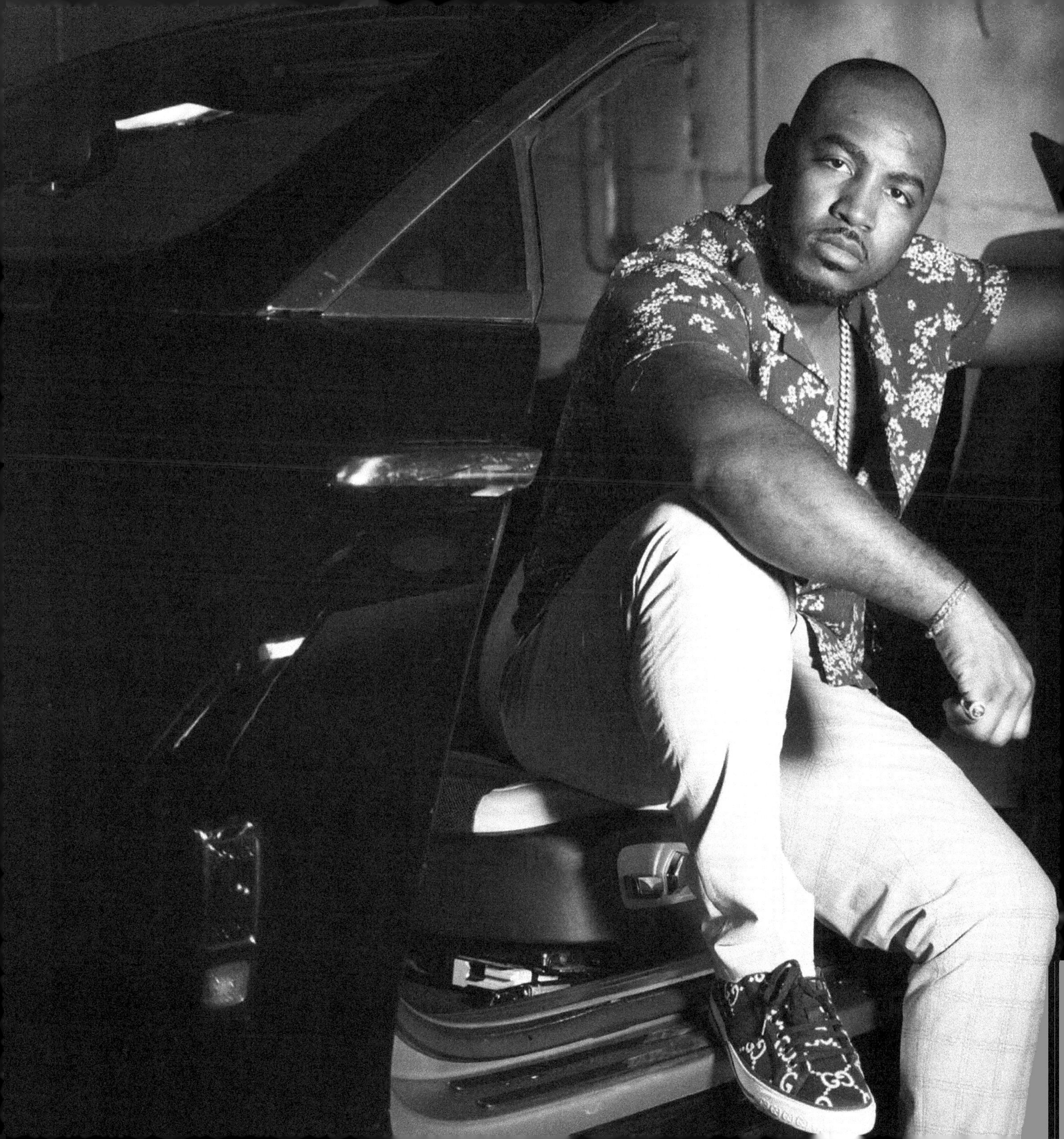

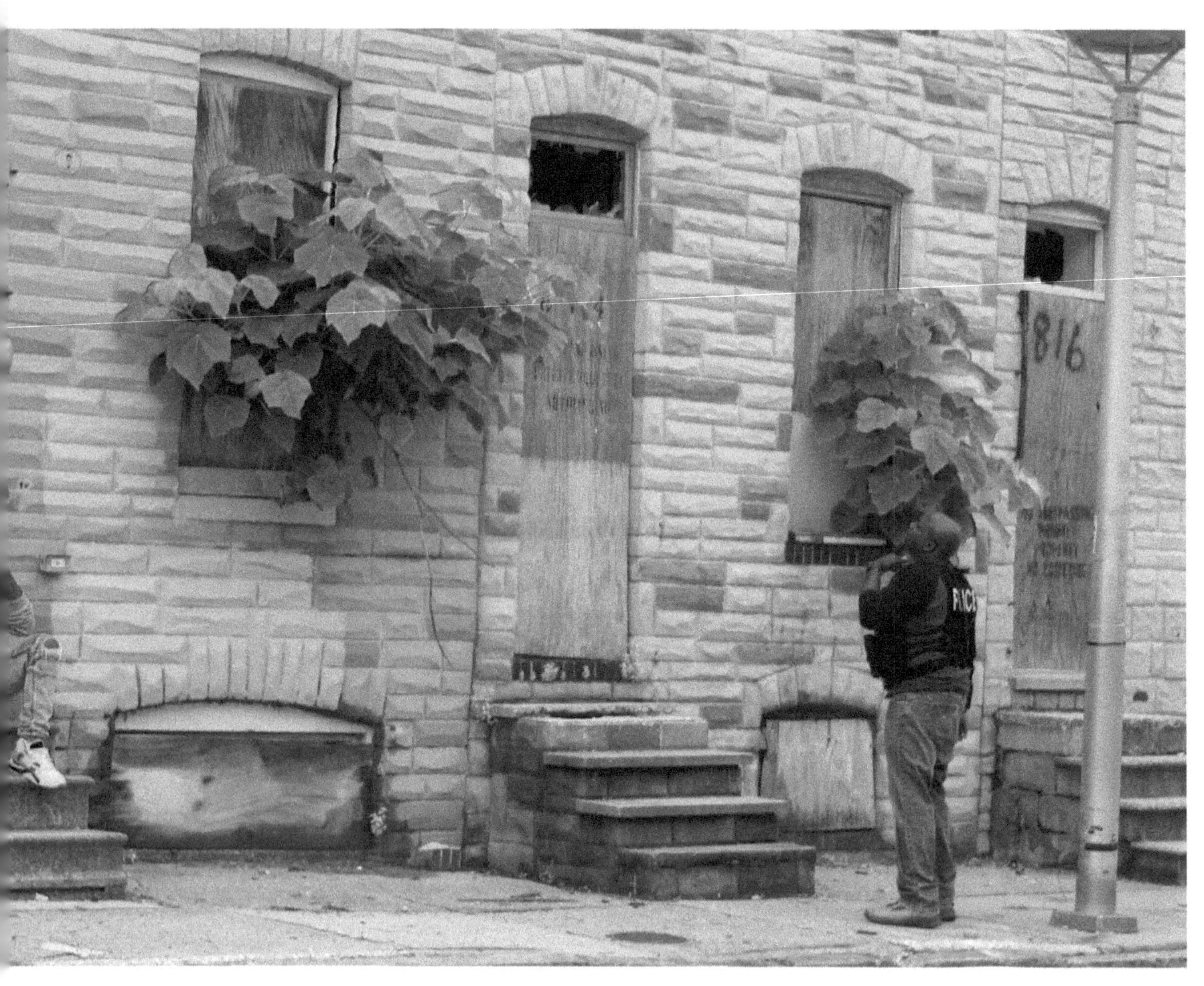
816

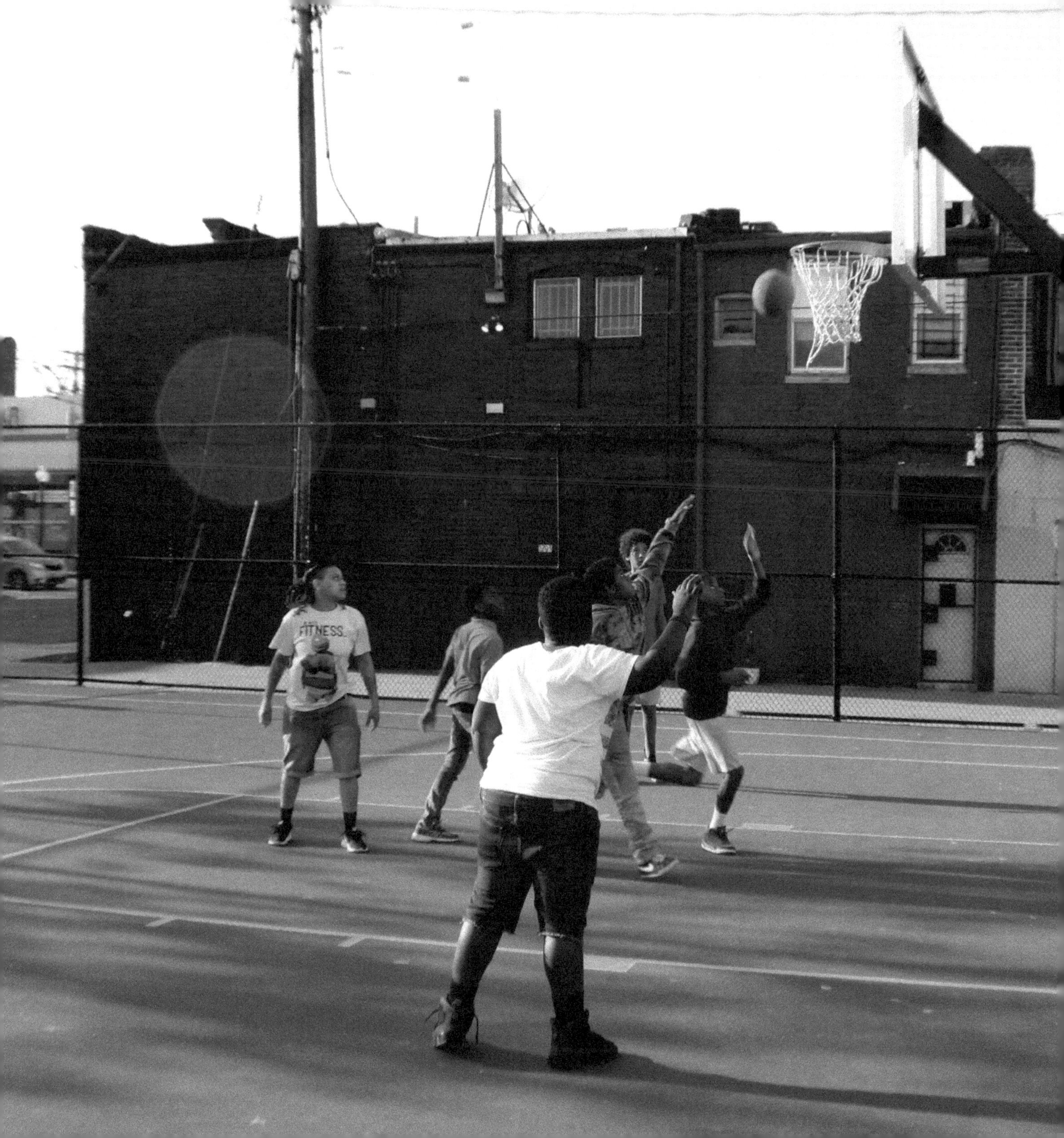
FITNESS

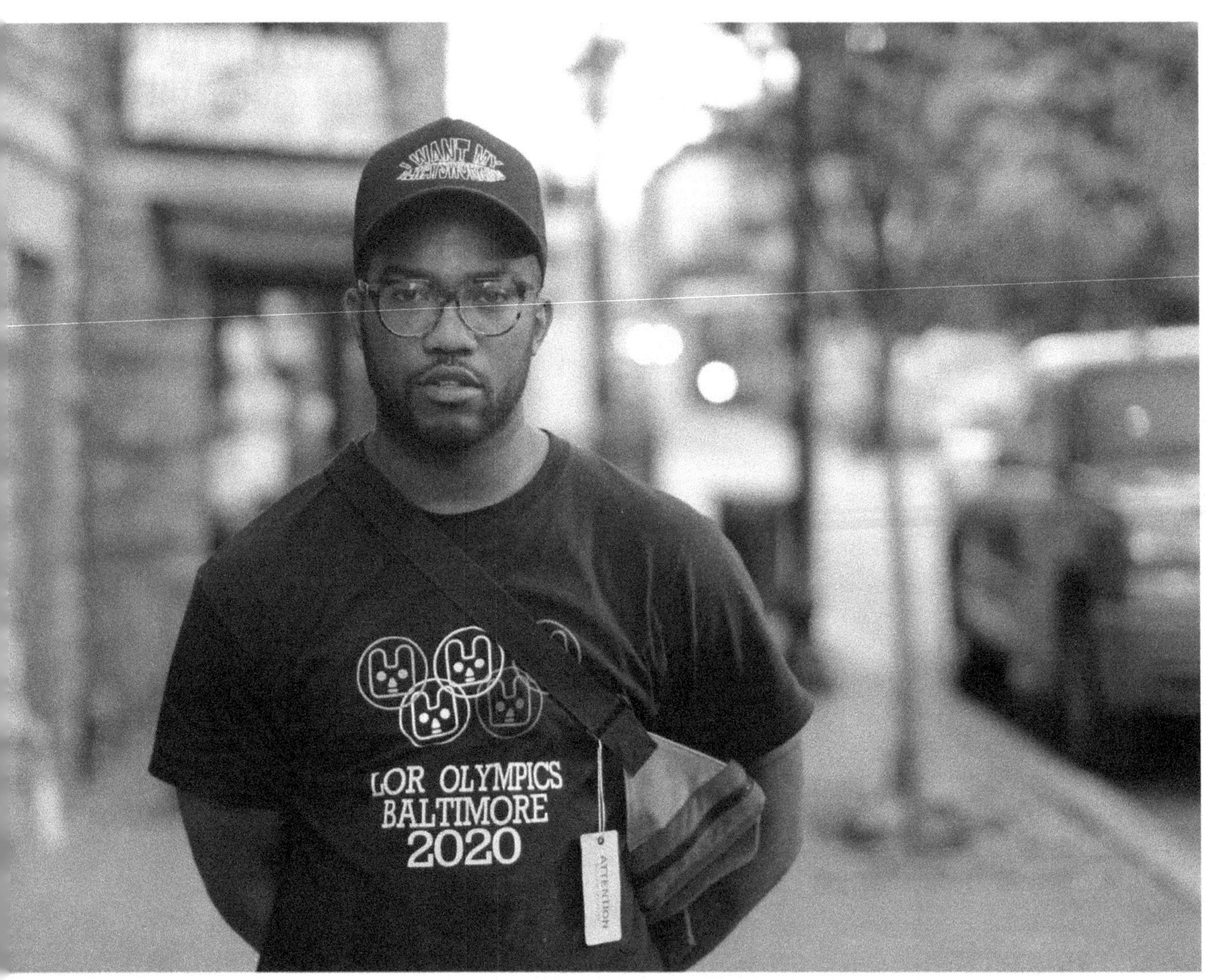
I WANT MY
LOR OLYMPICS
BALTIMORE
2020
ATTENTION

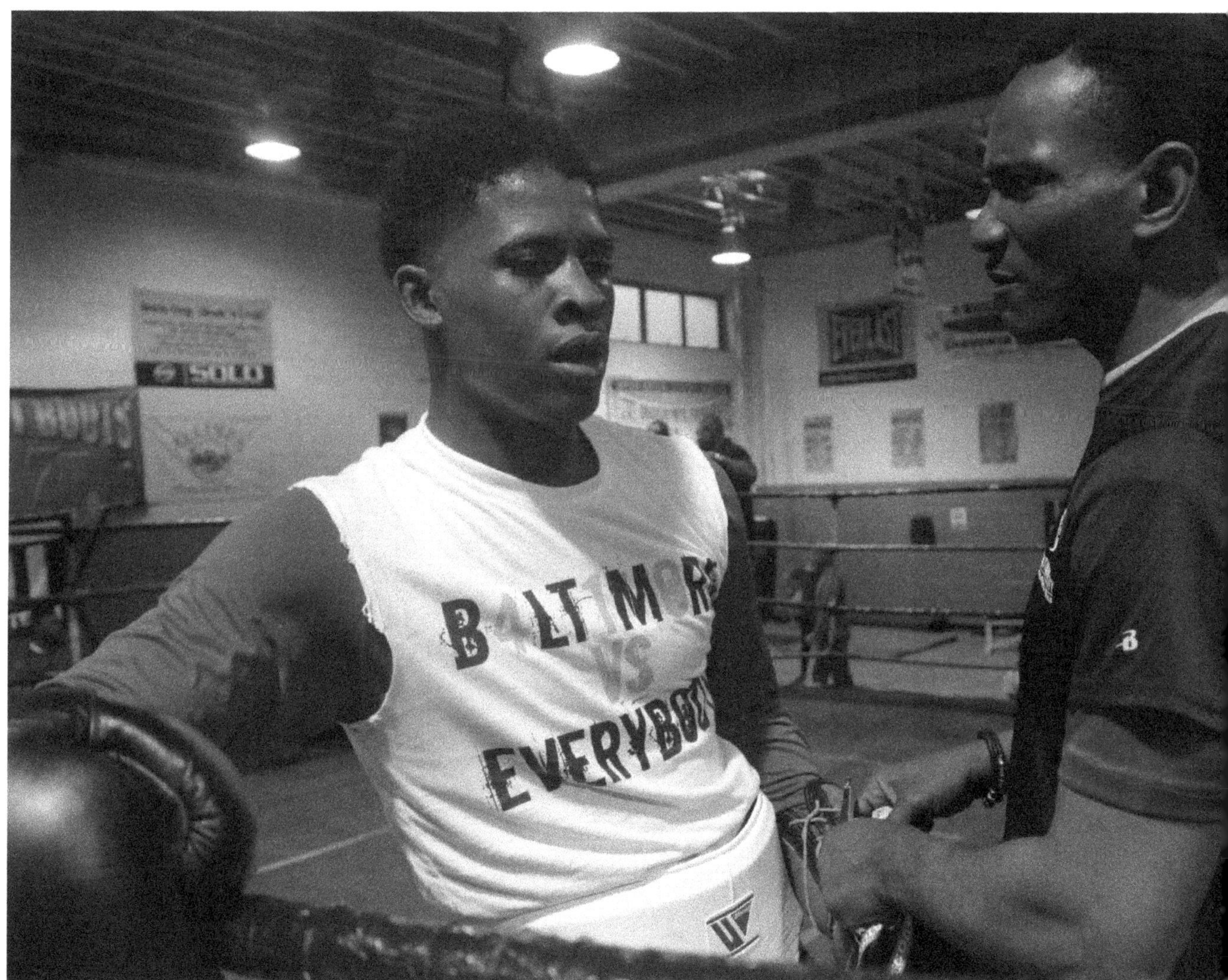
BALTIMORE
VS

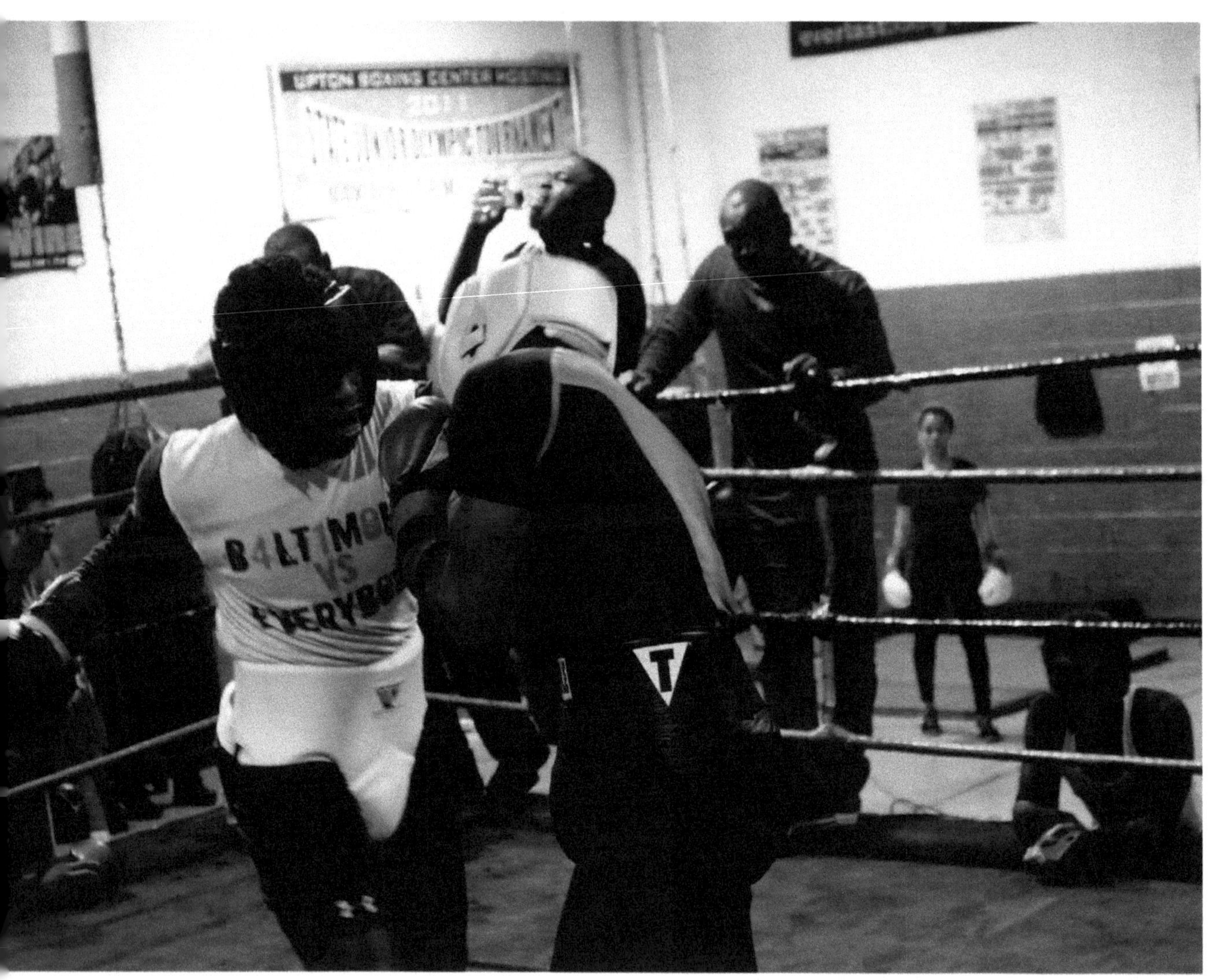
B4LT1MO
VS
EVERYBO

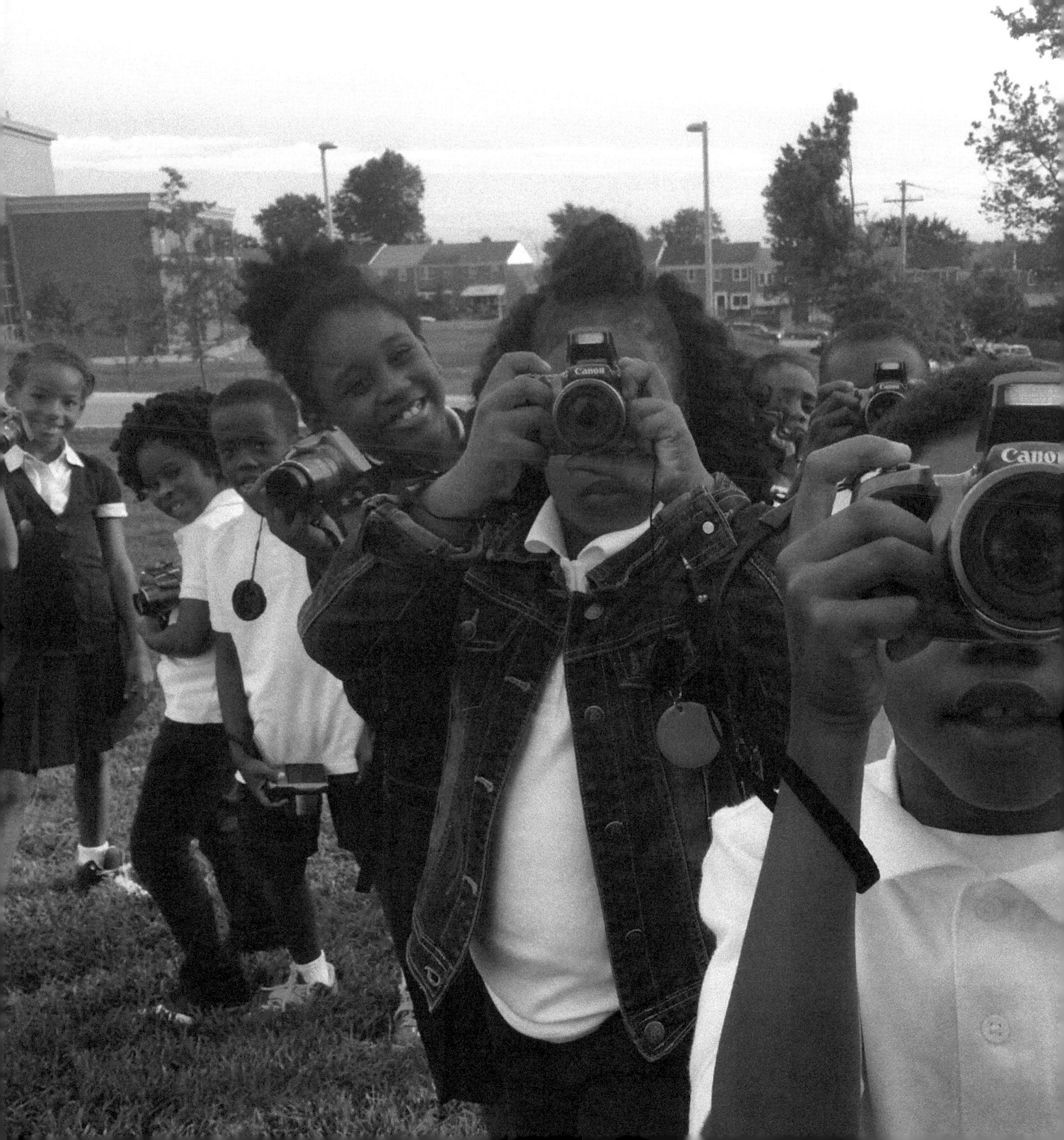
Canon

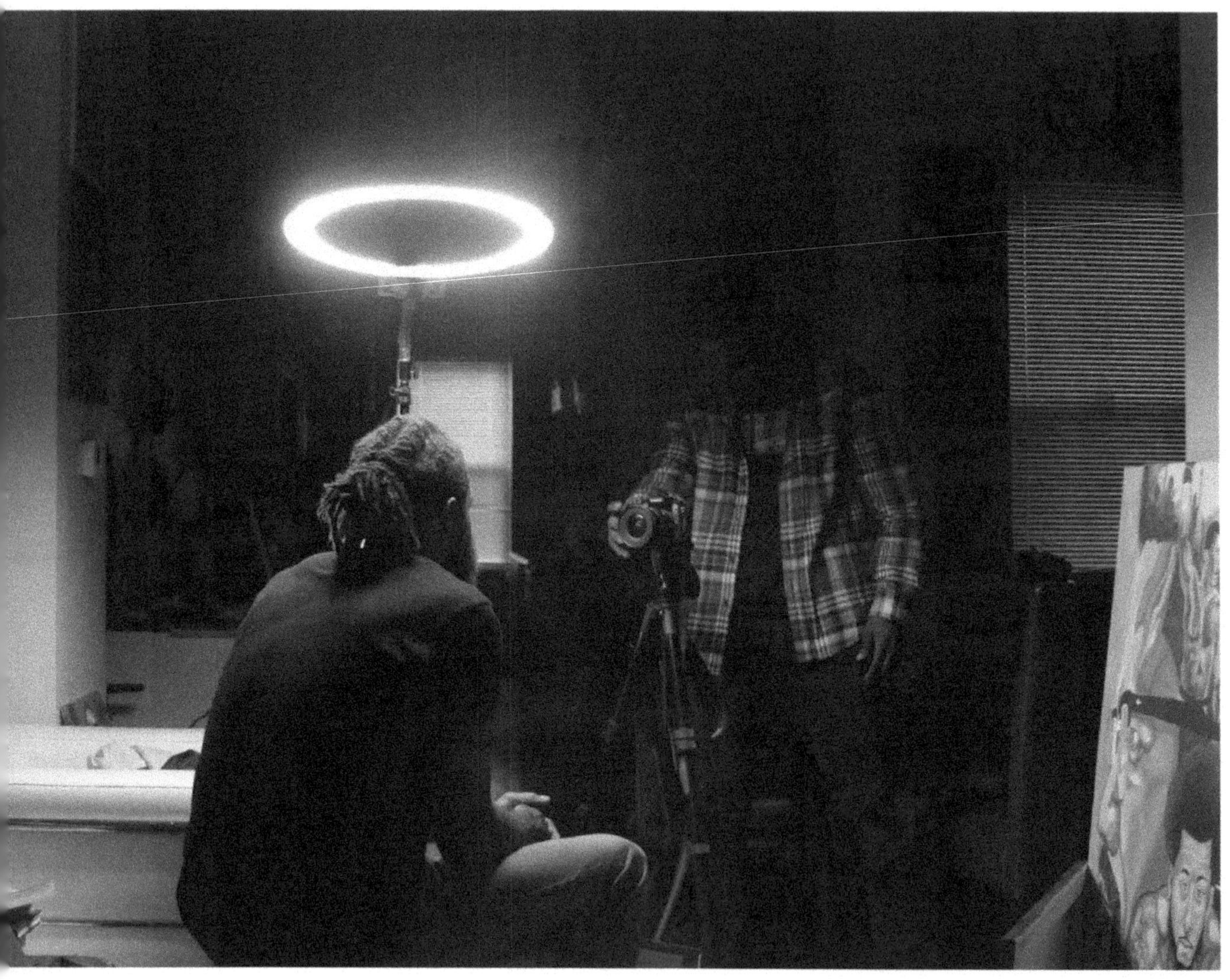

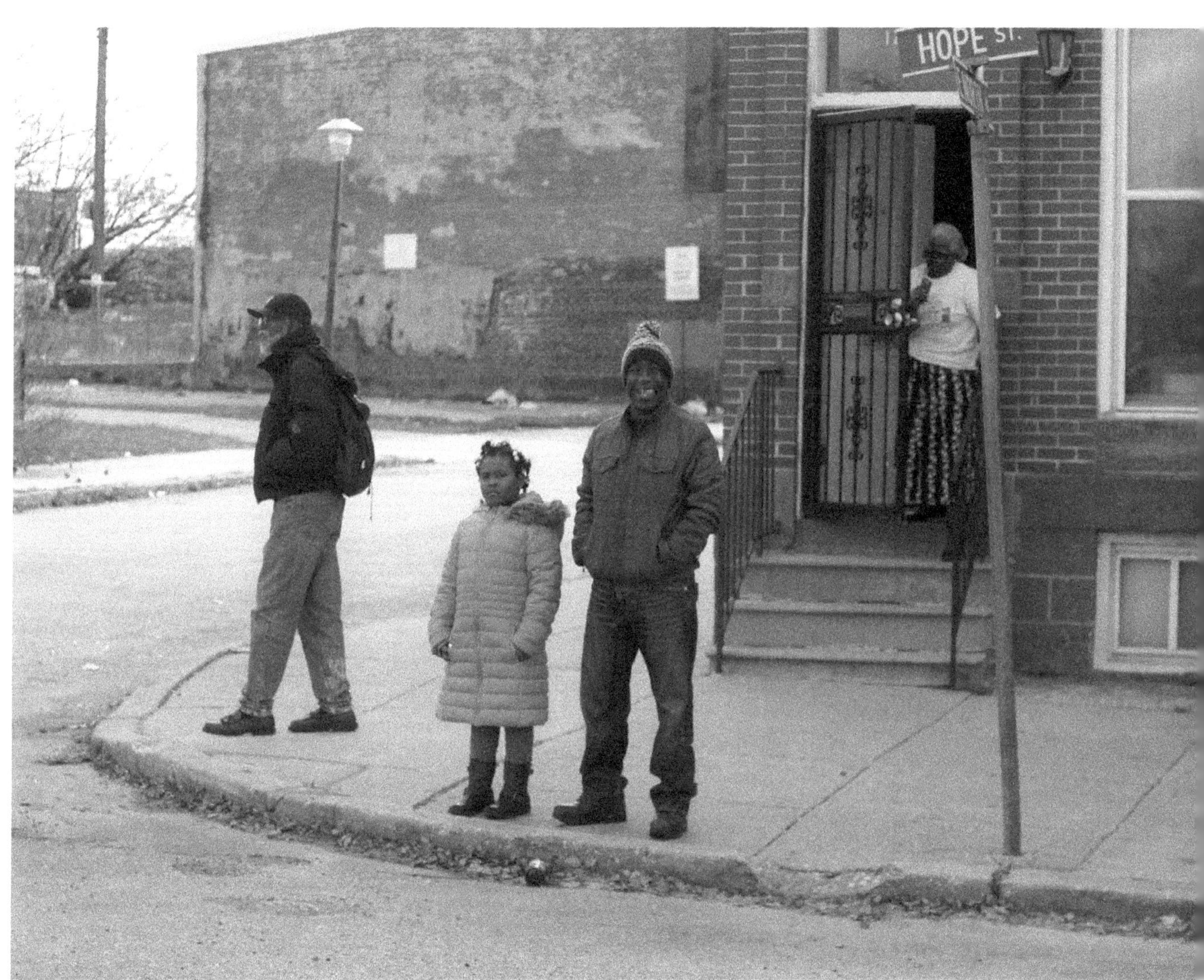
HOPE ST.

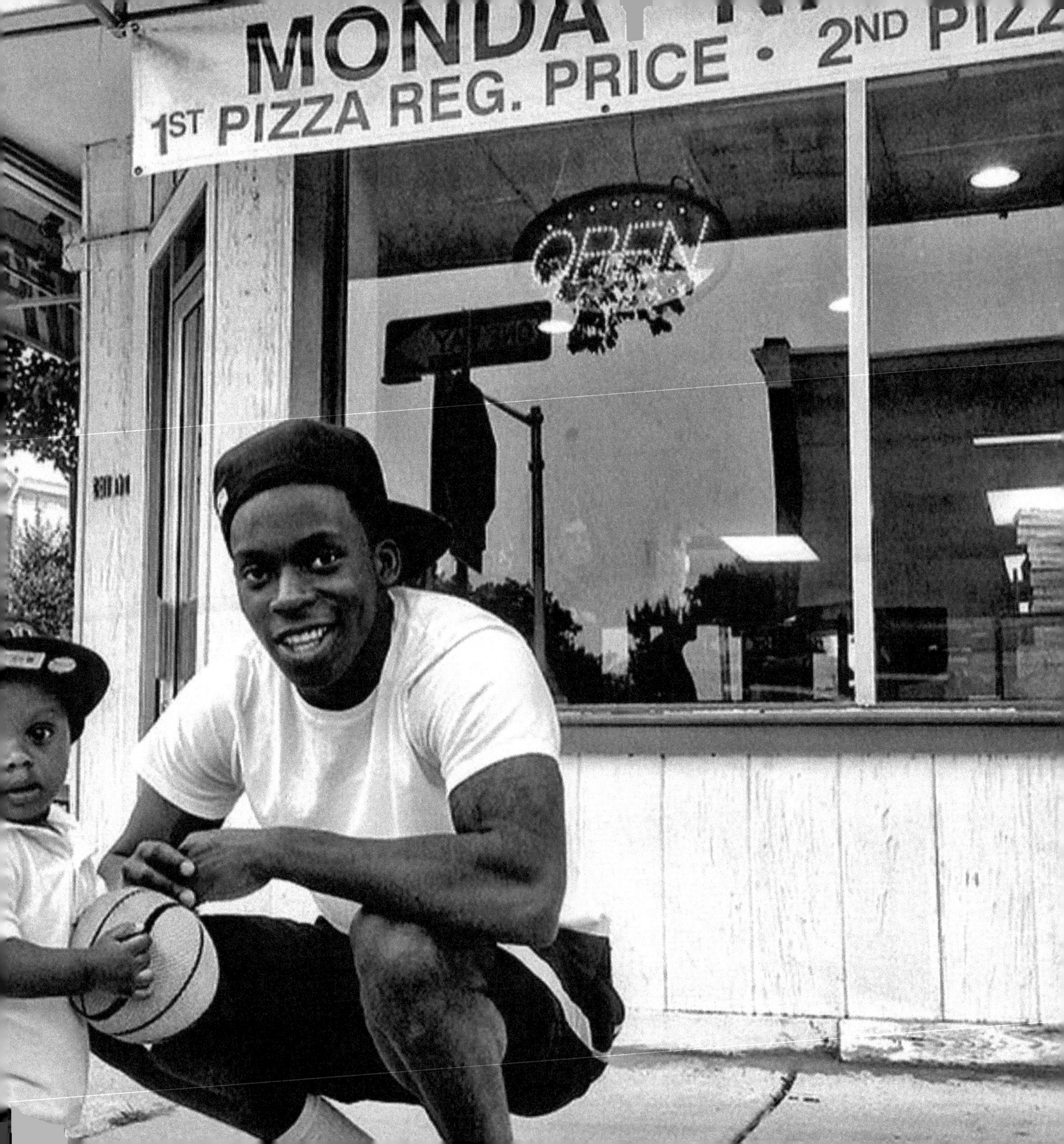
1ST PIZZA REG. PRICE
OPEN

ACKNOWLEDGEMENTS

This coffee table book, "Black Body, Baltimore in Black and White," is a testament to the collective effort of many individuals who have contributed to its creation.

First and foremost, I dedicate this book to my parents who have always supported my creative pursuits and encouraged me to pursue my passions. Their unwavering love and guidance have been a constant source of inspiration throughout my life.

I also want to express love to my brothers and all my family members who have been my pillars of strength and have always been there for me, no matter what. Your support and encouragement has been instrumental in shaping the person I am today.

To my friends, both old and new, who have cheered me on and provided me with valuable feedback and support throughout this project, I say a heartfelt thank you. To the designer, Nikiea Redmond, and editor, Kamaria Jones, who have worked tirelessly to bring this project to fruition, I am immensely grateful. Your enthusiasm and encouragement has kept me motivated and driven to see this project through to completion.

And last but not least, I want to dedicate this book to all the community leaders and organizers of the East vs. West Rally, the family of Freddy Gray and the city of Baltimore. Your resilient spirit has been a source of inspiration to me and has fueled my desire to capture the beauty and the complexity of this vibrant city in black and white.

Thank you to everyone who has contributed to this project in one way or another. Your support and encouragement has made all the difference.

COMPANIES & ORGANIZATIONS
Baltimore City Public Schools, 92Q Radio Station, Unruly Records, DTLR, Robot Films, Artllective LLC, The Manigault Film Company, Family Matters LLC, Keep It Equal, Manigault Empowerment Project, Thillery Group LLC, Destiny Productions, Manigault Enterprise LLC, G Food Truck, Peculiar Management LLC, Oliver Recreation Center, Madison Recreation Center, The Dome, FMG Records, More Life Seamoss, Taharka Brothers Ice Cream, Cashland and The Stokey Project.

SCHOOLS
Frostburg State University, St. Francis Academy, Dunbar High School, Mervo High School, Commodore John Rodgers Elementary and Margaret Brent Elementary.

CITIES
Baltimore, Los Angeles, DC, Miami and New York.

GOD.

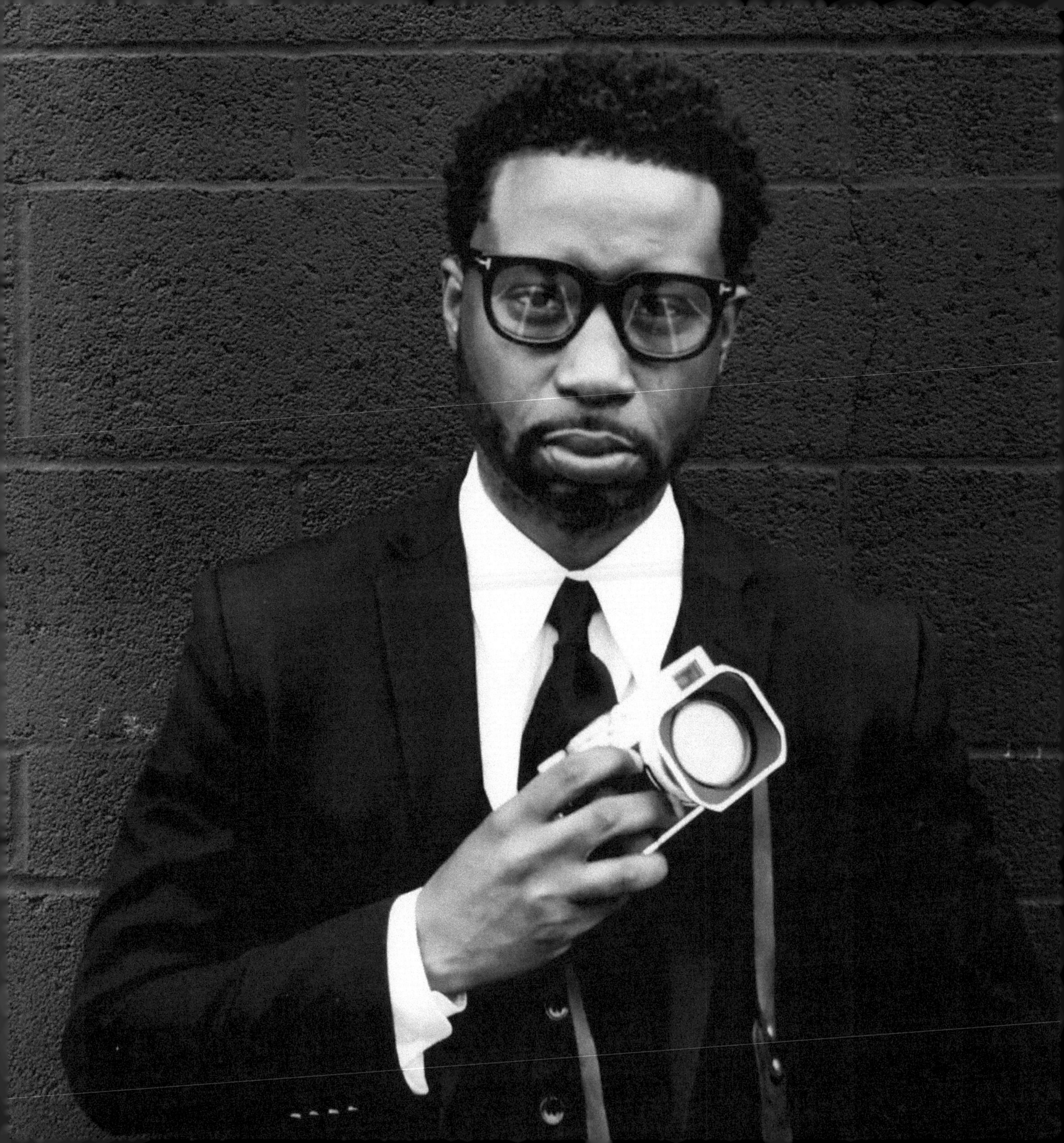

ABOUT THE PHOTOGRAPHER

David Manigault is a multi-talented actor, photographer and filmmaker based in Los Angeles. Born and raised in East Baltimore, Manigault grew up witnessing crime and drugs dominate his neighborhood, but somehow embraced the beauty and resilience from that environment. He parlayed his athletic success into a scholarship to Frostburg State University where he majored in Film/Television Production.

Manigault's work is characterized as Black celebration, Black empowerment, and he is known for introducing narratives about Black beauty and resilience through his films and photographs. In 2009, he made a basketball documentary 'Poet Pride" which follows the historic trials and tribulations of Baltimore City Dunbar HS basketball program. He later collaborated with HBO to create "Baltimore Boys," a documentary that explores the success of four basketball players from Dunbar H.S. The documentary garnered critical acclaim and was the first of many successful projects. Manigault has directed music videos for a variety of artist in the Baltimore/DMV area. Simultaneously, Manigault got his feet wet on the other side of the camera with appearances in music videos, including Jay-Z's "Roc Boyz" and Bone Thugs n Harmony's "I Tried.' He also landed the lead role in the acclaimed Bone Thugs n Harmony movie "I Tried" as Lethal. Not to mention a short film "Lost Path", and director of MTV's "Becoming a Pop Star" episode #2.

Manigault's photography work has been published in reputable outlets such as Baltimore Sun, Slam, The Afro, and Salon. Manigault's future goals are to continue exploring his creative boundaries and honing his craft with every project.

Manigault has been a visiting artist and lecturer at a number of Boys and Girls Clubs, High Schools, Youth Outreach Centers, Juvenile Facilities and Foster Homes spreading the message of self love and the power of artistic expressions.

www.manigaultglobalentertainment.com

For business inquiries and motivational speaking engagements

info@manigaultglobalentertainment.com

www.ingramcontent.com/pod-product-compliance
Lightning Source LLC
LaVergne TN
LVHW060640110826
845147LV00018B/1013

* 9 7 8 0 5 7 8 8 3 9 1 1 0 *